FOOTBALL

FOR THE SOUL

ALEX BYSOUTH

FOOTBALL
FOR THE SOUL

Rediscovering the Beauty
in the Beautiful Game

pitch

First published by Pitch Publishing, 2025

1

Pitch Publishing
9 Donnington Park,
85 Birdham Road,
Chichester, West Sussex,
PO20 7AJ
www.pitchpublishing.co.uk
info@pitchpublishing.co.uk

A CIP catalogue record is available for this book
from the British Library.

ISBN 978 1 83680 174 0

Typesetting and origination by Pitch Publishing

MIX
Paper | Supporting
responsible forestry
FSC   FSC® C010615

Printed and bound on FSC® certified paper in line with
our continuing commitment to ethical business practices,
sustainability and the environment.

Printed and bound in India by Thomson Press

Contents

DEDICATION

To my amazing wife, Hannah, thank you
for your patience and guidance. And to our
beautiful boys, Archie and Reggie; you are
my inspiration.

And in memory of my friend and team-mate,
Liam; I'll always be grateful for you first
giving me a platform to write about football.
Rest easy, mate. No doubt you're up there
winning headers and winding up centre-
forwards in the sky.

Prelude:

Hooked

WE HAD been married all of three weeks when I stumbled across an old vice, a football shirt-shaped craving that, however hard I tried, was impossible to kick. Like a recovering chain smoker caught in the swirling scent of nicotine, just the faintest echo of the words 'vintage jerseys' was enough to trigger pangs of desire.

Honeymooning in Tokyo as a couple of love-drunk newlyweds, caught in the glare of the city's neon lights and futuristic displays, we were blazing our way in equal measure through Japan's cultural treasures and its Instagram-friendly gimmicks – onsens overlooking Mount Fuji, real-life Mario Karting across Rainbow Bridge, chowing down yakitori on Piss Alley and slurping saké with strangers in Golden Gai. Then, one day, after observing the dizzying Shibuya Crossing, we found ourselves strolling through the neighbourhood when a sign for retro football shirts caught my eye. Just one little look wouldn't hurt, would it? The arcade entrance stood out because it wasn't very Tokyo. In fact, a weathered white-tile arch directing guests through a wooden front door below looked more like the entrance to a 1970s public bathroom in a small, forgotten UK town. Yet, in we went, intrepid adventurers as ever, up a narrow flight of stairs and through a heavy-set shop door to discover a treasure trove of jerseys in bold and clashing colours. Iconic Serie A numbers and international gems hid in the shadows as their J.League counterparts proudly flexed colour schemes and geometric patterns that would challenge even the most eccentric eye. It was honeymoon budget-busting heaven. The credit card braced itself in our travellers' bumbag. The wardrobe at home winced with anticipation at another never-to-be-seen-again shirt stuffed inside its already creaking doors. House to save for? But there's a 1995 match-worn, violent orange Shimizu S-Pulse jersey on sale.

Thankfully, for both our marriage and bank balance, after an internal (and external) talking to, I limped away relatively unscathed with a pink and white camouflage print Sagan Tosu number. Instead, at the checkout, it was my wife who experienced the unexpected moment that made her holiday. Standing by the till, its big bald head glistening under the lights of this stock cupboard crammed with shirts masquerading as a shop, was a Thomas Gravesen figurine sporting a full Everton kit. All two inches of him, plastic from head to base. The shop assistant, dazed by squeals of excitement and the surprise of coming face to face with a lifelong Toffees fan in Tokyo, gleefully un-BluTacked the tough-tackling Dane. The young lad, obviously not old enough to remember Gravesen's exploits at Goodison Park or stories of him nailing Robinho in Real Madrid training, remarked that he was previously unfamiliar with the player. He generously handed him over as a gift, free of charge. Pack your passport, Tommy, you're coming home.

Japan may seem like a strange place to start a book predominantly about European football but it is a country that struck me as full of love, creativity and enthusiasm for the game. It is modern and forward-thinking, yet embraces its heritage and is, in many ways, the perfect environment to forge and mould a burgeoning idea. Somewhere even the most optimistic projects can come to fruition. In that sense, it elicits the feeling that you can realise your dreams, footballing or otherwise. If you had to create your perfect football club from scratch, for example, what would you do? If you had to design the ideal fanbase, how would it look? What aspects would you cherry pick from other clubs, countries or cultures? That is exactly the proposition that faced Japanese fans when the J.League, the first fully professional football competition in the country's history, kicked off in 1993. Previously, football teams belonged to businesses or corporations and the main team spectator sport was baseball. One of the missions of the J.League was to establish cultural roots and communities by forming new clubs independent of their parent companies, who instead represented local towns or areas.

Nissan Motor became Yokohama F. Marinos, Toyota Motor SC became Nagoya Grampus Eight and Mitsubishi Urawa Football Club eventually dropped the company name to become Urawa Red Diamonds. As Japan experienced a 'soccer boom' and the league modelled its marketing strategies on those that had proved successful for US sports, the country became obsessed with football and the beautiful game threatened to knock baseball, as its traditional pastime, out of the stadium. J.League merchandise was everywhere; more than a million flags were sold in the first year and the brand appeared on everything from beer to bank cards and beef.

Fans flocked to stadiums that couldn't handle the demand for tickets, while a new wave of supporters, infatuated by the sport, sought to draw on the traditions and behaviours of their counterparts in nations where football had long been the focus of their weekend. As Sebastian Moffet explains in his brilliant book, *Japanese Rules*, one of the early influencers in this field was a man named Hiroshi Sato, who travelled Europe as a teenager to feed a burning intrigue for a game being played on the other side of the world. One with passionate crowds that he had so far only experienced via television. Sato posed for photographs with the likes of Johan Cruyff in Barcelona and Kevin Keegan in Hamburg. He studied fan culture and supporter chants on trips to Liverpool and Manchester. Years later, as general secretary, he was behind the naming of the aforementioned Mitsubishi Urawa Football Club, whose initials read MUFC, wore red shirts, white shorts and black socks and had the iconic Sir Matt Busby phrase 'play to the limit' inscribed on their jerseys. The influence of the Old Trafford outfit 6,000 miles away was anything but subtle; nor was that of British culture. Sato even helped devise a club song for the side from Saitama, north of Tokyo, to the tune of Rod Stewart's 'Sailing'.

Other clubs found different influences. At Kashima Antlers, where Zico was the star, they came up with Brazilian chants. At Kashiwa Reysol, who boasted another Brazilian in former Napoli frontman Careca, some of the most vociferous fans made homemade smoke bombs. Some ultra groups – who tended to be relatively friendly compared to those in Europe and South America, or at least less violent – borrowed chants or phrases they had heard watching Serie A, La Liga or Premier League matches on television. Others threw loo rolls and waved shirts above their heads like they had seen in Argentina. There were tifos, flags and mascots, making watching the game in certain parts of the ground intense and energetic. But crowds were also diverse and family friendly, with a large number of female supporters, and those traditions borrowed from around the world were sprinkled and entwined with local Japanese culture and behaviours to give the J.League a truly unique product.

My experience watching Japanese football was to discover an atmosphere like nothing I'd previously witnessed. Kyoto is well known for its more than 2,000 Buddhist temples and Shinto shrines. Its traditional gardens, palaces and charming, narrow streets transport you through time. It was spared bombing by the Americans during World War Two because of its cultural significance and, having previously been Japan's capital for more than 1,000 years, it maintains an essence of the country's imperial past. There are wooden houses, geisha and traditional tea ceremonies. It is also home to the most-relegated team in J.League history. Kyoto Sanga are one of the few clubs in Japan whose origins are not directly linked to a corporation, though since the formation of the J.League they have had the backing of big, local firms, including Nintendo. Until 2007, they were known as Kyoto Purple Sanga, incorporating the colour of their shirts, one befitting of the city's imperial past. They might not enjoy the prestige or nostalgic gratification of another Nintendo-sponsored side who play in purple, like the late 1990s Fiorentina of Gabriel Batistuta and Rui Costa, but can boast of having launched the career of a future Champions League winner in Park Ji-sung, who scored in the club's first and, so far, only Emperor's Cup triumph.

In September 2019, as Sanga found themselves enduring another stint in Japan's second tier, they were handed a Saturday evening kick-off against Machida Zelvia, a side known as the 'Brazil of Tokyo' for their small but passionate fanbase. Following a small stream of purple shirts from the train station through a dimly lit neighbourhood, we joined the crowds and felt confident we were on the right track for Takebishi Stadium. The athletics arena was built in 1942 and had long been Kyoto's home, although this would prove to be their last season at the ground before a move to the glossy, purpose-built, 21,000-seater Sanga Stadium 20 minutes out of town. Stalls outside Takebishi were selling shirts, scarves and horns. Inside, the athletics track kept the crowd at a distance from the pitch but in the curved terrace behind the goal, the chanting was relentless. Few fans sat down on the backless benches, instead standing and waving purple and gold scarves above their heads while seamlessly moving through a catalogue of songs. Some slow and harmonious, others with an obvious European influence. 'Allez, allez, allez, Kyoto!' At times, choreographed scarf-wielding supporters would spin one way and then the other. Among the many banners and flags was one in English reading: 'We love Sanga'. A handful of travelling Machida fans at the other end brought their own to drape over the hoardings. At one point, we were almost covered by a huge tifo and, when Sanga scored twice in the second half, fans in our section were quick to involve us in an enthusiastic exchange of high-fives. It was welcoming, engaging and wholesome. No one left the terraces for a good 15 minutes after full-time, celebrating the 2-0 win with conga lines and more singing as the players made their way over to applaud the home crowd. This felt like football as it was meant to be: fun, friendly and passionate without any of the toxicity that tends to follow the modern game around like an unwanted stench.

Visiting Japan got me thinking about football in different ways but it was also in the Land of the Rising Sun that one of the greatest footballers of a generation planted the seed for this book. The J.League has enjoyed its fair share of foreign imports over the past three decades with varying success, from Zico, Dunga and a raft of other Brazilians to Gary Lineker, Hristo Stoichkov, Diego Forlan, Lukas Podolski and Fernando Torres. But the one that intrigued me most was Andrés Iniesta. An hour down the road from Kyoto, just past the bright lights and food-fuelled avenues of Osaka, is Kobe. That is where the midfielder chose to spend five years of his career after leaving Barcelona in 2018, having won pretty much everything there is to win in football. A World Cup and two European Championships with Spain, four Champions Leagues and three Club World Cups on top of a plethora of domestic trophies with the Catalan giants. I was fortunate to interview him in 2021, when the Coronavirus pandemic was still making an impact on everyday life. He was modest, humble, understated, generous with his time. He came across very, well … normal. Sat in his living room in Kobe, only a club translator for company, curtains drawn to stop the sunlight reflecting off the computer screen, there was a romance to the way Iniesta talked about football that stirred the soul. Reminiscing about childhood kickabouts on makeshift pitches with an endearing innocence, stories punctuated with candid smiles, he continually referred to what he calls the 'essence' of the game. Iniesta never lost the same verve and freedom he enjoyed playing with friends in his hometown Fuentealbilla, whether it was clinching the J.League with Vissel Kobe or scoring the winning goal in the World Cup Final for Spain.

In Japan, generally, there is a sense that the whole experience of going to a game should be about enjoyment and entertainment. Perhaps that is why Ange Postecoglou fared so well there, winning the J.League with Yokohama F. Marinos. My brief but joyous interaction with football in Japan, as well as the wholesome and enlightening chat with Iniesta, got me questioning why I often allow myself to get so antagonised and frustrated by a game that should be, well, fun?

Football is, after all, a never-ending journey. It's the game itself, the goal, the assist, the perfect execution of a slide tackle on a drenched pitch. It's the result for a few days and then another one and another one. Without doubt, what's more important in the long term, though, are the people, the culture and the stories. Football is the world's great unifier. It can be reduced to stats and money and social media feuds but what really count above Super League proposals and unfathomable wage packets are the bonds and friendships. What stays with you are the memories, the feelings evoked when someone mentions Euro 96, Stuart Pearce's penalty celebration, Karel Poborský's lob, hearing your dad caught up in the passion while watching England at Wembley: 'Give it, Incey!' (Incey did give it and Alan Shearer scored.) It's getting transported to another, exotic, world with *Gazzetta Football Italia* on Saturday mornings, tracking the careers of strikers who bagged you a hatful on *Championship Manager*, playing with your grandad's hand-painted Subbuteo sets, flicking through old Panini stickers or having a binge on Premier League nostalgia. It's scorelines that mean everything and nothing all at once, the tears of defeat and the joy of Allan Nielsen heading a winner in the League Cup Final. It's watching Stevenage Borough draw 0-0 with Rushden and Diamonds on a freezing Boxing Day and creating chants to keep yourself warm. It's making tin foil FA Cups, high-fiving strangers in Japan, dodging firecrackers in Lisbon, walking with thousands of fans in Berlin and having Hugo Sánchez talk you through overhead kicks in Madrid before El Clásico. It's Tottenham Hotspur to Trafford FC and everything in between. The pint, the pie, the acca that nearly came in. It's the smile on your lad's face when he puts one past you in the garden.

Winning is important, of course it is, but it is not all about trophies (a Spurs fan *would* say that); rather the adventures you have along the way. Sir Bobby Robson put it best: 'What is a club in any case? Not the buildings or the directors or the people who are paid to represent it. It's not the television contracts, get-out clauses, marketing departments or executive boxes. It's the noise, the passion, the feeling of belonging, the pride in your city. It's a small boy clambering up stadium steps for the very first time, gripping his father's hand, gawping at that hallowed stretch of turf beneath him and, without being able to do a thing about it, falling in love.'

That is why I wanted to bring together some stories that prove football is more than just the outrage-baiting industry it can sometimes be reduced to, especially online and on social media. Stories that explore clubs, cities, cultures and people that perhaps offer a different, generally more feel-good, take on the beautiful game. This is not an exhaustive list of everything great in the sport, because scratch the surface a little and you'll find it almost everywhere, in every club or casual kickabout in every town and every city across the globe. These are stories and places that have, for one reason or another, resonated with me, as a football fan, journalist and now also a father.

And perhaps *that* is the real inspiration. Perhaps it is a message to my two boys that, however infuriating this wonderful, crazy, stupid game can feel at times (and, trust me, there will be moments that it really pisses you off), it can teach you so much about life and people and places if you enjoy and embrace it. So, if you've been feeling particularly disconnected recently from the sport you grew up adoring, I hope the tales in this book, this one tiny fragment in the vast footballing ether, help even just a fraction towards you falling in love with the beautiful game all over again.

Chapter One

A Sense of Belonging

FEW PRE-GAME rituals compare to the Txoko. But first you have to find it. That's a rite of passage in itself. Can't locate the Txoko? Well, you'll go hungry, thirsty and probably be the butt of an inside joke or two. A hop across the River Nervión from Bilbao's La Ribera Market, pacing the pavements on the waterfront trying to frantically decode an address, only the sight of two red-and-white-scarved men gives up the location, creaking open a large yet unassuming heavy door and ushering us up a staircase into a dining area decked in Athletic Club paraphernalia.

Warm faces glowing in the dint of winter sunshine appear familiar despite the fact we are meeting for the first time and the welcoming smell of grilled meat and seafood wafting in from the kitchen gives the charm of a traditional family meal. 'What took you so long?!' chime our hosts, joking and gesticulating in a heady mix of Basque, Spanish and English, posing a question that transcends merely pre-match dinner and drinks.

The designated chef for the day is serving enough traditional dishes and local delicacies, it seems, to feed half of Estadio de San Mamés. And that's before he wheels out the chocolate cake.

Traditionally, the Txoko is a cosy venue rented out by Basque friends, or cuadrillas as they call them locally, where they meet to cook, drink and spend time together. For the Mr Pentland Club, an international supporters' group, the gatherings are reserved for special occasions, this one being Athletic Club's 125th anniversary. Amid the food, so much food, old friends who have travelled from the United Kingdom and beyond reacquaint themselves with their companions in the peña and are treated to personal video messages from Athletic Club legends Andoni Goikoetxea, dubbed the 'Butcher of Bilbao' for an infamous tackle on Barcelona's Diego Maradona, and former left-back Aitor Larrazábal, who played more than 400 games for the club.

Bellies bursting and spirits heightened by lashings of Kalimotxo, a mix of red wine and cola, many then make the half-hour stroll through the bustling city to San Mamés, the stream of supporters gathering velocity as it reaches the streets approaching the stadium, where fans bounce out of bars after finishing their beers and pintxos, ready to take their seats for the pre-match anthem. 'Athletic, Athletic, eup!' they cry in spine-tingling unison, a 48,000-strong choir almost lifting La Catedral from its foundations. Among the many former Athletic Club heroes present in the crowd, most gearing up to play in an exhibition match against Porto later, is the legendary José Ángel Iribar, who featured a club record 614 times for Athletic and was honoured with the unveiling of his own statue outside the stadium before the anniversary game against Atlético Madrid.

If supporting Los Leones is like a religion, then San Mamés is a place of worship. Built next to the site of a chapel dedicated to Saint Mammes, a Christian orphan thrown to the lions by the Romans, fans have gathered here for more than a century to express their faith in Athletic. The new ground, opened in 2013, can proudly boast of being one of the most iconic in Europe. A landmark and point of reference for so many, its nickname, 'The Cathedral', is apt. As former coach Luis Fernández put it: 'Bilbao without San Mamés would be like Paris without the Eiffel Tower.'

Athletic Club contrive to make it a memorable occasion for Iribar and the raucous capacity crowd inside San Mamés, with Gorka Guruzeta's goal and a sublime finish from the unstoppable Nico Williams sealing an emphatic victory. The bars that fell silent for a couple of hours fill up again to the point fans spill out on to the streets with their drinks in hand. Joyous chatter and an occasional chant ripple through a pleasantly balmy December evening in the north of Spain. Once you have experienced football in Bilbao, immersed yourself in Athletic Club, the culture and all its charming idiosyncrasies, it is hard to view the sport through the same prism you once did.

Locals call it a city of former players because it is common to see Athletic Club icons wandering the streets but perhaps Bilbao is the city of current sports stars, too. The morning after the victory over Atlético Madrid, reigning Masters champion Jon Rahm is casually strolling the quiet neighbourhood next to the stadium and happily, or perhaps out of politeness, stops for a chat with my brother and I about the game. Rahm was invited to take a ceremonial kick-off before the win over Atlético and was expected to don his Masters Green Jacket for the occasion but instead opted to complement a red and white scarf with the vintage goalkeeper shirt of the legendary Iribar, who joined him in the centre circle. Somewhat hoarse in the aftermath of the previous day's festival atmosphere at San Mamés, where Rahm could later be spotted cheering and chanting with friends in the stands, the former world No.1 curiously asks what a couple of English lads are doing walking through Bilbao at such a time on a Sunday morning. Casually dressed and typically understated, you would be surprised to learn Rahm signed a deal with the Saudi-backed LIV Golf a few weeks earlier to the tune of more than $500 million.. The golfing superstar just sees himself as another fan when it comes to football.

He is a proud exponent of Basque culture, too. When it came to picking his menu for the annual Champions' Dinner at Augusta, an honour bestowed on the defending Masters champion, Rahm, born near the sea on the outskirts of Bilbao in Barrika, treated the world's best golfers to a veritable Basque feast. It began with a mix of tapas and pintxos – Ibericos, Idiazabal cheese and black truffle, Spanish omelette, Basque chorizo and potato, his mum's classic lentil stew and croqueta de pollo, creamy chicken fritters and potato. There was a Basque crab salad, followed by a main of either Chuleton, a ribeye steak or turbot and white asparagus in a pil pil sauce. The only surprise, especially as an Athletic supporter, was that Rahm opted for turbot; he doesn't like the more traditional Basque salted cod. Bacalao, the local name for such a cod dish, is synonymous with Athletic Club and shouted by local radio commentators whenever the team score a goal. This began in the 1980s and was made fashionable by Radio Popular's chief football commentator, José Iragorri, whom the press room at San Mamés is now named after. In fact, you normally know when Athletic have scored because fans' WhatsApp chats fill up with fish emojis.

Athletic have always been one of the marvels of world football because of their unique philosophy. They are both a global phenomenon and the heart of the local community. 'Athletic Club plays only with people of the land,' explains Galder Reguera, project manager of the Athletic Club Foundation. 'One of the consequences of this is that the people feel that the players are part of the stands. When we see the team, we see our brothers or sisters play. The relationship with them is very different than at other clubs. They are not idols, they are part of the community, and they have this very special link with the fans and the city.'

With around 350,000 inhabitants, Bilbao is the largest city in the province of Biscay and the wider Basque Country region, Euskal Herria as it is also known, which contains a number of territories in northern Spain and also the south-west of France. The club's philosophy dictates that they may only field players born or essentially raised in the area ('formardo' is the word the club use). The idea of being 'raised' in the Basque Country can be a little ambiguous and sometimes creatively moulded to incorporate a young prospect with high potential, such as Aymeric Laporte, who, despite having Basque heritage, was born outside the region in Agen and sent to play in Bayonne. But it effectively means a player who was trained in the Athletic academy or that of another club in the Basque Country.

'We represent more than a football club. We represent a region,' says director of football Mikel Gonzalez, referring to Euskadi, the Spanish Basque provinces. 'We have this feeling that we have to defend our culture, the Basque Country, our history. So, it is more than football. Football is our way of representing our culture and our way of living.'

There is a sense of belonging to being Basque. Euskera, the Basque language, is thought to be the oldest living language in the world and bears no relation to any other. Its origins remain largely a mystery to linguists yet around a million people in the region now speak it. A century ago, Basque was in danger of disappearing, an issue furthered when the Franco regime forbade the teaching of it in schools or its use in the workplace. Some suggest migration to Bilbao was also encouraged in a bid to dilute Basque culture, although the region's role as Spain's industrial powerhouse of the time meant workers were naturally drawn to the Basque Country, too. Instead of replacing Basque culture, they embraced it. 'In the past 40 or 50 years, the Basque governments and the social movement in schools have done lots to recover the use of the language,' explains Reguera. 'But this is sometimes too much associated with work and studies by children.' The club's foundation is doing its part to try and make learning the language more engaging for youngsters. 'You must bring it to their social lives, too, and football is a part of this,' adds Reguera.

As well as community projects, Athletic Club provide Basque language lessons for all players and employees. The club is an embodiment of Basqueness, celebrating its history and culture, but also a vehicle through which the Euskadi people can present their proud heritage on a global scale. As one taxi driver suggests: 'Ninety per cent of people here support Athletic Club but Bilbainos who live away feel they have to protect the Basque heritage even more so than locals.'

'It is something that you feel since you are young,' says Gonzalez, explaining how kids learn Athletic songs in schools, that their first football jersey is typically the red and white stripes of their local club and that the first ground they visit is, of course, La Catedral. 'The first history you hear about football is about your parents or your grandfather's first time in San Mamés or the first time they saw Athletic win a title,' adds Gonzalez. 'Since you are very young – family, people, school, everywhere – you start receiving a lot of input about Athletic. It is something you feel that is a lot of you; about your family, your friends, everything. It is not about football – of course, it *is* football, 11 v 11 – but a lot of times we don't speak about *just* football here.'

Athletic have become a Basque institution in their own right. But they were not always a club for exclusively Basque players. Football first arrived in the city via Basque students returning from their studies in the United Kingdom and through British miners and shipyard workers who brought coal, and a ball, to the docks with them. Indeed, there was an Englishman, Alfred Mills, among the founding members of the club in 1898 and Athletic featured a number of foreign players in the early years. However, their unique philosophy has stood since 1911, when Andrew Veitch became the last non-Basque player to represent the club. The birth of the now-renowned tradition was not a slight on Veitch, rather a way of sticking up two fingers at Athletic Club's rivals from the rest of Spain, who complained about them winning the Copa del Rey that year with foreigners in the team. The club were initially stripped of the title before being reinstated as champions. Their headstrong reaction to the criticism was inherently Basque.

'Stubbornness is what defines it and it is probably part of Basque character,' concedes Basque journalist Beñat Gutiérrez. 'I guess now, even if Athletic wanted to stop being stubborn, it wouldn't make sense. The identity is blended with this idea of just signing Basque-born or raised players because this is what makes them unique in the world. You need to have a positive narrative; you need to have a message that brings people together and I think Athletic has a perfect one.'

It is a philosophy, rather than something written into the club's statutes or agreed on between Athletic Club socios (Athletic are one of four clubs in La Liga, alongside Barcelona, Osasuna and Real Madrid, who are still run by members) and is, therefore, one open to interpretation. A description of the policy on the club website is what tends to be taken as gospel. 'I know some people who want to have a proper debate between the members of the club and write down what they agree on but it feels like the kind of topic that would create more tension than anything else,' adds Gutiérrez. The interpretation has changed over time, though. At first, it just incorporated players born in the region of Biscay, then the wider Basque Country and now, of course, stretches to players raised or trained there. Some suggest it should include all players of Basque heritage and in the past, usually when presidential candidates are jostling for power before club elections, rumours have circulated about tweaking the model to attract high-profile players with Basque heritage. Such stars to be discussed have included Uruguay's Diego Forlán and Argentina forward Gonzalo Higuaín.

'It is true that now there is a bit of an attempt to add some nuance to the signing policy, maybe consider signing players from Basque heritage,' explains Gutiérrez. 'I think it is really difficult to put that on paper.' Gutiérrez uses Mexican side Club Deportivo Guadalajara, better known as Chivas, who only play with Mexican players, as an example. 'It's easy to know when a player is Mexican. Can he hold a Mexican passport? We don't have a Basque passport. So, to refine what Basque is and be like "Okay, the son of this person can sign because he has Basque heritage" is really difficult. And, right now, it is lax enough that if you want to bring in a player that is good, there are ways to do it and natural ways. If you have your son playing for a big academy and you want him to play for

Athletic and you're a Basque man, you probably have some relatives there, so send him [to Bilbao].'

It is a method that has proved sustainable and successful. Athletic have never been relegated from Spain's top tier and they are the third-most decorated team in Spain in terms of trophies won behind Real Madrid and Barcelona. They have won eight La Liga titles and, as of 2024, have won the Copa del Rey 25 times. The first cup success in 1902, however, is disputed. It is not recognised by the Spanish football authorities because it was a combined Athletic Club and Bilbao FC side and was played as an invitational tournament. The sides merged under the Athletic Club banner the following year and the trophy is proudly displayed by the club in their phenomenal museum at San Mamés.

Restricting the pool of players Athletic can pick from means there have been fallow periods without silverware and times where the club have finished lower in the table. Indeed, they narrowly avoided relegation in 2007. But, sticking to their principles, Athletic ended a 40-year wait for a trophy when they won the Copa del Rey in 2024 and have regularly qualified for Europe since that nervy campaign in which they battled the drop. 'To stay 125 years in the first division, without relegation, with 25 cups, with eight leagues, three Super Cups, just with Basque players … pff!' says sporting director Gonzalez. 'In one year in 125 years, normally you go to the second division. To have 125 years of success and not make big mistakes, I think that is the biggest strength for Athletic.'

Reguera, a lifelong Athletic fan before he began working for the club, believes the club's sustained success is underpinned by their use of local players. Not because they produce world class stars but because Athletic continuously produce a succession of role models for the next generation. 'Because we only play with people of the land, talent is something there is and something there is not,' he says. 'If you are lucky, you may find five very talented players in ten years. But if you are not lucky, in the next ten years maybe you only have one? The rest are people who give 150 per cent every match and [this] behaviour is like a disease. It is there in the room, it is contagious. It is a spirit. If you have in your team one guy, two guys, three guys that give 150 per cent every match, you will have this in all the team. If you have three talented players, okay, give the ball to them and maybe you are lucky … like Real Madrid!'

Of course, when Athletic do not have a good season, there are arguments in the newspapers and local media that maybe the club should change philosophy or relax the restrictions to some extent. 'You never know what will happen in 50 years,' says Gonzalez. 'But in this moment, you can't imagine Athletic playing with Basque players plus players from other countries.'

Gaizka Garitano has experienced it as a fan, a player and a head coach. He was born in Bilbao, came through the club's youth academy and was first-team manager for two years. 'We all are very proud of our philosophy,' he says. 'It is the reason we feel something special about our club and we will continue this way. I know it is difficult to achieve trophies, to achieve titles with this philosophy, because we can't sign foreign players, but if you ask every single supporter of the club, all of us agree with the philosophy. We are proud and it is for this reason we are very special. It is not about money, it is not about business, it is about *feel*. We feel different for that reason.'

Ander Herrera, the former Spain, Paris Saint-Germain and Manchester United midfielder, was one of those eligible to play for Athletic Club thanks to being born in Bilbao. His father, Pedro, is a huge Athletic fan and played his youth football at the club but never made it as a first-team member at San Mamés, instead enjoying a career in the Spanish top flight with Salamanca, Real Zaragoza and Celta Vigo. It was while his dad was working as general manager at Zaragoza that Herrera fell in love with football, enjoying the chance to kick a ball around with players after training and, thus, becoming a lifelong Real Zaragoza fan. Herrera progressed through the Aragonese club's ranks before living out his father's dream by joining Athletic. In fact, he has joined them twice, either side of spells in Manchester and Paris. That was before he fulfilled another dream by moving to Boca Juniors in January 2025, inspired by stories of his father's travels to Argentina.

Herrera is a football romantic. Even as an outsider, in the sense he is not a diehard Athletic fan like many of his former team-mates in Bilbao, he is a staunch believer in the club's philosophy. 'In my opinion, that should never change, because that makes the club so special,' he told me before the Copa del Rey Final against Mallorca. 'You have to experience this feeling of being part of this group, of this club, how important it is for society as well.' Herrera says he would come across people in the city who are not necessarily into football but care deeply about Athletic Club. There are people who have been season ticket holders at San Mamés their whole lives, yet they have no interest in watching any other football or seeing any other team. Herrera, for example, recalls being stopped in the street by pensioners who would insist to him that Athletic win the cup and qualify for the Champions League.

Athletic are such a huge part of everyday life for people in Bilbao and the Basque Country. They are visible everywhere, from the many flags flying from buildings in the city to Athletic-branded crisps and pictures of current stars and club legends in bars and restaurants. In 2023, they sent a bib commemorating the club's 125th anniversary to every baby born in the region. Newborns are regularly showered in Athletic gifts and even maternity wards are decked in red and white. Most kids here are Athletic fans from birth. They have the passion and desire to represent their hometown club. Athletic's challenge is just moulding enough of those enthusiastic youngsters into elite talents who can compete in La Liga and Europe. And that work is done at Lezama.

Around a 40-minute train ride from the centre of Bilbao sits the sleepy village of Lezama, nestled in the tree-lined foothills of Monte Ganguren amid the vast, fertile Basque countryside where fresh air and spectacular views meet in a marriage of peace and tranquillity. A short stroll from the station and the silence is punctured by the voices of young men shouting and the slap of synthetic leather. Since 1971, Lezama has been the venue for Athletic's training ground and home to its esteemed academy. The 13-hectare complex boasts four grass pitches, one with a 3,200-capacity stadium and the magnificent arch from the old San Mamés, four outdoor artificial pitches and another inside, plus a state-of-the-art gym, medical facilities and even a goalkeepers' cage. Howard Kendall famously stayed at Lezama with caretaker and former player Jesus Renteria when he was manager in the late 1980s and, since 2021, the club have been able to host young players on the campus after building a residence with 30 double rooms.

Getting the right players to Lezama ready to start their journey with the academy at the under-11s age group is one of the most important parts of the process. Athletic Club invest a lot of money and resources in scouting for the cantera, the word Spanish clubs give their academies and which translates as 'the quarry'. Athletic have 20 designated academy scouts, plus another 20 working across their partnership clubs, of which there are more than 160 in the region. Before the age of 11, Athletic believe that every football-playing boy in the Biscay region will have trained with the club at Lezama at least once. Each season they put on around 45 sessions to get a look at more than 1,000 kids.

'It is their first filter to enter our academy,' explains sporting director Gonzalez in his office at the training base, which opens into a communal workplace where members of the recruitment staff are busy beavering away on their laptops. 'When they are 11, 12, 13, 14, we invest a lot of time and a lot of resources to know 100 per cent of the players that we can pick. Then we have a lot of physical tests, investigations, because they are going to be the future of the club and if we make a mistake with one of them, this mistake in the future can be terrible. In other clubs, you can make I don't know how many mistakes in the academy, because you go to the first team, you invest money and you sign a good player. Here, you make a mistake when this kid is 12 years old and he goes to another club, maybe you can't correct this mistake. And in the future, you are light because of this mistake. It is a big pressure working in the academy in the small ages, because it is the moment you can't make mistakes.'

Athletic's dominance when it comes to recruiting youth from the region can be a source of frustration for their rivals. Real Sociedad abandoned their own Basque-only policy in 1989 to try and be more competitive, with John Aldridge their first foreign signing, yet they still boast a productive youth academy at Zubieta and regularly feature among the clubs to have fielded the most homegrown players. Gonzalez calls it a 'beautiful fight' for the best young talent. In 2023/24, no club in Europe's top leagues featured more academy graduates than Athletic and that route to the first team is something that can be attractive when speaking to prospective young signings and their families. 'It is very difficult to get into the first team,' says Gonzalez. 'We have very good players and it is not easy to have space. But, for sure, it is the easiest club in the world or in the five big leagues. We are playing with eight or nine players formed in the academy every weekend. So, when you go to an agent or to a family, [you say] we have great facilities, we have a great stadium, for sure we can make you a good contract but, also, and this is the most important, if you want to arrive in professional football, here in Athletic you have doors more open than everywhere.'

Still, abiding by the club's philosophy brings its own challenges. What happens if Athletic need a centre-back, for example? Their options on the transfer market are far more limited than other top clubs and if there is not a suitable Basque option available, the solution must come from within. The club, therefore, work towards having a line of succession, projecting what players aged 15, 16, 17 years old need to reach first-team football and how long it will take them to get there. Young players are put on a programme with the performance department to meet their physical, mental, psychological and nutritional needs. Then, whether it is six months or three years down the line, they hope one of the three or four designated players from the B or C teams will be able to make the leap to senior football. And for those who don't, because not every youngster in the academy will go on to enjoy a career as a professional footballer, Lezama is set up to develop good people, not just good players. Many take university degrees or further studies and all appreciate the idea of Athletic being one big family.

It helps that most people working at Lezama, whether it be players, coaches or backroom staff, are predominantly Athletic Club fans. 'Here in Athletic, we go further and further because it is like our dream,' says Gonzalez. 'Since we are young, we dream to play for Athletic. When you are not a football player, you dream to work for Athletic and when you are working for Athletic you dream to make history and to win every game and to try to explain our philosophy.' They are also essentially playing or working for friends and family that support the club, alongside team-mates they have known, in many cases, since the age of 11. 'That is huge because it gives people from Bilbao the chance to support groups of players that tend to be really close together, this idea they are a group of friends,' adds fan and journalist Gutiérrez.

Athletic are, and have for a long time been, the main social organisation of the Basque Country, explains Gutiérrez. Yet the club are not complacent about their role in society. In fact, many inside the organisation see it as their duty to be more than just a football club to local people.

The Ibaigane Palace sits in the heart of Bilbao, in many ways situated between the old and the new. It is 500m one way from the eclectic Café Iruña, opened more than a century ago with its distinctive tiles and Mudejar-inspired decoration, and 500m the other from the modern and contemporary Guggenheim Museum that dominates the waterfront. If you stroll down the Nervión in one direction, you reach Bilbao's old town, Casco Viejo, with its quaint cobbled streets and bustling plazas lined with bakeries, restaurants and bars. Head the other, past the Guggenheim, and you find peaceful parks, old shipyards and, eventually, San Mamés.

Ibaigane is as much a part of Bilbao's past as it is its present. Steeped in history, the grand, neo-Basque building was constructed in the early 20th century by Ramón de la Sota, who was one of the wealthiest businessmen in Spain and given a knighthood by King

George V. De La Sota admired Athletic Club, was a member of the Basque Nationalist Party and a patron of Basque culture. Because of this, when General Francisco Franco took power following victory for the Nationalists in the Spanish Civil War in 1939, the dictatorship seized De La Sota's assets and turned Ibaigane into a military barracks. Under the regime, Athletic Club were also forced to change their title to Atlético de Bilbao, as Franco imposed a 'Spanishisation' on foreign names. Following Franco's death, Ibaigane was returned to the family and Athletic Club reached an agreement to purchase the property and restore it. Since 1988, it has been their headquarters.

There cannot be many other, if any, of the biggest clubs in world football with a head office like Ibaigane. Inside, the building is split over three floors with large, wooden pillars as support. Wooden balconies flank the whole perimeter of the upper two, meaning that, whichever level you are on, you can peer down at the grand, open inner courtyard. The real treasure, however, is in looking up. In doing so, you witness an incredible stained-glass ceiling created by renowned Basque artist Anselmo Guinea. On the ground floor, a huge Athletic flag flies and players come here to pose for photographs after signing new contracts. In the basement, fondly known as 'The Txoko', there is a bar and several boardrooms, covered with iconic pictures from throughout Athletic Club's history, that have recently been converted into office space for staff. It is down here that English manager Howard Kendall delivered his famous, emotional goodbye press conference in November 1989, calling

Athletic the best club in the world. It says a lot about Athletic that Kendall was invited to the next home game after his resignation for a meal in the directors' box and received a standing ovation from the home fans before kick-off.

Members of the public can also stroll through Ibaigane's grounds if they wish, again showing the openness between club and fans, while a postbox was set up by the front entrance for young supporters to send letters to the players before the Copa del Rey Final against Mallorca in April 2024. The club took them down to Seville for the players to read.

Galder Reguera's office with the Athletic Club Foundation is inside the main building. This is where many of the club's finest ideas come to fruition, many of which are more impactful on the community than anything the first XI do. That is, of course, when Reguera is not coming on as an impact sub for the Spanish national team of authors and writers in their own European Cup equivalent. 'I only play the last five or ten minutes,' he laughs. 'But the experience is wonderful.'

Reguera's work with the foundation began almost two decades ago, when the philosophy graduate pitched the idea of hosting an event for football writers to showcase their work and meet with readers. The initial response was lukewarm but now Athletic Club's Thinking, Letters and Football Festival is a fundamental part of the calendar and includes players and staff at the club who share the belief that football and culture are an entwined and important part of the community.

Every year, the club invite authors to the stadium to share their work. They come in many forms, from novelists, poets, journalists and columnists, to scriptwriters, musicians, cartoonists, film-makers, rappers and more. They all discuss life and sport from their perspective. 'Normally it is people who don't have a voice in the world of football,' explains Reguera. In the past, it has even included Athletic Club players. In 2019, the club published a story by defender Óscar de Marcos which detailed the high and low points of his first year with Athletic and how a visit to Togo in West Africa helped put his life as a young footballer in perspective. De Marcos, as well as having played almost an hour of a league win over Real Zaragoza with a tear in his scrotum that required 25 stitches, is well known for his regular visits to local hospitals and for his charity work in Africa and South America. At the same time, the club published a Basque-language book by women's goalkeeper and captain Ainhoa Tirapu called *Bizitzu Eskukadaka*, while Igor Porset from Athletic Genuine, the club's team for people with intellectual disabilities, wrote a biographical piece. Athletic distributed 13,000 copies of the players' work to schools, local clubs and bookshops before hosting discussions with the writers. Club legends such as Iribar, Andoni Zubizarreta and Andoni Iraola, as well as former Real Madrid and Argentina striker Jorge Valdano, an admirer of the club, have all been known to join in the discussions, too.

'There is a very beautiful thing that we make book clubs with players from the first team of the men's and women's team,' explains Reguera, referring to another initiative, the Athletic Reading Club. Here, fans put forward books they enjoyed and one is selected for the players to read. They have a month to finish it. Then they come together with the readers to discuss the book and sometimes make suggestions of their own. 'When you finish a book, in the first moment you think of your friends and you share it with the people you love,' says Reguera. 'To share a book is a very social experience. It is great to see a professional player of the Spanish league share two hours talking about the book with "normal" readers. It is very good for the people but it is more important for the players, because the players must always remember they are "normal" people but in a strange world. They are very young, they have no experience in life, they are at the top at 20 years old and surrounded by lots of people and they can lose their perspective.'

Reading the same book, sharing the same experiences and interpreting the story in their own individual ways is a wonderful leveller between players and fans, as well as a means of keeping the Athletic stars grounded. 'When you bring the players into a social project, the atmosphere changes and the people are very happy and a lot of beautiful things can happen,' explains Reguera. The players are undoubtedly the club's biggest ambassadors; what they do and say resonates. Generally, Athletic's stars are also very happy to volunteer their time; whether that is for a book club or to play corridor football with children in hospital. 'One of the incredible things about football is it is like an animal, it adapts to any space,' beams Reguera. 'Most games have not got 11 v 11. It is six v six or ten v five, if you play with the kids! We almost never play in a full team. We play in the square, we play in the streets and it is one of the most powerful things. Football is the best sport and it is so universal because you hardly need anything to play, even a ball. You can play with paper or the heart of the enemy!'

One day, a fan came to Reguera's office and explained how he had witnessed lots of children in hospital who wished to play football, whether that be with a soft ball or a pair of socks, but they were unable to leave the hospital to do so while having treatment. He suggested a championship of corridor football. 'I thought "wow, this is so powerful",' says Reguera. 'These children are going through pain and they spend all day in their bed. We went there, we talked with the hospitals, said we would bring some players to play with the children in the corridor and one of the beautiful things is we don't want to announce this, it must be a secret. One day, some players will come here, they will take a ball, go to the room and say to a child "do you want to play?" and the child says "what!" This kind of project is wonderful to a child but it is wonderful to the players, too. Many times, clubs say, "Just go to this [kind of] project and shut up, stay there, sign some autographs; if anyone asks you any questions, talk with the press officer and he will send you what you need to know ..." We go to the locker room and say, "We are going to organise a football corridor championship, who wants to come?" It is incredible and it is so beautiful. The players who have done it before just say to their team-mates it is very beautiful and they go happily. I think this relationship with the players and the experience of the people is the secret of the Athletic Club Foundation.'

The foundation, and the players, are involved in a number of similar projects; working with people with disabilities around inclusion in the community, for example. They also work in Basque hospitals with more than 600 adults who have mental health problems, providing hospitals the materials to play football and putting on coaching sessions. They then host a championship between the hospitals. 'Our model of the project is to be there every week with them,' says Reguera. 'They feel they are part of an important question for them, which is the club. They play with the emblem, they represent us when we go to play another club and we do a lot of things with them.'

Another of the most successful projects is the Thinking Football Film Festival, which has been running since 2013. Every year, the club screens around 14 films and follows these up with forums for the audience to discuss the topics, often social or political, with representatives from the film. It often attracts well-known names from the game; Ossie Ardiles, Ledley King, Thomas Hitzlsperger, Bob Bradley, Georgios Samaras. The list goes on. And then there are the Athletic players themselves, who are regular attendees. 'There was one moment I thought "Okay, we are doing a great job,"' says Reguera. 'It was to see Mikel Vesga waiting with the people to go into the cinema. He was just like anyone. I said to him "What are you doing, you can just go in!" And he said he didn't know, he just wanted to see the film. The star of the team, waiting with the people to go into the cinema, and he came because he wanted to see the film! He was so happy. At this moment, he was not a star of the club, he was just part of the community. It was wonderful.' One year, the festival even concluded with a rendition from Orsai, the band made up of Athletic Club footballers at the time – Vesga, De Marcos, Mikel Balenziaga, Iñigo Lekue and Asier Villalibre. Their most popular song is, of course, 'One Club Men'.

Previous winners at the film festival have included *Kenny*, which documents how Liverpool legend Kenny Dalglish's life became entwined with his adopted city; *Democracia em preto e branco* (Democracy in Black and White), a film about how football and music helped in the search for a more democratic Brazil; and *Next Goal Wins*, the story of the American Samoa national team, who once lost a game 31-0. 'It is very useful to the club in terms of thinking about the role of football in contemporary society,' explains Reguera. 'Because one of the problems for clubs is that they don't think too much about *why* football is so extraordinary. You feel your feelings are extraordinary, you feel they have always been there, you don't need to think too much [about why]. We have a very special club, I usually say we are a club of philosophers, because when you talk to a fan of Athletic Club, we are always thinking of who we are, where we are going and where we come from. They are the three big questions of philosophy. We are always thinking about the role of the club, what is the role of the club in the contemporary world, "Maybe this change in the world will be effective for the club ..." The film festival is a very good tool for a club to think about what their role is.'

One of the most unique projects, however, is something that encapsulates the passionate and unprecedented Basque rivalry between Athletic Club and Real Sociedad. It is a derby like no other, where fans mingle in the streets beforehand and in the stands, regardless of whether the stripes on their shirts are red or blue. They are clubs with two distinct identities but with a shared culture and heritage. 'Bertsolaritza' is the tradition of singing improvised songs in Basque; it's somewhere between improvised poetry and a rap battle. Before the Basque derby, Athletic versus La Real, you will find Bertsolari competing against one another, three versus three, a 'fight between poets' where they criticise, mock the other club or sing about relevant topics. It is all in good humour, of course. And organised by the clubs. The artists have even performed on the pitch at San Mamés before kick-off. 'We are very close rivals. We hate each other very much,' says Reguera. 'But only in the stadium. We go together to the stadium. We are friends, them with their shirts, us with our shirts. We discuss a lot but we are friends. There have never been problems in the stands. You can go with your Athletic Club shirt and stand with Real Sociedad fans and there will be no problem. This kind of rivalry shows what football has to be. It is a symbolic rivalry. As fans, there is a beautiful bond when there is a rivalry. I saw one of these [Bertsolaritza] and thought it was very similar to a football rivalry. If you don't understand the symbolic question, you may feel they hate each other.'

Indeed, one of the biggest travesties in Basque football in recent years is that the Coronavirus pandemic denied fans the chance to witness the first Copa del Rey Final between Athletic Club and Real Sociedad in 112 years of rivalry. The match was due to be played in 2020 but was delayed by 12 months to give supporters the best chance of being able to attend. Come April 2021, restrictions in Spain meant that was still not possible and the game took place behind closed doors at Seville's La Cartuja Stadium. Back in Bilbao, a minority of fans clashed with police who tried to prevent them gathering in groups to watch the game together near San Mamés. La Real won 1-0, clinching a first major trophy since 1987. Athletic got another shot at ending their own drought two weeks later, when they faced Barcelona in the final of the 2021 edition. Back in Seville, however, they were beaten in a sixth successive final, and second in as many weeks, as the Catalan giants ran out 4-0 winners.

Three years later, Athletic earned another chance to end their trophy drought. 'It would mean a lot because a lot of generations have never seen Athletic win a Copa. It is a dream for all the lads that have come up through the ranks,' Iñaki Williams, one of the team's stars alongside younger brother Nico, told me before the final, as Athletic hosted a packed pre-final media day at Lezama. The anticipation in Bilbao was tangible. A city decked in red and white, from metro stations kitted out like San Mamés to bridal shops with Athletic Club scarves draped around the shoulders of their wedding dress mannequins, and everything in between. Back in Seville, with fans allowed to travel this time, more than 100,000 descended on the city by plane, train or epic drive from the north of Spain to the south. They laughed together, sang Athletic songs and hundreds even serenaded a newly married couple in one of the city's picturesque squares. The most magical thing was just being there together. 'I went to the final with my son,' explains Reguera. 'It was two days, 18 hours of car journeys. But the important thing was to share the moments we will remember for all our lives – this first trip together to a final. And it was incredible. The important thing was the travel!'

The journey back was made sweeter by the fact Athletic won, on penalties, fans travelling deep into the night or, in fact, even the early hours of the following morning by the time the final concluded. 'Thank you to our extraordinary fans for their faith and unwavering devotion,' professed manager Ernesto Valverde afterwards. 'They've shown the world what Athletic is about. If there's anyone out there, wherever you're from, who now wants to support Athletic, we'll welcome you with open arms.'

That was a poignant message. Athletic's critics suggest the club's policy of only selecting Basque players is xenophobic or racist. The club refute that, of course, and it is a policy only applied to the playing squad. Managers and fans are welcomed from around the world. Indeed, Howard Kendall, Marcelo Bielsa and Fred Pentland, one of Athletic's most successful bosses and whom the international supporters' club is named after, are all celebrated honorary sons of Bilbao. The club's uniquely endearing nature can captivate even the most hardened football souls, Basque or otherwise.

Born in Mexico, it was curiosity about his Basque heritage that led Gaizka Atxa, one of the Mr Pentland

Club's founders, to support Athletic Club. Now, he lives in Bilbao and was in Seville for the final. And, of course, two of the club's biggest stars are the Williams brothers, whose parents are Ghanaian. Atxa says it has been rewarding to see how Athletic Club have evolved over time. 'Athletic is a reflection of our society here and seeing the Williams brothers flourish means that any immigrant or son of immigrants has a decent opportunity to play for our club,' he adds.

The Williams brothers' story is in itself remarkable and inspirational, never mind the barriers they have broken by becoming the first black players to star for Athletic, following in the footsteps of one-time Angola international Jonás Ramalho, who played a handful of games for the club after his debut in 2011. 'We had to suffer a lot,' Iñaki told me. 'But thanks to God we are all here together now, living a really good life. My parents are getting to watch their sons prosper, which is why they came here. Everything we do is for our parents. We have to be grateful to them, and we thank God that we have such a good life now.' Their mother, Maria, was pregnant with Iñaki when she left Ghana with his father, Felix, and crossed part of the Sahara barefoot. Felix burned his feet on the scorching hot sand and the couple had to jump a border fence at the Spanish territory of Melilla in North Africa to find safety. They were advised by a lawyer to say they were from war-torn Liberia and seek political asylum. The couple wound up in Bilbao and were introduced to Catholic priest Inaki Mardones when Maria was seven months pregnant. He found them an apartment, took them to the hospital where Iñaki was born and he became his godfather, even introducing the young boy to Athletic, gifting him a red and white football shirt. Iñaki donned the same classic jersey, with Kappa print down the arms, while lifting the Copa del Rey trophy in Seville.

'If you look at the latest signings for the youth teams, you have a strong number of black players,' explains journalist Beñat Gutiérrez. 'It was just part of the historical process of the country. The Basque Country got a lot of immigrants but they were coming from other parts of Spain, therefore they were mainly white. And then African immigrants started coming in the late 80s, early 90s, probably the bigger influx in the 2000s. It was just younger adult men who were not ready to start a sports career here. It has been a process until we are seeing the sons or even the grandsons of those new Basque citizens that are starting to be really important for Athletic.'

Nothing highlights the new face or globalisation of Bilbao more than the incredible celebrations on the River Nervión five days after the Copa del Rey Final. Videos and pictures from the early 1980s, when Athletic won back-to-back La Liga titles and the double in 1984, portray an industrial city with shipyards, steelworks and factories billowing out smoke as a backdrop to the celebratory boats cruising through murky waters. 'Bilbao was dirtier!' exclaims Gutiérrez. Now, with the gleaming Guggenheim on a clean and attractive waterfront, it is a renewed and revitalised city of services and culture, with input from renowned architects across the world. On the day of this Copa del Rey celebration, because there were many impromptu ones in the week prior, including veteran Iker Muniain dancing on fans' shoulders in an old-town street party that brought a ticking-off and a fine from local police, there are a million sets of eyeballs locked on the Nervión. La Gabarra holds almost mythical status in Bilbao. Fans, players and media alike were all wary of mentioning the barge on which the 1980s team celebrated in the build-up to the final for fear of jinxing proceedings, adding a seventh successive loss to the pile and extending the 40-year wait for a major trophy. But, finally, the blue barge with a red bottom earned its day in the Bilbao sunshine. Athletic players sporting tailored red-and-white smart shirts with crisp collars, matching the 1984 team, board with the Copa del Rey trophy, shaking hands and high-fiving fans on the way. Iñaki Williams wears his shirt unbuttoned, white vest beneath, shades on, uber cool, shaking the trophy to the sky. Members of the 1984 team join them, along with legend José Ángel Iribar, of course.

Fans line the route from the beginning of the estuary at Bartola, others hang from balconies with flags, waving and cheering La Gabarra along its two-hour journey, past San Mamés to the Bilbao City Hall steps. Many follow on the water in 160 boats and all manner of vessels, anything that will float. They include Barcelona defender Iñigo Martínez, who spent five seasons with Athletic. Some players scatter red and white petals in memory of those who are no longer around to witness the celebrations. Tears of joy and remembrance among the watching fans run both red and white. Ultimately, it is a day that solidifies the idea that Athletic Club is about much more than just football. Being an Athletic fan is a sense of shared identity. Winning, losing, crying, just being together. It is a unique, collective belief.

'It is important to understand that, always, football is secondary,' concludes Galder Reguera. 'There are a few people who go to the stadium alone, they go to meet people they only know from the stadium. When we changed from the old San Mamés to the new, there was the possibility to choose your place with your friends you met in the old stadium. Two guys forgot to put their names together and they didn't know anything about the other, apart from going to the football! They were trying to find the other one, talking with other people, "Do you know this guy? He hates Fernando Llorente? He has two feet!?" They knew nothing about each other.' Somehow, Athletic fans, obliged by a sense of care to their elderly companions, managed to connect the dots and reacquaint the old friends. Now, they sit side by side again in the new San Mamés. 'In the end, they are together,' smiles Reguera. 'It is a very special relationship.' Perhaps that is the power of 'The Cathedral', the unifying force of Athletic Club. In the end, it is about belonging.

Chapter Two

The Mighty Penguins

IT WAS while in Bilbao that Dan Parry – who, if we are talking about the most generous and genuine people in football, must be right up there – mentioned a project that has touched his heart and that of many others. A few months before our visit, Parry and Galder Reguera were part of an Athletic Club entourage who welcomed Brentford Penguins to Bilbao. Parry, who works in Athletic Club's communications department, calls it 'one of the best weekends of my life'.

The Penguins are a very special team, a not-for-profit organisation set up in 2017 for children with Down's Syndrome who are coached every Sunday morning by former Brentford and Tottenham midfielder Allan Cockram. Flying to Bilbao and travelling on Athletic Club's first-team coach, getting waved at by fans as they passed through the city, was a long way from sessions on 'Dog Shit Park', as Cockram jokingly calls their usual home. As was Athletic's training base at Lezama, where the Penguins faced Athletic Genuine, a team representing the Basque club that is made up of players with intellectual disabilities and who usually compete in La Liga Genuine. There was Cockram with his team, president Ollie, captain Charlie, 'Special K', coach 'Big D' and the rest of the gang, donned in red and white stripes, names on their backs, proud smiles that would transcend any language barriers. And on the other side, with his kids in Athletic's changed light blue strip, Igor Arenaza, who bore a striking resemblance to Cockram in both looks and personality. 'I called him "Bilbao Al",' laughs the Englishman. The kids celebrated every goal in front of their parents in the stands – captain Charlie performed the Cristiano Ronaldo *Siuuu!* – and fans watching a youth team game on the adjacent pitch found themselves, instead, drawn in by Athletic Genuine versus the Penguins. 'You had the mums and dads of the next generation of Spanish superstars watching our match,' says Louis Myles, director and producer of *Mighty Penguins*, a documentary about the club that was being shown at Athletic's Thinking Football Film Festival that weekend.

Myles, whose uncle has Down's Syndrome, has created a film that is raw, powerful, emotional and funny, all at the same time. 'My pitch to all of them was I want to tell this as it is,' adds Myles, talking about what he said when approaching Cockram and the parents. 'This should not feel like it is on Comic Relief. "Oh wow, isn't this sad." I want to enter your worlds and show that it's shit but also brilliant at the same time.' And that he does, with unerring authenticity.

The Penguins' story is an incredible journey that began with just four children at a school sports hall in West Ealing and has since taken them to the big screen, not just in Bilbao but also New York, where they watched the documentary premiere at Robert De Niro's Tribeca Film Festival. 'We had a message from Ted Lasso the other day; he was in bits watching it,' adds Myles. They have appeared on NBC Sports' live Premier League coverage in Chicago, formed a guard of honour at Brentford, where they high-fived stars Bryan Mbeumo and Yoane Wissa, been for lunch with Gordon Ramsay and hung out with David Beckham and his son, Romeo, who presented Cockram with the Unsung Hero prize as part of *The Sun*'s Who Cares Wins awards. 'The whole thing was crazy,' laughs Cockram, reflecting on the 'Father Christmas moment' when he met one of England's most legendary midfielders. 'I could smell him! I turned around and he and Romeo were there. For two hours, the pair of them were amazing, down to earth, very interested in the children and knew how to handle the kids. He said, "Whatever you need, just ask …"' Beckham followed that up by sending Cockram a signed Inter Miami shirt, as the coach considered what he should request. In the end, he decided to ask Romeo to be an ambassador. 'We got the kids, Louis and Charlie, to send him videos. He said he loved it. We have had videos from him and he's been to see us. It's a two-way thing, because even though you are a Beckham, you need your identity as well, otherwise you're just David's son. As a father, I understand that. And now, with the Penguins, he's found a bit of himself in that as a young man.'

Then, at the end of 2024, they took part in *Miracles,* the TV Christmas special by magician Steven Frayne, aka Dynamo. 'It took me days to recover because I could not work it out,' says Cockram. 'I love all that. I like to believe in certain things because it is transcendent of being a kid again, you know? He is showing me stuff up close and I'm still like, "What the fuck has just gone on there?" The reaction of the children was "What!?"' Cockram even had a chance meeting with the magician on his way to the toilets, where he asked to see a quick trick. 'He got a £2 coin and it levitated from his bottom hand to his top hand from about 2ft away. He's just pulled it out his pocket. What he did blew me away!'

The Penguins might now be mini-celebrities in their own right but the real magic, and the most important thing of all, is how that initial group of four kids has blossomed into a huge community of more than 50 players and hundreds of family members and carers, who support each other and spend time together for a couple of hours every Sunday morning with Cockram, his wife, Vickie, and their team of volunteers. 'Without the volunteers, we don't have a club,' insists Cockram, though it is he who has inspired the project.

Cockram spent ten years at Spurs after signing as a schoolboy, breaking into the first team and making two appearances in the 1983/84 season in a midfield that also included Glenn Hoddle and Ossie Ardiles. He was released the following year and a nomadic career saw him feature mostly at Brentford and St Albans City. He was something of a maverick, with locks as flamboyant as his footwork. That made him a fans' favourite. Cockram, however, ultimately feels his refusal to conform cost him his professional career. There followed coaching spells with St

Albans, Chertsey Town and the San Francisco Flyers, as well as an attempt to break into the US market alongside ex-Wimbledon forward Gary Blissett, a former team-mate at Brentford, with their bespoke training sessions choreographed to a backbeat of house and dance music. Other drills used blindfolds to help improve the senses and awareness of players, something they devised after working with England's national blind team.

Between those ventures, Cockram worked as a firefighter and then a taxi driver. 'I was brought up on football, so you don't think you'll do anything different,' he explains, able now to talk about the harsh reality that comes when you are thrown on the 'scrapheap'. Going from the endorphin-fuelled highs of scoring goals and wowing fans to no longer making money from playing football – and facing the mental and emotional challenges that come with it – is tough. 'Sometimes, life throws curveballs at you and you have to be malleable,' he says. 'And, the truth is, when I join the dots backwards, it is all meant to be. It is bizarre, you can't predict the forward path of your life. But when you join the dots of major events, you can see how it has all ended up, good and bad.'

It was while working as a taxi driver in the 1990s that Cockram met Phil, a teenager with Down's Syndrome. Phil would sit in the front of his cab. They would sing and dance together on the journey to school and get out to have a kickaround. One day, however, Cockram got the message that Phil had passed away. It was then that he vowed to find a way to provide youngsters with Down's Syndrome the opportunity to participate in the game together. Years later, that ambition came to fruition.

Cockram visited professional clubs to see how they were working with Down's Syndrome children but it was only when he began training them himself that he realised he needed to rip up any planned drills and just go with the flow of the kids. 'From the beginning, we decided there was no age group minimum and no disability maximum,' he explains. 'Whereas, before I started, I looked at pro clubs and what they were doing. It was cool, we can get the kids playing football … and then, in my first training session, I kicked all the cones away and winged it for 18 months, because the truth wasn't really being told about Down's Syndrome. People were only taking the upper echelons of comprehension rate.' Cockram has a team of older kids he trains who he says 'get football'. 'But honestly,' he adds, 'I would say 85 per cent of our children will never play in a game. So what has happened to those 85 per cent in all the bigger clubs? How do you have discrimination within disability? You can't, so we don't! It's any age, any disability and we have tailored the training sessions to each group.'

With the number of players signed on, they have also trained a team of volunteers to help. 'They are amazing,' says Cockram, who alongside wife, Vickie, also runs an over-55s men's mental health walking football team and a women's over-40s walking football team. Not all the Penguins make it to every session; the most Cockram has counted is 38. 'A lot of the kids get ill. Or they'll have not slept. A lot of them have sleep deprivation. A lot don't recognise hours. One of our kids will read all night under the covers and then, in the morning, he is knackered and needs to sleep.' But, as he points out, organising a session for 38 kids at academy level would be hard enough. 'To have 38 children of mixed disability and mixed ages is nigh on impossible,' he explains. Instead, Cockram thinks of it as building a community where football is the glue. 'It is the hardest coaching session in the world,' he beams. 'But it is the most rewarding coaching session I have ever done.'

And, despite being a wonderful environment for the kids to enjoy, the project has, perhaps, an even bigger impact on the parents. They have confidence in Cockram and his team that they can disappear for a coffee and a chat for a couple of hours while the youngsters are playing football or they can discuss any problems that arise with other like-minded parents, from issues at school to which specialist doctors can treat certain ailments. 'The kids are the kids. It's like any group or team or whatever; they only see what they see and they just get on with it,' says Cockram. 'It is the parents that are the second team and the siblings, the nans, the carers, all of them, that can finally not have to answer for their child. We are in a bigger group than most every Sunday – there are over 100 people – and they feel part of something that is a little bit bigger than themself. They know that the myriad of problems they go through, they are not on their own, because all the other parents preceding them have been through that problem, no matter how hard that problem is. I think, really, it is the parents who get the biggest deal out of this. And a lot of brothers and sisters get a bad rap; they grow up very quickly. They are really amazing children, they seem to have adulthood before their time. They love joining in, the fun of it. Because that's what it is at the end of the day – fun.'

'Al's not created a centre, he's created a community, and that's the point,' adds Myles, who shot the documentary over a three-month period with the Penguins. 'It works because every football team in the Premier League has some sort of special needs team but most of them do it professionally. Al just wings it. His jokes are very close to the bone! It's not a politically correct place. I am not saying that is the reason it works but it is that attitude of permitting people to be okay, if that makes sense? It comes with emotion. You just wouldn't get it if you had an allotted hour where people are actually trying to get you to do exercises. Al gets that he is there to make the kids' lives better but he is also really there to help this community. All those kids have broken parents, a fair amount split up because it's difficult, and for the ones that don't, it is still just hard.'

In the documentary, Charlie's mum explains: 'He has always known he's got Down's Syndrome. He recognised very early on when he used to watch things on television. He'd go, "That's my brother, he looks like me." I went to Penguins so he could actually have friendships. And it wasn't just that *he* got friendships. I had friendships where I didn't have to explain my son. It was just like being with family.'

Down's Syndrome children are born with an extra chromosome, which often leads to some level of learning disability, although the impact of this varies widely. During the Coronavirus pandemic and the resulting lockdowns, many of the kids Cockram coaches at the Brentford Penguins struggled to understand why they were no longer allowed to go outside or had to keep a certain distance from their friends. 'They were putting their Penguins kit on and then there was no training and they couldn't understand why,' he explains. 'A few of the kids had to be taken to the GTech [Brentford's stadium] to show them it was closed on a matchday. And why *would* they understand?'

Cockram also found the restrictions challenging. He was diagnosed with ADHD during the pandemic, which he felt helped explain a lot about his life up until that point. 'I have been through some bad stuff but Covid was up there because of me rattling about like a caged lion,' he adds. 'I lost the plot. But I was getting frantic phone calls from parents because the kids are similar to me, in a way. My brain is quite formulaic. If I don't understand something, I try to find out why, because it doesn't make sense to me. And the children are the same.'

They tried online training and other methods to get the kids engaged. Cockram, an incredible artist, says he missed the children like a parent would and drew pictures for them. Restrictions meant they were not allowed back inside the school gym but, after taking a pleading call from a parent, they decided to take the project outside. 'I took personal responsibility for three or four of the kids losing all their hair,' says Cockram. 'I just went "fuck this". In the end I was like, "I ain't having it. You know what, fuck everyone, let's go outside." We just had to bite the bullet and think "What is the scale of this?" We put it to the parents and they said "No, get them out." We went to the park and it is where the Penguins really took off, because we had socially distanced training and educated the parents in training their children.' But not everyone was happy. 'We got abused,' laughs Cockram. 'Me and my wife got abused by people in the park! The kids did not understand social distancing. Well, why should they? They're jumping all over me – and I didn't give a shit anyway – and the parents were just like "I can breathe". To have children of a certain age locked in all day is one thing but then to put disability on top of that – and disability where they don't understand why they can't go outside – is a whole new ball game.'

Getting outside was a relief for the parents, the players and, also, Cockram. In many ways, he needs the kids as much as they need the Penguins. 'Because of my brain and what I have been through in the past, it kind of focuses me,' he admits. 'I have been through my own journey as well. I felt with the film, I trusted Louis because of his uncle, who had Down's Syndrome, and I knew he was on point. I felt I had to bare my soul a little bit, because the parents were. It was cathartic for me. It has taught me to meditate and calm down and discover the way my brain works and how to handle myself. It has been my journey, as well as the kids', and they have kind of run parallel. It was the perfect storm at the perfect time and that is why it is unique.'

Interestingly, Myles feels the same about the time he got to spend with the Penguins while filming. 'Someone would have made that film and I'm glad it was me,' he says. 'It helped me. It will be the best thing

I ever do. I didn't know I needed it but I did. It's been amazing.'

And that is because, as Cockram explains, spending time with children with Down's Syndrome is like being around your best friends. It's a privilege. 'All these kids are on a different timeline to ours and we don't know their timeline,' he adds. 'Unless I get a terrible illness, I am dead in, say, 20 years … let's put it that way. But they are not like that. They are on a different timeline because of the way Down's Syndrome works. I am seeing people like "Special K" and the only way I can describe her is like an angel, because that evokes something in your brain; it is like she has been here before. She is 16 but it's almost like she has got her nan in her and her great nan. When she cuddles you, it is bizarre – it's just this crazy feeling.' Cockram describes the children as 'gurus'. 'If you go blind, your hearing comes into play more,' he says. 'With these kids, because they are deficient in certain areas, they seem to have this thing of what we should all be – there is no filter. They say it as it is and there is no kidding them. You can have a kid who can't communicate but if he doesn't like you, he tells you in his own way. It is almost like they are the best of human beings without knowing it. We always say "I try to be myself …" but the truth of the matter is, you are never always yourself, because you are always saying certain things to your boss or your wife. You will be one thing to one person and one thing to another. And these kids aren't. It is just being around amazing human beings. You can never be down! If I have a blip of 20 minutes, all I think of is "Special K", how did she get to training in her wheelchair? And it's gone, that's the reality of it. You haven't got time to feel sorry for yourself or be down or negative, because these kids just aren't. And they have the right to be negative but they're not.'

For the Penguins, the experiences they have been able to enjoy, from meeting Brentford manager Thomas Frank and his players to attending film premieres across the world, have been special. But there is a deeper meaning to the publicity awarded to them off the back of the documentary. For Cockram, that is to highlight Down's Syndrome to the wider population and provoke conversations about facilities and funding. 'I didn't do it to go to Bilbao,' says Cockram. 'I didn't do it to meet the Beckhams or get awards. Because if you said to me tomorrow it's all finished and you're going to go back to the same four kids, I would do exactly the same thing. My job is to highlight to the masses these children and if people can help me fast-track that, then I will use that. I'm trying to help you lot! Because, unless you have met Down's Syndrome children and been privy to them, you are missing out. They are so amazing. I'm fortunate. I live in Down's Syndrome world and I see the benefits of it all. It is my happy place.'

It just so happens that for players, parents and siblings, Sunday mornings spent with the community created by Cockram and the rest of the Penguins is their happy place, too.

Chapter Three

A Parisian Derby

SATURDAY LUNCHTIME in the northern suburbs of Paris and tourists are getting lost in the labyrinth of alleyways, stalls and small units that make up the Saint-Ouen flea market. Heading in from Porte de Clignancourt, either side of the bridges under the Périphérique, Paris' dual carriageway ring road, lurk stalls selling knock-off designer gear, football shirts and flashy trainers. Beyond an outer ring of counterfeit goods, the old market unfurls like an onion. Each layer of narrow spellbinding lanes and treasure-packed cul-de-sacs reveals rare antiques, vintage furniture and second-hand ornaments you never knew you wanted. Over one shoulder, an ancient Japanese samurai suit; over the other, grand pianos, chandeliers, silks and woollen rugs. Each corner opens up a new world: bric-à-brac, toys, glassware, art. More than 2,500 traders congregate here across 12 covered markets and five designated streets, along with many other stalls flanking the pavements, to make Saint-Ouen the largest flea market in the world. Some five million visitors are attracted each year to a spot that traders first claimed in the late 1800s but some of the goods on sale date back even further. It is vast but also hidden, an endearing maze of magical trinkets that can prove hard to escape.

The market, however, may just be the second-biggest attraction on this particular Saturday in September, with another of Saint-Ouen's historic institutions garnering significant attention of their own. Neighbouring the sprawling maze of stalls and sellers is the Stade Bauer, home to France's fourth-oldest football club and the longest-running team in Paris. Red Star are preparing to host local rivals Paris FC for the first time in more than five years. In fact, it has been almost a decade since this derby was played at their iconic home ground. The clubs sit geographically at opposite axes of the French capital, Red Star in the north and Paris FC to the south, and, traditionally, their fans are on opposing ends of the political spectrum. They share a city but their identities could not be more conflicting. Today, though, they take to the same pitch.

Red Star Club Français were founded in 1897 in a small Parisian cafe by a group of friends that included one Jules Rimet. Rimet was a devout Catholic. His father, a grocer, moved to Paris when he was a child, initially leaving the young Rimet with his grandfather in the small village of Theuley-les-Lavoncourt, in eastern France, where he was an altar server and choirboy. By age 11, Rimet followed his father to Paris and was exposed to the harsh, working-class conditions of the capital. Yet, Rimet defied the class boundaries of the time to become a lawyer. He was not overly interested in football, rather fencing and running, but the sport was growing in popularity – albeit somewhat looked down upon by the French bourgeoisie – and was seen by Rimet and his friends as a way of promoting social harmony. Crucially, with Rimet a self-made man, Red Star were formed on the basis of equality and inclusion, a sports club that did not discriminate based on class. With Rimet behind them, Red Star can, perhaps, claim to have laid the foundations for what would become the most recognised football tournament on the planet, the World Cup. Rimet, of course, would go on to become one of the founders of the Fédération Internationale de Football Association – or FIFA, as we know it – and serve as president for 33 years from 1921 to 1954. He is widely credited as the architect of the World Cup, taking it to Uruguay for the first edition in 1930, and the trophy was later renamed in his honour.

There are different stories about where the name Red Star emerged from. Despite many fans' left-leaning stance and the club's reputation for being working class, it does not derive from communism. One tale links it to the red star of Buffalo Bill but the more widely accepted version is that it stems from the Red Star Line, a famous shipping route, and was suggested by British governess Miss Jenny, who took one of the Red Star Line steamers from the UK to work for Rimet in Paris and became an almost matriarchal figure to those at the club. But Red Star's rich and unique history goes beyond just the name. They were hugely successful in the Coupe de France between 1921 and 1942, winning it five times. Then, during World War Two, during German occupation, a number of Red Star players joined the French Resistance and the stadium was used to stash weapons. One of those players to join the resistance was 19-year-old winger Rino Della Negra, the son of Italian immigrants, who joined the Manouchian Group led by Armenian poet and activist Missak Manouchian until both were, along with 20 of their comrades, captured and executed by the Nazis in 1944. Before he died, Della Negra was able to send a letter to his brother in which he said: 'Send farewell and hello to all of Red Star.' Thus, he has become a legendary figure at the club and someone Red Star honoured with the unveiling of a plaque in 2004, 60 years after his death.

Since 1909, Red Star have played at Stade Bauer, itself named after a member of the Resistance from Saint-Ouen, Dr Jean-Claude Bauer. The ground, which also hosted football at the 1924 Olympics, was previously known as Stade de Paris but became known locally by the street it adorned, the one named Rue du Dr Bauer, following Paris' liberation. Now, redevelopment works are in full flow on a new-look 10,000-capacity arena that will meet Ligue 1 standards. The plans are not universally adored among the Red Star faithful but there is an acceptance they are needed. Over the past decade, Red Star have had to play elsewhere because their ageing home did not even meet Ligue 2 requirements. They played first at Stade Jean-Bouin, next to the Parc des Princes, and then at Stade Pierre Brisson, an hour's drive away in Beauvais. Relegation to the third tier, where there are more relaxed ground regulations, meant that Red Star were able to return home in 2019. They have been able to stay there after winning promotion back to Ligue 2, thanks to the opening of an impressive new 4,700-capacity stand as part of the renovations.

Wandering around the corner from the flea market, Stade Bauer is partially hidden by the ongoing construction work; just the peeping heads of floodlights give away its location. Across the road is L'Olympic de Saint-Ouen, a meeting place for Red Star fans. The green banner wrapped around the outside of the pub matches that of the club's jersey. It claims to be a cafe and hotel, although the clothes hung out to dry from the windows above suggest those rooms may be lived in now. Nevertheless, it is certainly a popular watering hole. A couple of hours before kick-off, fans are already starting to mingle outside. One of them is George Boxall, who has been following the club since he moved to Paris in 2019, attracted by the stories and the atmosphere at Stade Bauer. 'I don't think you generally go to Red Star for the quality of football on show,' he laughs, 'especially around the time I started going, when they were struggling at the bottom of the third division. I was kind of fascinated by the visual aspect of what Stade Bauer used to be. You'd walk in that place and really feel a sense of historical presence. It's like when you're a kid and watch your first match; you have that same kind of feeling. Then I was inspired by the atmosphere the supporters created and their values, as well as the stories of Rino Della Negra and Jean-Claude Bauer. I was just fascinated by the political and social side of the club.'

Inside L'Olympic, the decor is slightly fading, vintage perhaps, and the walls punctuated by nods to the football club across the road. Red Star posters line the bar and supporters in green and white edge in to buy a round before shuffling back out to serve their friends on the street. Yasin, the barman, pours us a Picon. It's a pint with an extra kick, one accompanied by a shot of an orangey liqueur. It warms you from the inside out. 'It's a massive part of my life now,' adds Boxall, talking about his matchday ritual rather than just the Picon he is sipping. 'That is all part of the experience, the community aspect of going down to L'Olympic. And at first you don't know everyone. I would just go down for the atmosphere, because it was something amazing, but now it's almost on another level.'

Boxall, tall, broad-shouldered and English, is hard to miss in the crowd. But he is also fully embedded in Red Star and Saint-Ouen culture, having written his dissertation on the identity of the club and the supporters. He's lived in Saint-Ouen and seen the rate of change. Walking through the neighbourhood now, the area is a blend of old and new, with cranes mapping the skyline as the gentrification continues. 'All of the changes happening in the city are also kind of reflected in who's now coming to games and reflected in the fact that the renovation is happening,' he explains. 'The rate of change around the club is so, so quick. Sometimes it's hard to imagine that only a year and a half ago we were still in that old stand.'

Once considered a rough and working-class area, with predominantly social housing, families are now moving out of the city to Saint-Ouen, where there is more space and affordable homes. 'You go to one part of the town and it's kind of new-builds, families in their 30s or 40s moving out of Paris, and all very quiet,' says Boxall. 'It feels like a separate place to another side of Saint-Ouen, which is just the flea markets and bits that have lasted a bit longer but have seen a lot of change. That division is funny. I can talk about the city of Saint-Ouen but that applies directly to what is going on around the club.'

Red Star have become something of a cult club because of their passionate fanbase, community values and hip, uber-cool demeanour. They are well known across the world, not just in France, in part because of their trendy, sought-after merchandise and creative marketing. David Bellion, the club's former striker and creative director, remembers being stunned when he saw someone in Tokyo wearing an extremely rare orange Red Star shirt. The club had only produced 20 of the jerseys, to be sold at a shop in Paris. Despite a long and distinguished history, movements since the turn of the millennium have shaped the way the club are seen today. Relegated to the fourth tier in 2001, Red Star lost their professional status. Then, saddled with debts of €1.5m, they spiralled further down the French football pyramid and ended up playing in the sixth tier between 2003 and 2005. They climbed back into Ligue 2 for the 2014/15 season and missed out on promotion to Ligue 1 by a point. They have since yo-yoed between the second and third divisions. That meant being in and out of Stade Bauer, until 2019. A prolonged period back home has brought the crowd back, too, with many fixtures sold out. 'It has completely changed since I came to the club in 2015,' explains Paul Ducassou, the club's communications director. 'We have spent so much time on "How do we bring people to the stadium?" Now it is completely insane that it is no longer a topic. It shows how the club has developed and how the club can be noisy in our area and even more in all of Paris.' Now, even football fans visiting from out of town want a glimpse of Red Star. Ducassou recalls finding two Real Sociedad fans at the ground when they were in the city for the Basque side's Champions League clash with Paris Saint-Germain. 'They found their way to my office with an old picture of Real Sociedad against Red Star,' he laughs. 'During the Olympic Games, many people came from everywhere to take a look at the stadium.'

On derby day, police vans line the streets and officers in riot gear form a human dam to direct the flow of away fans into the correct end. At one point, around 30 blokes in black tops with hoods pulled up and tightened around their jaws bounce past on their tiptoes in a hurry. The heavy police presence dilutes some of the bloodthirsty energy and the moment is defused. There are reports of earlier scuffles elsewhere but, around the stadium, the supporters seem to be kept at a good distance. 'When it comes to the rivalry it is very localised between the ultra groups,' explains Boxall. 'You are not going to have a random group of Red Star supporters and Paris FC supporters fighting. It is within the ultra groups, the real hatred between each other.' There is the obvious geographical rivalry but also a political difference of opinion. 'Red Star fans are more left-wing and Paris FC fans are more right-wing,' explains French football journalist Raphaël Jucobin. 'Or at least that's the general perception and that's where their respective ultra groups have leaned in the past.'

The majority of home fans pack into the main stand, with Red Star's more hardcore following congregating to one end in the raucous Kop. The small contingent of away fans are sent into the far corner, behind the goal in the Tribune Sud, where there is room for 800 people next to the VIP and hospitality boxes. Behind the terrace stands the iconic, diagonally rising apartment block that has become a recognisable part of the Bauer landscape. The far side of the ground, opposite the main stand, is still a building site, with TV camera crews picking their spot on the mounds of earth running parallel to the pitch. At the north end, work is well under way on what will be the new Rino Della Negra Stand and a community space behind it, with offices, collaborative workspaces, shops and health services.

In the Kop, huge flags are unveiled. One sports an image of Rino Della Negra, another a skull and crossbones wearing a Red Star cap. One flag has 1897, the year the club were founded, sketched on it. Banners are draped over the front barriers and green flare smoke wafts over a crowd packed tightly together as if wanting to share their collective warmth on a chilly afternoon. Kids with oversized green and white scarves dangling by their knees look for a foot up. Grown men perch on the railings to rally the masses. Then, a rival flag is unfurled. Red Star share a friendship with Ligue 2 peers Grenoble Foot 38 and fans have been known to go and support the team from the south-east of France when they have previously played in the capital against Paris FC. Boxall says it was on one such visit that Red Star ultras managed to pinch the flag of rival group

Ultras Lutetia. 'No one knew about it until on the day against Paris FC,' he explains. 'They weren't going to bring out the flag originally because it is a derby game but we don't necessarily hate them that much. But then there were a lot of Paris FC fans opening their mouths on Twitter and that kind of thing, so there was a decision made to bring out the Lutetia flag upside down. That signifies you have taken a banner from another group and is a big shame on them. They burnt it down the bottom of the stand with a flare.'

Of the three main clubs in the French capital, Paris FC are perhaps the most curious. What Paris Saint-Germain stand for is obvious, especially since the investment of Qatar Sports Investments in 2011. They are a huge brand who transcend French football, endorsed by the past signings of some of the game's biggest names; Lionel Messi, Kylian Mbappé, Neymar Jr, Zlatan Ibrahimović and so on. 'If you're born in Paris, you're going to support Paris Saint-Germain if you want glory and all of that,' says Boxall. In many ways, PSG are the perfect opposite to Red Star. 'They have got the Eiffel Tower, we come from the neighbourhood,' adds Ducassou. As David Bellion, the former Manchester United and Sunderland striker, puts it: 'PSG are a blockbuster movie, Red Star an indie film.' But Paris FC? One Red Star fan describes them as 'PSG from Wish'. 'They are a club who have what Red Star don't have and Red Star have what Paris FC don't have,' adds Boxall. 'The identity of Red Star is built a lot differently from Paris FC and Paris Saint-Germain.'

What Paris FC do have is formidably wealthy backers. The family of Bernaud Arnault, named by

Forbes as the richest man in the world in 2024, bought a majority stake in the club in late 2024. They also have the nous of the Red Bull Football Group to call upon after it purchased a smaller, minority share of the club. 'Red Bull is by our side because we know what we're good at and what we're not. We have management skills but none in football operations,' said Antoine Arnault when the agreement was announced. Antoine is the son of Bernaud and represents the family on the Paris FC board. 'This is a family project we started with my brothers and sister,' he added. 'We thought it was a good idea to venture into something more thrilling than our usual activities. Football has been my passion since I was ten years old.'

Previously, between 2020 and 2024, the Kingdom of Bahrain held a 20 per cent stake, so Paris FC were hardly up against it. But the involvement of the Arnault family has the potential to blow other clubs out of the water. 'There was never going to be a PSG-like project there for Bahrain,' explains Jucobin. 'The only time they started spending properly was last summer and you get the feeling that was because they knew the current takeover was going to happen and were preparing for that.'

Arnault is the chairman and CEO of LVMH Moët Hennessy Louis Vuitton, the luxury goods company which boasts an extensive armoury also including Fendi, Givenchy, TAG Heuer, Christian Dior, Dom Pérignon and many, many more. 'Paris FC have been around for a while but it does feel like the dawn of a new project that is going places,' concedes Boxall. 'They've had the investment from Bahrain, they have used that to get in the position they are in and now they are going to take that next step with Arnault.'

If Paris FC are more akin to PSG than Red Star, it is because they were once the same club. Founded in 1969, the following year Paris FC merged with Stade Saint-Germain to form Paris Saint-Germain. But in 1972, they split. Paris FC kept their place in Ligue 1, playing at the Parc des Princes, and Paris Saint-Germain were sent to the third tier. That all changed within a matter of years as the clubs trended in opposite directions, PSG reaching Ligue 1 and Paris FC slipping away, last playing in the top flight in 1979.

While PSG have the profile and Red Star the history, Paris FC have struggled to find something original to attract fans to their games at the 20,000-capacity Stade Charléty, a ground they rent from the city council and share with third-tier side Paris 13 Atletico, rugby union team Paris Université Club and a number of athletics clubs. In November 2023, they started giving away home tickets for free, although the season's average attendance remained at just under 5,500. 'From what I've seen, for the big games, it's brought in a lot of people,' explains journalist Jucobin. 'It hasn't really impacted standard league games. But I think, especially with how well the team's doing this season, it is seeing attendances growing.'

In the derby, Paris FC prove how much further they are along with their project than Red Star with a 3-1 win that delights the away support. 'They want to be a club with lots of young players,' says Boxall. 'You can see it in their style of play and the players they are bringing through. They have got a very good academy and their whole thing is bringing through young players, attracting young people to games. It feels like a very youthful project.' There is certainly enough talent on their doorstep, with the Île-de-France region that surrounds Paris one of the most prolific on the planet for producing young stars.

Victory in the derby sends them top of Ligue 2 and on course for a return to the top tier of French football for the first time in 45 years. That would mean a first Parisian derby in Ligue 1 in a quarter of a century since the days of Matra Racing, whose existence essentially condemned Paris FC into obscurity after businessman Jean-Luc Lagardère bought the second division club in 1983, renamed them and filled the squad with expensive stars such as Uruguayans Enzo Francescoli and Ruben Paz, West Germany winger Pierre Littbarski, France international and PSG captain Luis Fernandez and a young French prospect named David Ginola. The entity Paris FC had to pick up from the fourth tier.

Whether the club will draw in big crowds in the top flight, however, is up for debate. 'They are now trying to build a supporter base that they didn't really have before,' explains Boxall, who says a portion of Paris FC's support comes from disaffected PSG fans. 'The trouble is, for a long time they didn't really represent anything.'

There is also the question of whether there is room for more than one 'big' club in Paris. 'It's a general pattern in France,' says Jucobin. 'I can't think of any city in France that has two major clubs. That's mainly down to the fact very few clubs actually own their stadium. It is always owned by the local council, so they only rent it out to one club and that means that only one club can thrive sustainably over a longer period of time.' Indeed, PSG president Nasser Al-Khelaifi has previously said the club want to leave the Parc des Princes, which is owned by Paris City Council, as they are unable to expand the stadium and increase matchday revenue as they wish. Interestingly, there is talk that Paris FC want to move to Stade Jean-Bouin, the home of Top 14 rugby union outfit Stade Francais, which would place them right across the road from PSG and the Parc des Princes. Jucobin adds: 'France, in general, is quite a centralised country. There is not really much scope for having more than one club. It doesn't really have that culture like you see in the UK or Germany, where people go out and support their local club. Attendance figures in, say, League Two in the UK are pretty much on par with the best clubs in Ligue 2 and you are not going to get a fourth or fifth division French club drawing in thousands of people.' Bordeaux, he points out, are a rare exception after the six-time French champions ended up in the Championnat National 2 following bankruptcy.

At Stade Bauer, buoyed by their side's performance, the Paris FC fans have their own banners to unfurl. They poke fun at the Red Star fans as 'hipster bobos', a term originated from an amalgamation of the bohemian bourgeois, suggesting the home crowd are champagne socialists and that 'no one from Saint-Ouen supports Red Star'. That has become a point of contention in recent years, as the club look to grow the brand and attract more fans, while also maintaining what makes Red Star unique. 'They were kind of insulting the wrong crowd,' laughs Boxall. 'A club of hipster bobos and stuff like that? Well, yeah, the main group are fighting against that.'

A lot of what has made Red Star noticeable outside of France has happened off the pitch, such as partnerships with Vice and LinkedOut, a project that plays on the business-focused social platform LinkedIn and, instead of high-flying employees, helps homeless or disadvantaged adults find work. They have worked with artists, musicians, directors, creatives and photographers on a whole host of unique projects. There have been clothing collaborations, both with what Bellion would call 'indie' local brands and more well-known ones such as Highsnobiety, Lack of Guidance and streetwear label Daily Paper. Red Star's popular shirts have featured customisable Velcro badges, with messages including 'Refugees Welcome', and portrayed historical landmarks from the area, as well as images of Rina Della Negra. They've taken football shirts from sports shops to high-end Parisian boutiques. It was the creative eye of Red Star president Patrice Haddad, himself a film-maker, that attracted then-Bordeaux forward Bellion to drop down the pyramid and join Red Star in 2014, before continuing at the club after his retirement in 2016. The club maintain that, however big and in whatever direction the brand goes, their ultimate goal will continue to be helping provide opportunities for local Saint-Ouen youngsters. In football or otherwise.

Behind the main stand, a tall wire fence separates match-going fans from an all-weather pitch and a long two-storey building painted red, white, green and yellow. On one corner is etched the Red Star badge and below it the stencilled letters of 'Bauer'. Red Star LAB is a project that puts the club at the heart of the community. Created in 2008, when Haddad took over the club, it provides a valuable learning hub for around 500 kids from Red Star's under-6s all the way up to the reserve team, the majority of whom come from the local neighbourhood. Through football, it allows the children to learn or discover other vocations, hobbies and talents. 'Of course we think about football, of course about school, but also the third pillar is the culture,' explains Ducassou. 'At the club, all the kids want to be professional footballers but, for sure, they will not all 100 per cent be able to do that. So, with this programme, if we can help the kids who are going to miss a professional career and just discover some new topics, new things, then maybe the kids will say "Okay, I did an architect workshop with Red Star and want to be an architect …" That is the idea.' The projects are fun, varied and imaginative. The club recently took 12 youngsters to London for a photo rally in which they could practise their English. Others have seen young players create podcasts, design their own football shirts and produce hand-made boots. Working with a local craftsman, they called the collection 'Made in 93', the area of Paris in which Red Star reside.

One project celebrated the 50th anniversary of hip-hop by getting the young players to produce their own music, while at the same time learning about how the genre crosses geographical borders, social aspects and cultural barriers. Another saw guest chefs judge a pre-match meal cooking competition, helping to raise awareness and understanding of nutrition. There has been a comedy club and cinema workshop, while former France international, World Cup winner and anti-racism activist Lilian Thuram was involved in one of Red Star's history projects. As well as helping youngsters learn new skills and opening their eyes to alternative potential careers, Ducassou believes the work the club are doing off the pitch helps forge a bond between them and the youth team players. 'Maybe the kids get Red Star in their blood and they are going to stay at the club, play in the first team, win games and make this career,' he suggests. 'Ajax, for example, have made that on a very high level. Lyon also. The sense of belonging.'

It is important Red Star hold on to the things that make them authentic, because contentious ownership issues have driven a wedge between those at the top of the club and the fans. In 2022, much to the disdain of supporters, American private equity firm 777 Partners bought the club from Haddad, who remained as president. 'That was the real banter era of Red Star,' laughs a resigned Boxall. Former Barcelona and Spain defender Gerard Piqué also announced that his company, Kosmos, along with a group of entrepreneurs and French players, was close to buying the club. But they entered negotiations too late, pipped to the sale by 777. The Americans were in the process of hoovering up a number of assets; Genoa, Vasco da Gama, Standard Liège, Melbourne Victory, Hertha Berlin. They tried and failed to purchase Everton. 'It was right from the off,' says Boxall about the opposition of the fans, who were furious the club had been sold without them being consulted, especially into a multi-club ownership model. 'That was when the club and the supporters really fell out. All the worries people were talking about were more to do with the player trading side of things, more to do with losing your identity a bit. But, actually, the reality was a lot worse.'

Even before the deal was made official, Red Star's home clash with FC Sète 34 was abandoned when fans held up a '777 not welcome' banner and threw fireworks and smoke bombs on the pitch. Similar banners followed throughout the 777 tenure and, as the Miami-based firm's investments came under increasing scrutiny, fans dished out fake bank notes in protest. At the time of writing, the immediate future is still to be resolved. The fans just want to move on. But has a brush with multi-club ownership tarnished the Parisians' unique and principled reputation? 'I feel like the fact fans distanced themselves from it has maintained that image as a hipster club,' says journalist Jucobin, looking at the situation from the outside.

Indeed, 777 have not been the lone focus of their rage in recent seasons. There was outrage at having to play on Monday nights in the third tier and general grievances throughout the French football pyramid over scheduling games outside traditional slots for television. 'No one watches the third division on a Monday night anyway,' laments Boxall. That started a movement that saw supporters of many different clubs effectively go on strike, refusing to sing, chant or make any noise at all during live broadcasts. During one match at Stade Bauer, laser pens were shone at the TV cameras. Other games, including in Ligue 1, have been interrupted by fans throwing tennis balls on the pitch. Supporters at different stadiums have found unity in displaying banners reading 'Football is for the weekend'. Others have aimed criticism at the French Professional Football League. 'That's been a big feature of the supporters' identity,' adds Boxall. 'All these little battles they choose to take. They're quite organised now because they've been doing it for a few years and they've got a growing supporter group. Especially with the new stand, there's a bit more space to grow as an ultra group. And not just an ultra group but people like me who sympathise with the supporter group but aren't necessarily part of it.'

The supporters crave a Red Star that remains true to them and Red Star need that primary fanbase, who have helped put the club on the map through passion, politics and a healthy dose of pyrotechnics. 'All the values of the club have been reappropriated by the supporters,' says Boxall. 'Even if the club is changing, there's always that core supporter base there. But the difference now is, because of the club's marketing model and the way it wants to present itself as a kind of hipster, alternative club in Paris, it is attracting new fans who don't necessarily hold the same vision of what football is or don't necessarily interact with football the same way.'

It is true, however, that even within that central hub of matchgoers who all desire the same thing from their football club, there is a range of personas and profiles. 'They're not all just part of this big lefty kind of ultra group,' explains Boxall. 'There's this core that's been there for a while and even that is made up of different generations of Red Star fans from when they were playing in different leagues and from different subcultures.' Boxall describes one group known as the Perry Boys, who began as a collection of mainly skinheads from Saint-Ouen's diverse suburbs and were into reggae and ska. 'Then there's the guys who are more inspired by the Italian style of ultras and other guys that are inspired by mod culture. And they all get on,' he adds, explaining that the different ultra subcultures all tend to come together under the Rino Della Negra banner. 'The rest are newer fans that have come and they don't get the club in the same way,' he explains. 'Even internationally, I think Red Star is a bit misunderstood.'

If Red Star are to fill the new, 10,000-capacity Stade Bauer, though, they can expect a range of fans wanting different experiences from their matchday. After all, the club is built on the values of Jules Rimet, of not discriminating by class or any other metric. After their 3-1 defeat by rivals Paris FC, the fans shuffle down the concourse to clap the players off, past pillars plastered with stickers reading 'Old School Bauer', 'Tribune Rino Della Negra' and 'Une Ville, Un Club, Un Stade', before pouring out via the bottleneck created by Saint-Ouen's ageing apartment blocks on one side and cranes working on the ground on the other, back on to Rue du Dr Bauer. The heavily armoured police stop them turning right, towards where the Paris FC supporters have been filtered out. But most want to go left anyway, gathering once more outside L'Olympic to grab a smoke, debrief and pint of Picon for the road. There are men, women, kids on their parents' shoulders, a diverse cast of fans young and old. 'You get so many different people,' says Ducassou about the Red Star fanbase. 'Some people are men or women who knew the club 50 years ago. You have the ultras, where the movement was created around 2010. The kids from the club, young kids from District 93, who just love football and want to follow the club. Some new people who have been in touch regarding what we have done on the brand development, with Vice, with the collaboration on the clothes. When you are at Bauer, you get a small quantity of people – 4,600 is not an amazing attendance compared to Ligue 1 or other clubs around football – but you get everything, every kind of people. People who come from Saint-Ouen, people who have just arrived at Saint-Ouen because the price in Paris for real estate just goes too high. When you visit the stadium you see everything and if we think about who lives in Paris, at Bauer you have got all the different people. Red Star walks as the heart of a famous place where everybody can be able to be together. I think if Red Star didn't exist, some of the people would not be able to be in the same place. That is the magic side of football.'

New ownership should, Red Star hope, bring stability and even the platform to build in Ligue 2 and beyond. Perhaps, after a generation of PSG dominance, French top-flight football will have three Parisian clubs in the future. The new Bauer is taking shape and Red Star's training complex at the historic Parc des sports de Marville has also been undergoing renovation works. Ducassou believes the club are well placed for the long term, even if the everyday pressures of professional football often don't allow for such perspective.

'I don't speak for every single Red Star supporter,' adds Boxall. 'But I just want the club to be in good hands, nothing to do with multi-club ownership. In five years' time, I want a solid owner, who has money, and the stadium will be finished by then. We are realistic; we are not going to be in the Champions League. But, you know what, if Red Star can stabilise in Ligue 2, maybe even go down and come back up, I would be happy with that. A club that can also stay true to itself, a club that doesn't need to make AI-generated shirts for people to be interested in them.'

What Red Star will always have is authenticity, a unique place in French football and beyond. A club forged by history, principles, politics and their role at the heart of the diverse and multicultural Saint-Ouen community. 'All the people who work at a club are going to say "my club is the best",' concludes Ducassou. 'But some clubs get something different. When you have fans, a huge atmosphere, we have got that, and you can't create that. You get it or you don't. That is what makes the club different.'

Chapter Four

Going Dutch

THE STIFLING humidity gave way to a torrential downpour and then it was just hot. The kind of searing heat that prickles at your bare neck and leaves you reaching for the Factor 50. Berlin was sweltering. And it was orange. Thousands of replica shirts glimmering in the July sunshine turned the streets into an eye-wateringly resplendent portrait of Dutch fandom. It was vibrant to the point of needing sunglasses, the accompanying techno backdrop prodding the temples to a rhythmic, repetitive beat. Alongside Turkey, thanks to the large Turkish diaspora in Germany, the Netherlands could place a strong argument for being the most vociferous travelling fanbase at Euro 2024. They were certainly the most recognisable, standing out like bright-coloured traffic cones in shirts that can date their origins back almost 500 years to William of Orange and the House of Orange-Nassau, the Dutch royal family.

The beginning of the now iconic Netherlands fan march is something that is harder to trace. One supporter claims he has been doing it for more than 40 years but in this current guise, it is a tradition that goes back to the start of Euro 2004. Officially, the march celebrated its 50th journey before Ronald Koeman's side's opening game of the tournament against Poland in Hamburg, when more than 30,000 fans joined. Now, before a meeting with Ralf Rangnick's rock 'n' roll Austria in Berlin to round off the group stage, a river of orange was snaking through the sun-kissed streets as far as the eye could see.

The night before, a message went out, instructing fans to meet at Hammarskjöldplatz. As I arrived there the following afternoon, there was a scramble to dash out of the metro stations nearby, no one wanting to miss the double decker orange bus leaving for the stadium at 2.30pm. The Oranje Bus has earned mythical status at major tournaments. After making its debut in Portugal in 2004, the vehicle has been everywhere from Brazil to Budapest and Cape Town to Qatar, becoming a four-wheeled Pied Piper for Dutch supporters at World Cups and European Championships. In the absence of Total Football, the Dutch have at least cultivated a fan culture phenomenon that has inspired other nations.

Hammarskjöldplatz is just under two miles from the Olympiastadion, less than a ten-minute drive if there's no traffic. But when you're leading tens of thousands of fans, with foam busts of Johan Cruyff, Ruud Gullit, Marco van Basten and Dennis Bergkamp bobbing behind, and with a haze of orange flare smoke wafting above the crowd, it becomes a leisurely two-hour cruise. The stream of supporters showcase a catalogue of Dutch shirts from throughout the eras, orange hues melting into one another, the pavement a paint palette committed exclusively to one colour. The most prominent, of course, is the Euro 88-winning jersey, once likened to goldfish scales but now well loved.

As the bus and the dancing, swaying army in orange pass through usually quiet residential streets, owners dip out of their apartments to wave from balconies and are greeted by thunderous cheers and enthusiastic fist pumps in response. You might think you can bob along and join the procession for a few stops but once you're in, you're in – both physically and emotionally invested in this journey. I planned to dip out along the way but the whole experience is completely intoxicating. Leaving before the climax would be like escaping a stadium five minutes early, only to hear a goal being cheered on your way to the train station.

By the time the Dutch reach their destination, there is still enough energy in the tank for a sweaty, sun-seared rendition of 'The Bounce'. And you'd better bounce along with them. Snollebollekes are a Dutch party act, led by comedian Rob Kemps, who have enjoyed almost accidental success. Their first hit was a carnival song they jokingly performed on Dutch radio that gained traction and reached No.11 in the chart. Since then, they have sold out Vitesse Arnhem's GelreDome, receiving a tile on the Walk of Fame outside the stadium, and have played at the Johan Cruyff ArenA in Amsterdam. If you have heard of them, it will likely be for the now-viral anthem 'Links Rechts'. 'Oh, it's going to get messy!' the lyrics state, before requiring partygoers to all jump from left to right. Dutch regional broadcaster Omroep Brabant reported that during a Kings Day show by Snollebollekes in Breda in 2019, the crowd performed the dance so enthusiastically that houses in the neighbourhood began to shake. 'I suddenly felt my bed moving up and down,' exclaimed a shocked 27-year-old resident named Sandy. So, when you get caught among almost 40,000 football fans bouncing en masse along the streets of Berlin like a huge orange tidal wave, you either jump along or get your toes trodden on.

'Football should be a festival,' professed former Netherlands winger Bolo Zenden about the craze. The feel-good factor at Euro 2024 swept up the current players, too, carrying them all the way to the semi-finals. At the Olympiastadion, after a 2-1 quarter-final win over Turkey, the Netherlands squad performed the dance in front of a magnificent orange wall of support in one corner of the ground – arms around each other's shoulders, jigging left and then right in tandem with the fans. 'We hear what is happening in the Netherlands and see all the movies,' said defender Stefan de Vrij afterwards. 'The song is also very popular now and the whole team knows it. It's nice to see that football can bring a country together.'

Chapter Five

Berlin and the Bench

BERLIN IS a thriving hub of migration and constant flux. A city of many identities and one of complex historical contrasts. One of postcard-worthy sights that hold a thousand stories and bear a thousand scars. Visit the East Side Gallery and its memorable artwork, get out early enough and you can beat selfie-seeking tourists to Erich Honecker and Leonid Brezhnev's kiss or a Trabant bursting through the wall, walk in the shadow of the Soviet television tower at Alexanderplatz, explore the cathedral and a plethora of architecturally intriguing museums, climb the Reichstag, cross Checkpoint Charlie, pass through the Brandenburg Gate or confront and contemplate the terrors of the past at the Memorial to the Murdered Jews of Europe. Few cities bear such era-defining and salient significance. Few have witnessed such division and turbulence over the past century. Berlin's football scene is moulded by that past but also by its creative, varied and liberal present. It's a complex, often confusing, tangle of beliefs, identities and rivalries, influenced by a diverse and multifarious population. 'Berlin, without its immigrants and without its foreign influence, is not the city we know today,' says Hertha Berlin fan Max Mueller, who was born in Germany but spent 20 years in the United States.

Among the complexities is the Olympiastadion. It is an undeniably impressive structure and the main feature of the Olympic Park, cultivated and tapered to keep the imposing arena in view. It dominates the horizon, whether you take the S-Bahn or U-Bahn from the city centre to reach it … or walk with 40,000 Dutch fans. Limestone-capped concrete columns give it an intended air of the Colosseum in Rome. Just like any ancient amphitheatre, it carries a long and complicated history.

In the affluent suburbs of Charlottenburg, on the edge of Grunewald Forest and surrounded by the greenery of West Berlin, the site was originally used as a horseracing track and then became the large, open-air and multi-use Deutsches Stadion, which could stage athletics, swimming and cycling. It was earmarked for the 1916 Olympic Games and inaugurated with the release of 10,000 pigeons, with more than 30,000 spectators present and another 30,000 men, women and children parading and performing in front of Kaiser Wilhelm II. The outbreak of the First World War meant those Games never happened. Instead, Berlin hosted the most controversial Olympics in history on the same site in 1936, the first Games to be broadcast on black and white television and an event used to fuel the propaganda machine of the Nazi regime and its ideals of racial supremacy. By this point, Adolf Hitler had ordered the construction of the Reich Sports Field complex, with a new Olympiastadion at its heart – a 110,000-capacity arena complete with Führer's Box, a balcony where Hitler and the Nazi elite would congregate. There, Hitler would host Benito Mussolini, the founder of Italian fascism, the following year to watch a night-time rally. Then, in May 1938, two months after Germany invaded Austria and with the spectre of wider conflict in Europe looming, an England side including Stanley Matthews went to Berlin and beat the home team 6-3. It is a match that is instead remembered for the English players giving the Nazi salute before kick-off – something many later said they were angry about but were requested to carry out as a formal, respectful gesture towards their hosts. Something it was believed would help maintain relationships. Within two years, the countries were at war.

Almost 90 years since that fixture, the same stadium, now a listed building, hosted England's 2-1 defeat by Spain in the Euro 2024 Final. Where Hitler and Mussolini once stood, the balcony has been lowered to reduce its 'historic effect', part of a discreet de-Nazification in the years after the war which also included removing swastikas from around the complex. There is a sleek new roof and the inside of the stadium has been completely refurbished. But 70 per cent of the original arena, designed to showcase Germany's might and supremacy to the rest of the world when it was built, has been preserved and renovated. It is breathtaking, with an eerie presence – an arena bearing the weight of the darkest epoch in German history. And that is the intention.

The Germans use a word, *vergangenheitsaufarbeitung*, which is essentially accepting that such a past did exist and that the people are going through a process of working or learning from it. To an extent, the Olympiastadion, like other landmarks in Berlin, is part of that. In front of the stadium, the Olympic rings still hang from two stone pillars, while statues and relics from the time are dotted around the park. Fans take selfies in front of the iconic rings; some stop to read educational information boards about the history of the site. The bell from the original Olympic Bell Tower, weighing more than nine tonnes, was later used for target practice by occupying troops and now sits outside one of the stadium entrances. The athletics track and football pitch have been lowered further to sit 15m beneath ground level, something that can catch you by surprise when first entering the arena to find your seat. Then, at the open end of the ground, by the Marathon Gate, is a plaque prominently bearing the name of Jesse Owens, the black American athlete who won four gold medals in 1936, delivering a hammer blow to Hitler and the Nazis' myth of Aryan supremacy.

Following the reunification of Berlin, there was scrutiny over the stadium's future. Renovate or leave it to ruin? 'You can't overcome history by destroying it,' one of the architects involved in the restoration, Volkwin Marg, told the *New York Times* before Germany hosted the 2006 World Cup.

The stadium now has a history that goes beyond its Nazi foundations. From Allied occupation, to a famous Rolling Stones concert that every local of the right vintage claims to have attended, to West Germany overcoming the Total Football of Johan Cruyff and the Netherlands in the 1974 World Cup Final, Zinedine

Zidane's headbutt in France's 2006 final defeat by Italy, Usain Bolt's 100m and 200m world records, Barcelona's Champions League triumph in 2015 and now Euro 2024. It means different things to different people these days, while always acting as a reminder of the past. During Euro 2024, supporters sporting different national jerseys mingle together, pass through the stadium's narrow concourses and buy snacks and beer at the food and drink outlets just outside. Some may grapple with the juxtaposition of the stadium's past and present, feel conflicted about its complex and complicated history. But come kick-off, whether Dutch, Swiss, Italian, Austrian, Turkish, English, Spanish or German, any such feeling is reduced to the euphoria and agony of following a football match.

For Hertha Berlin supporters, that is every other weekend. Since 1963 and the dawn of the Bundesliga, this has been home. One of the alterations to the stadium was to make the athletics track blue, in line with the club colours. Despite that, Hertha do not own the stadium. It is further away from their old Die Plumpe ground, towards the north-west of Berlin, than many would like. And bigger, too. Hertha's average home crowd was 50,000 in the second tier during the 2023/24 campaign. Seriously impressive, albeit only the third-highest in a league of fallen giants behind Schalke and Hamburg that season. But in a stadium that can hold 75,000, and with an athletics track between the crowd and the pitch, there is room to move. Unless you're packed into the 17,000-strong Ostkurve, that is, where pyro, flags and choreography are regularly found. Plans for a new 50,000-capacity ground of their own are due for approval in 2025 on another part of the Olympic complex, just off Jesse-Owens-Allee, the street renamed in the sprinter's honour in 1984. 'On one hand, every fan would agree the running track is not ideal in terms of your distance to the field,' explains Mueller, part of the Hertha Inters fan club, who can see the top of the stadium from his apartment in Charlottenburg. 'The financial component of it is not great. We start every season with an €8m deficit in rent. But, at the same time, the Olympiastadion is revered. It is iconic, unique, it speaks to Berlin. It's not just another cookie-cutter German football stadium like we'll probably get if we build a new one. Yes, other clubs rib us a bit for not having our own stadium. But every time they come here, they are in awe. In an age where everything is conforming into this monoculture, we have something unique and that is a huge value proposition and something I really enjoy about going to Hertha.'

Indeed, it carries plenty of clout. Hertha are one of only four club teams to play at a ground that has hosted a World Cup, European Championship and Champions League final. Roma and Lazio, at the Stadio Olimpico and Real Madrid at the Santiago Bernabéu respectively, are the others. 'We are a second division team and that's our stadium?' smiles Mueller. 'We are blessed, if you view it from a certain way.'

Playing at the Olympiastadion, the club can cater for a vast and varied fanbase from across Berlin and beyond. Supporter Antonio Folger says that in the 1970s and 80s, members of groups like the Hertha-Frösche, likened to 'Frogs' because they jumped up and down in the stands to keep warm, were linked to right-wing extremism and violence but that their influence waned with the rise of a more organised ultra scene. The current leading group, Harlekins Berlin '98, are regarded as more apolitical and the group's former capo, the person holding the megaphone, Kay Bernstein, was made club president in 2022 until, sadly and unexpectedly, he passed away in 2024 aged just 43.

In fact, the club's roots were laid in a borough of Berlin once known as 'Red Wedding' for its communist, working-class population. '[It was] one of the only holdouts, even in Nazi times, of socialism and communism,' explains Folger, who has been following Hertha since the early 2000s. 'In a grander scheme of things, I'd say Hertha's fanbase is rather left-leaning compared to most clubs. I think the fact that some of the most diverse parts of the country are squarely in Hertha territory just makes everything else near impossible.' That, Folger says, is mostly a reflection of the current political climate in Berlin, with the right-voting districts in the city tending to fall in the former East, where Union Berlin are more popular. He also dismisses the idea that Hertha are somehow a more affluent club than their neighbours. 'In reality, both have more roots in the working class and now cater to all,' he adds. 'As they should, I guess.'

Really, given their size and scope, Hertha could and perhaps should be a force both domestically and in Europe, yet they were last German champions in 1931. 'Hertha is never boring,' says Mueller. 'It mirrors the chaos of the city in a lot of ways. Berlin is always going through these false dawns, right? We think it is going to be so great and then it's kinda shit. In that sense, Hertha is a very Berlin club, in that it shares the chaos.'

At the time of writing, Hertha are not even in the top division. 'Berlin must be the biggest city in Europe without a major club,' another Hertha fan tells me. Union Berlin followers may disagree. Or maybe they wouldn't.

Twenty years after dropping into the fifth tier, Union were playing Champions League football. It is an incredible rise but one that leaves fans and officials at their iconic Stadion An der Alten Försterei, to the south-east of the capital in Köpenick, juggling with how to maintain their identity as a local, working-class institution. Even before they became the first club from the former East Berlin to reach the Bundesliga, one who were regarded as anti-establishment during the Cold War, Union were beginning to attract an alternative following who were intrigued and encouraged by their unique initiatives. They have even given blood for the cause. In 2004, as part of the Bleed for Union campaign, supporters earned money through blood transfusions and donated the funds to help the club stave off bankruptcy. In 2008, almost 2,500 fans spent 300 days and 140,000 working hours volunteering to rebuild the stadium when it was deemed the club would otherwise not be able to afford to modernise it. And in 2019, during Union's first game in the Bundesliga, fans held up photographs of their loved ones who had not lived to see the club reach the highest level of German football.

Then there is Union's Christmas tradition. Since 2003, supporters have gathered at the club's stadium in the forest to sing carols together on 23 December. It began with 89 fans, frustrated by a disappointing start to the season, who jumped the fence to access the ground, armed with flasks of Glühwein, stocked up on biscuits and ready to stretch their vocal cords. It was Torsten Eisenbeiser's idea, after disgruntledly leaving a game without wishing the friends he stood with a merry Christmas. It has grown into a huge annual celebration, endorsed by the club. More than 30,000 people now attend each year. A choir and brass band set the tone, with fans handed a candle and songbook, in exchange for a small donation to the club's youth work. It is popular across different generations of fans and even those from different clubs like to attend.

They may be the two biggest clubs in Berlin but Hertha and Union have long shared a mutual respect, offering companionship in a once divided city. Hertha in the West, Union in the East. After the wall went up in 1961, at the height of the Cold War, those living in East Berlin were no longer able to pass freely to the West. Many longed for a united city, to see friends and family again. Those living in the West, however, were able to attain visas to cross to the East. There are stories of Hertha fans passing to the other side of the wall to go and watch Union, where it was said subtle rebellions would take place against the Soviet regime. Likewise, Hertha fans who found themselves in the East and, thus, were unable to attend their own club's matches would supposedly go to Union instead. 'They weren't really fans of Union. It's just that Union had established a fanbase of people unhappy with how the authorities treated them, which obviously attracted loads of people with the same mindset,' says Folger, whose family were torn apart by the regime. Folger's father wished to flee to the West. But he was shopped to the authorities by his own father, a member of the secret police, and spent two years imprisoned at Bautzen. It may be almost 40 years since the fall of the Berlin Wall but many still speak of the 'wall in the head' in regard to the psychological effects that remain.

In that sense, stories have been passed down and forged into legend about what it was like to attend Union games in the German Democratic Republic (GDR). Most tell of a stadium full of punks, rebels and political dissidents, who during the 1980s would chant 'the wall must go' every time there was a free kick. Gerald Karpa, Union's club chronicler, believes this to be a myth, however. He suggests there is a misconception because of Union's rivalry with BFC Dynamo, formerly Dynamo Berlin, the club of much-feared Stasi chief Erich Mielke and the most successful in East German football. Backed by the secret police, Dynamo could recruit the best players in the country and influence referees. Naturally, they dominated, winning ten successive titles between 1979 and 1988, and played regularly in the European Cup. Like many clubs from the former East, they have struggled since reunification.

From the 1991/92 season, clubs from East Germany's Oberliga were merged into the footballing pyramid in what was West Germany. Most had been backed by companies or government organisations. Some sought alternative investment, while others struggled financially after being exposed to the capitalist system of the West. Dynamo lost that backing and state-supported power in a unified Germany, as well as a majority of their star players, who were snapped up in a free market transfer system Dynamo were previously not exposed to. Rebranded FC Berlin and then BFC Dynamo, the club soon found themselves playing amateur football and running out of money. Millions made in player sales in the early 1990s were frittered away and, because of the club's Stasi past, new sponsors were hard to come by. In 2002, following insolvency proceedings, they had to start again in the sixth tier.

Nevertheless, Union fans still see Dynamo as old foes. 'Hardly anyone considered Union supporters to be anti-establishment,' historian Karpa, who has been attending Union games since he was a 13-year-old in 1979, tells me. 'They were perceived and portrayed as normal football fans – in both good and bad contexts. The fact that Berlin had a much more politically charged club, BFC Dynamo, as its direct competitor does not change this. Union was also always a solid and reliable part of the sports system, the political system and, thus, an element of the dictatorship. Some older Union supporters today probably interpret the competition with Dynamo as a kind of resistance behaviour. This is deceptive, their role as a socialist club was known to everyone back then. There is no record of dissident behaviour. Dissidence in the GDR existed in church, artistic and academic circles, not in sport, not in the stadium.'

So, what of the stories about Union fans following Hertha when they played in continental competitions in Eastern Europe? Legend has it, half the 30,000 fans in attendance for a UEFA Cup quarter-final at ASVS Dukla Praha in 1979 travelled from either side of Berlin. 'On the occasion of some matches between Hertha teams in the late 1970s in Bratislava and Prague, some Union supporters travelled there,' explains Karpa. 'As well as to Dresden, when Hertha played there in a match as part of the so-called "German-German sports calendar", an agreement between the two states.'

What is clear is that any camaraderie was not always shared among the playing squads, with Union's effectively amateur stars witnessing their Hertha counterparts enjoy the fruits of an increasingly popular sport following the formation of the Bundesliga. 'We became pretty jealous of the Hertha players,' Lutz Hovest, who was delegated to Union Berlin in 1979 after 18 months' military service, told *FourFourTwo* in 2022. 'In those days, we'd watch Bundesliga coverage on TV and see our peers in the West climbing into their Porsches after matches. We went home on a public bus!'

Days after the wall fell, with any friendship now able to be shared openly, thousands of East Berliners were given free tickets for Hertha's second-tier promotion clash with Wattenscheid at the Olympiastadion. Two months after that, in January 1990, Hertha hosted Union in a reunification friendly. It was the first time the Berlin sides ever played each other and more than 50,000 fans showed up, singing songs of solidarity and unity. But that euphoria was hard to sustain. Karpa says not even 4,000 turned up for a return match the following summer. 'The relationship between Union supporters and Hertha, and vice versa, changed very soon after the border was opened towards a lack of interest,' he adds. 'Because what united them was what divided them.'

That is until they began meeting more regularly. It was once unthinkable that Hertha and Union would feature in the same division but in September 2010, they met for the first time in a competitive game in the second tier. Since then, Berlin derbies have often stoked emotions and demanded a large police presence. Especially after Union overtook the 'Old Lady' as top dogs in the city, finishing above them in the Bundesliga for the first time in 2020/21. 'Among the younger generations, the relationship can be described more as hostility,' says Karpa. Hertha fan Folger agrees the rivalry has 'gone sour'. 'There's still somewhat of a generational divide in regards to how that relationship is viewed but the traditional derby character is winning out,' he adds. 'In the Union pub I go to sometimes when visiting my aunt, for example, the barkeeper in his 60s once brought out some Hertha–Union friendship memorabilia. At the same time, there's a reason why it's not up on the wall anymore. And instances of violence, if caught with the wrong kit in the wrong neighbourhood, are picking up.'

Mueller, however, feels the narrative around a 'loathsome city derby' is something that is pushed by international media. Hertha, he says, have not had a proper local rival since the days of regional leagues, before the Bundesliga began in 1963. West Berlin's other sides have since dropped way down the pyramid. 'Then Union came. The plucky upstarts!' he laughs, accepting their story is often viewed as more romantic than his own club's. 'Hertha fans were so desperate to fill that hole and Union was such a natural fit: East v West, red v blue, old v new. Their fans built the stadium, we play in the Olympiastadion ... everything lined up so perfectly. But a lot of Union and Hertha fans I know feel it is forced and that it is the media outside of Berlin putting us together and going "fight!" Yes, when we play on derby day it gets heated. But I would say most Hertha fans don't have Union as a top three rival.' Instead, he sees Schalke, Stuttgart or Kaiserslautern as Hertha's biggest enemies, the latter two because of a long-standing fan friendship with Karlsruher SC. 'There is the desire to have rivals but, in my view, it is not really registering,' adds Mueller about the relationship with Union. 'If anything, if I could have my way, I would say how wonderful would it be for Berlin as a city to have a friendship between these two teams? To buck the trend. Because Berlin is not like any other city in Europe. Do something no other city would do, have two teams who actually quite like each other. If they do well, I am happy for my Union friends. And if we play, I want to beat them.'

After all, for Mueller and the Hertha Inters fan club, football is about meeting people, making friends and offering a social support network. Part of the reason they started the group was to help people moving to Berlin connect and integrate. 'We wanted to show people that if you are an international living in Berlin, you don't just have to watch the Premier League on a screen on Saturdays, you can come into a stadium and be a part of something,' explains Mueller, who believes many expats find adapting and settling into everyday culture in the city a different proposition to those who arrive as tourists just for a good time, not a long time. 'For millions of people, Berghain is not interesting. They are born and raised Berliners; they live here, work here, they don't view Berlin the way internationals view Berlin as this party city, this place to go to. A lot of people struggle to arrive in Berlin. Seeing that side expressed through football can help people feel very settled – or it has done for a majority of people in the group. We offer a chance to experience real Berlin culture with real Berliners. We're not promising results but we are promising a good time!'

The group meet at the same bench outside the Olympiastadion two hours before every home game, bringing beers, snacks and a speaker to play music. 'I cannot overstate how important the bench is to our group's identity,' laughs Mueller. The bench has even made its way on to their official merchandise, featuring on stickers and scarves. Whether it's minus nine degrees Celsius in February or glorious sunshine in May, there's always a group meeting at the bench. 'I am a fan. I want the club to do well. I want the club to be financially secure,' says Mueller. 'But everything outside of that … I am here for a good time. If we stay in the 2.Bundesliga for ten years but do it in a way that's fun for the fans, I would rather be proud of the club in the second division than go on another big city club adventure trying to get somewhere where, at the end of the day, what does that mean for me as a fan? Other fans might have different feelings, more traditional success. But, for me, it's about the community.'

Beyond the top two, Berlin's football scene is as eclectic as its varied, characterful, edgy and diverse neighbourhoods. It's packed with as much history, too. Türkiyemspor Berlin and Berliner Athletik Klub 07 are both heavily influenced by the area's large Turkish diaspora. Berlin is, after all, the home of the modern döner kebab, introduced and popularised by Turkish immigrants in the 1970s. Berliner AK 07, along with former Oberliga champions SC Union 06 Berlin, play at the historic Poststadion, where England drew 3-3 with Germany in front of 45,000 fans in 1930. Meanwhile, Tennis Borussia Berlin, also referred to as TeBe, spent two seasons in the Bundesliga in the 1970s. They were once Hertha's rivals but are more well known these days for being a cosmopolitan club who promote inclusivity and anti-discrimination and boast a large youth sector. All the above clubs are now well down the league pyramid. 'Unlike London, where you have teams in every division, it is really just Union and Hertha and then the drop-off is really serious,' explains Mueller, pointing to Berlin's geographical position in the east of Germany as a factor. 'Relative to the rest of West Germany, West Berlin was not wealthy at all. The other clubs in West Berlin struggled to compete with clubs in West Germany, so Hertha pulled away to such a large degree that it became unfeasible to continue to have rivalries with regional league clubs that we never played. Over time, some of them went insolvent.'

One of those was SC Tasmania 1900 Berlin. A club who may have folded in 1973 but whose legacy lives on. In bizarre circumstances, Tasmania, named by founders who shared a wish to emigrate to the Australian island, found themselves promoted to the Bundesliga just two weeks before the 1965/1966 season in place of

Hertha, who had their licence revoked for breaching player salary cap rules. At the height of the Cold War, German authorities deemed it politically important to have a club from West Berlin in the top flight. Tasmania were actually the third choice, after TeBe and Spandauer SV. But after the other two passed up the opportunity, they were plucked from the regional leagues to compete against West Germany's best.

An opening-day 2-0 win over Karlsruher, in front of a remarkable 81,000 at the Olympiastadion, proved a false dawn and was one of just two victories all season as Tasmania instead racked up a host of unwanted records, making them the worst team in the league's history. They earned eight points in the days of two for a win, scored just 15 goals and conceded 108 times in 34 games, while crowds dwindled to such an extent that they were playing in front of a record-low 827 people by January. When the main club folded, members of the youth and amateur teams formed SV Tasmania Berlin. They still have a presence at amateur level and play in Neukölln, next to the old Berlin Tempelhof Airport, which itself carries a weighty history as the site of the Berlin Airlift in the late 1940s.

Now, just as in pre-Bundesliga times, many of Berlin's rivalries play out in the regional leagues. It was the cup, however, that threw up a particularly intriguing clash in November 2024. BFC Dynamo, as previously mentioned, are one of Berlin's most historic and decorated clubs. They have worked hard to shed any association with a section of the fans who were linked with violence and labelled by German news outlet *Spiegel* as 'Stasi, hooligans, Nazis and Hell's Angels'.

Nowadays, the club take a stand against racism and extremism and are trying to tap into a new generation of more liberal supporters with their diverse youth set-up. A complex past, though, can still weigh heavy in the eyes of some. In contrast, in the last 16 of the Berlin Pokal, they came up against a club with a blank history whose fanbase is generated online. Despite sitting in the district leagues, social media upstarts Delay Sports Berlin boast 140,000 YouTube subscribers and have posted videos with more than 800,000 views. The club have 551,000 followers on Instagram, almost 200,000 more than both Hertha and Union. Co-founder, streamer and influencer Elias Nerlich blows them all out of the water with 1.5 million. That popularity has even seen him launch an indoor competition called the Icon League with German football legend Toni Kroos. BFC Dynamo's Sportforum Hohenschönhausen was a 4,500 sell-out for the much-anticipated clash, with Replay bringing 1,200 away fans for a grey November lunchtime kick-off. The hosts, however, made the five-division difference tell in the scoreline, easing to a 12-0 victory. But the match highlighted that, despite the rough-around-the-edges and sometimes ramshackle feel of the city's regional football scene, there remains plenty of interest in the old and the new.

Delay Sports aren't the only club bringing a modern feel to football in Berlin. FC Viktoria 1889 Berlin can legitimately claim to be different to any other club in the city. The men and boys' side boast the largest football department in Germany, with 65 teams and more than 1,600 members. However, it is on the women's side that the club are making waves.

Inspired by Angel City FC in the United States, who in 2020 were founded by a blockbuster all-female cast that included Natalie Portman, Serena Williams, Jennifer Garner, Eva Longoria and many former USA national team players, an all-female consortium in Germany decided to spark their own 'revolution in football' by taking over the women's team at Viktoria Berlin, a club who previously had a good women's structure but were without the resources to progress further. The founders include: Germany's two-time World Cup winner Ariane Hingst; entrepreneur and investor Verena Pausder; the CEO of Vattenfall Wärme Berlin AG, Tanja Wielgoß; former TV presenter Felicia Mutterer; co-founder of BRLO Craft Beer, Katharina Kurz; and marketing expert Lisa Währer. It provides them with a wealth of experience across different sectors and the power to run the club like an innovative start-up.

Beginning life in the third tier, Viktoria's five-year goal is to reach the Frauen-Bundesliga by 2027. But it goes much deeper than that. The co-founders want to bring more equality and fairness to the sport as a whole. They want lasting change and hope to use the club to ensure more visibility, equal pay and recognition for women's sport in Berlin. 'Who thinks of women's teams when they think of Berlin, the sports capital?' said Kurz, when the movement was launched in 2022. Wielgoß added: 'We no longer want to just talk or wait for women to conquer their place in football. We want to be the accelerators for fair play in sport ourselves.'

The project has proved popular with both investors and fans. Crowds have swelled, sponsorship has grown tenfold, seeing Viktoria bring in six-figure sums, and games have been broadcast live on TV. Franziska Giffey, Berlin's governing mayor at the time of the launch, said: 'The sports metropolis of Berlin is exactly the right place to break new ground in football. In the public perception, top-level football is still often dominated by men. I, therefore, support the idea of making football in our capital – and throughout the country – more female.'

At the time of writing, however, the only representative Berlin has in the women's top flight are FFC Turbine Potsdam, Champions League winners in 2005 and 2010 and six-time Frauen-Bundesliga champions, making them the only club from the former East Germany to win the competition. They were relegated in 2023, only to bounce straight back up and, despite their former success, seem destined to flit between the top two divisions.

On the Berlin football scene, it seems, there is a place and a club for everyone, whether that's at arenas fit for World Cups and world records, stadiums deep in the forest or pocket-sized grounds with crumbling concrete concourses. Even for those who are passionate supporters of one particular side, there is scope to experience and enjoy others, too. 'There is this allowance, almost, because of the separation between the teams and the fact they are not competing really in the same world of football, that you can be a Hertha fan and you can be a Union fan but you're also allowed to have a regional league team you go to when your team plays away and you can't go,' explains Mueller. 'My friends and I go to a lot of Babelsberg and TeBe games, because we live in the west, we're not a political group but lean more towards feeling comfortable at Babelsberg than we do at BFC.'

And Babelsberg, it turns out, are something of a hidden gem.

Chapter Six

A Groundhopper's Paradise

POTSDAM IS a place of huge cultural and historical significance. It is part of the Berlin metropolitan region but is a distinct city in its own right in the state of Brandenburg. In fact, it's the perfect escape from the hustle, bustle and general business of Berlin. Hopping on a train at Friedrichstraße in central Berlin, it is a half-hour ride, beyond the Olympiastadion and out into the leafy suburbs. You could get satisfyingly lost trying to discover Potsdam's grand palaces, architectural gems and elegant gardens. It's Germany's answer to Versailles. Once the residence of Prussia's royal family, the city is now a UNESCO world heritage site, protected and revered for its elegance. Even on a dreary, wet morning, the quaint Dutch Quarter is endearingly charming and all the city's palaces breathtakingly beautiful. The steps of the Sanssouci Palace, built by Prussian King Frederick the Great, spill out like a royal carpet into its impressive grounds, Babelsberg Palace perches proudly by the Havel River, Cecilienhof resembles a Tudor manor, Charlottenhof a Roman villa and, arguably the most commanding of them all, the New Palace imposes itself on one end of the huge, marauding grounds of

Sanssouci Park. Opposite is the University of Potsdam, making it a quite inspiring backdrop for any student.

Potsdam is also home to the original Brandenburg Gate, completed in 1771, two decades earlier than its namesake in central Berlin, by order of Frederick II to celebrate his victories in the Seven Years' War. But the real reason to trek out here is, of course, football. Babelsberg is the largest quarter in Potsdam, most widely known for Studio Babelsberg which, opened in 1912, is the world's oldest film studio and still one of Europe's largest. In its pomp, the large-scale studio was essentially the Hollywood of Europe. Some of its more recent productions include *The Bourne Ultimatum*, *Inglourious Basterds* and *The Grand Budapest Hotel*. Now, it also boasts a theme park.

Yet, the real thrill-seekers congregate in the north of the town. Navigating the leafy, quiet neighbourhoods, via Karl-Marx-Straße if you want to take the scenic route, is a small but thriving football community. One a million miles from the glitz and glamour of Hollywood and where the only thing scripted is the ultras' choreography.

SV Babelsberg 03 play in the Regionalliga Nordost, the same league as BFC Dynamo, Viktoria Berlin and Hertha Berlin's second team. But there is a distinct difference to the club, a reason why they have become a cherished stop for European groundhoppers.

First, there is the history. With Babelsberg falling under Soviet occupation following the Second World War, they were briefly known as SG Karl Marx Babelsberg, and later BSG Motor Babelsberg, and continue to play at the Karl-Liebknecht-Stadion, a ground shared with women's team FFC Turbine Potsdam and named after the anti-war revolutionary who was one of the founders of the Community Party in Germany. Liebknecht was later captured and assassinated, along with Rosa Luxemburg, by Germany's right-wing Freikorps, becoming a martyr for the socialist cause.

Then, there is the fans' Antifa stance. The club don't assign themselves to any one political party but are staunchly anti-fascist and anti-racist. Outside the ground, someone has spray-painted 'stop racism' on the wall and a bin is plastered with stickers. One pays homage to FC St Pauli, with an image of Che Guevara next to the Ultra Sankt Pauli group, who Babelsberg supporters share a close friendship with because of their beliefs. Indeed, they are often referred to as 'the St Pauli of the East'.

'There are St Pauli stickers all over the place and you see a lot of St Pauli shirts,' explains a fan, who wishes to merely be known as Mike. 'You used to see quite a lot of Celtic shirts, too. But that friendship is maybe over now, because Celtic and St Pauli are not so friendly anymore.' Mike, who has been attending games for the best part of two decades, adds: 'Even in the ultra scene, there are a lot of St Pauli flags. It is a pity they don't come and play a few friendly games. They sent their second team about four or five years ago and that was good – there was a big crowd. It would be good for the money coming in.'

St Pauli, although only modestly successful themselves, have always been the bigger of the two but Babelsberg's evolution as a cult club shares a lot of similarities to that of their friends in Hamburg. St Pauli emerged as the rebels they are today renowned as during the 1980s, a heady mix of squatters, social activists, punk rockers and disillusioned Hamburger SV fans gradually drawn to their rivals situated by the docks and near the city's Reeperbahn. Over the next decade, St Pauli built a left-leaning, socially active, alternative fanbase that adopted the skull and crossbones Jolly Roger flag as its emblem. Crowds at their Millerntor-Stadion have grown from barely 2,000 a game to 20,000 sell-outs.

Nowadays, a more affluent middle class resides in the area around Babelsberg's Karl-Liebknecht-Stadion but at the beginning of the 1990s, this was a working-class district which was shaped by its position in East Germany. Just over a mile away is the Glienicke Bridge, where captured spies and secret agents were exchanged during the Cold War. Football fans from the squatter scene in Potsdam wanted a place to congregate, a team to watch and found Babelsberg hacking about in the amateur leagues with very few supporters for company. The club provided a blank canvas in terms of a fan scene, so the new flurry of matchgoers created an environment inside the ground that became a platform for speaking up against fascism, racism, anti-Semitism and sexism.

'It was people from the squats,' explains Mike. 'They started coming to the games, bringing their own crates of beer, their dogs, just sitting in the terraces and watching the game for free, because it was a really low level at the time. And that's why the anthem they sing before the games today is aligned with that.' The lyrics refer to living in squats, which the song labels as a 'shithouse', and the changing face of Babelsberg after the fall of the Berlin Wall. The anthem is open to interpretation but generally reflects the unruliness and nonconformity some people felt at the time as they got to grips with their hometown merging with the West and the economic and cultural challenges that posed. It has become an anthem and source of pride, not just for the football club but for all locals.

'It's got an incredible amount of very local support,' says Max Mueller, talking about the crowds at Babelsberg. 'It makes no qualms to hide the fact it is a politically oriented left team. There are more of those in Germany than anywhere else. Football as a whole in Germany tends to be quite left, compared to maybe some other countries where the right feels more comfortable in the roles of the ultras and organising themselves. Babelsberg fits into a great tapestry of left-leaning clubs and for people who are also quite dejected by the commercialisation of football, they like the grassroots component of it all. So, you have a really interesting mix of Berliners who come down because it is a good time and it is a local team, maybe they are left, but it's cheap and it's nice and it feels very easy.'

During the summer, the gates to the stadium are open but the ground is empty. It's still, peaceful, with just a couple of groundsmen keeping busy in the stands. The pitch is guarded by a tall green fence and the terraces are covered in even more stickers. 'The atmosphere itself is interesting because they have two different ultra sections; they have had a split,' adds Mueller. 'The more organised, traditional fan scene doesn't sit behind the goal, they sit parallel to the field, and then you have this leftover other part of the ultras behind the goal, which is sometimes quite confusing. Then, for certain games, like Energie Cottbus, that was the Brandenburg derby, it's a sell-out. It feels like a proper atmosphere.'

The Filmstadt Inferno 99 are the club's original ultras but most prominent on the sticker front in this part of the 10,000-capacity ground are those in blue and white for Junge Ultras, whose logo is a floppy-cheeked bulldog wearing a baseball cap and studded necklace. Another sticker reads 'Skinheads Babelsberg', while Karl Liebknecht's face is dotted across the stone steps. 'The ultras sell loads of stickers with his head on. There must be a hundred different variations!' laughs Mike. On matchdays, it is a different scene. The tranquillity gives way to flares, smoke bombs and flags sporting the faces of Liebknecht, Che Guevara and Leon Trotsky. Especially in the Nordkurve, where a large section of fans congregate to choreograph chants and drape banners over the hoardings condemning fascism and homophobia.

'St Pauli and Babelsberg are the only two clubs I can think of in Germany who really have that Antifa stance,' adds Mike. 'The other left-wing clubs are different. They are either more centre left or hard left, more socialist. A lot of Antifa things revolve around racism and homophobia, whereas the other left-leaning clubs are more about fair working conditions and those kinds of topics. They are a bit different in that way. A lot of Germans really hate the Antifa movement, so it is not for everyone. There is a lot of needle in the games.

Because Babelsberg are this Antifa, left-wing club, it means that they have a lot of enemies. A lot of games are quite intense, which adds to the atmosphere. It feels like there is a lot underlying.'

The regional fourth-tier division Babelsberg play in is made up of teams from the states of the former East Germany and those from Berlin. In 2016, more than 200 people were arrested following far-right riots around Leipzig, with police describing them as mostly football hooligans.

Babelsberg leapt into the global consciousness in 2017 following a home game against Cottbus in which, according to local media, several away fans performed Nazi salutes and made chants referencing Auschwitz and other Nazi concentration camps. However, it was the hosts who were hit with a €7,000 fine as punishment for what the local football authorities deemed 'crowd trouble' after responding to the visitors' actions with their own chants of 'Nazi pigs out'. Babelsberg, often known by their nickname 'Nulldrei', refused to pay the fine, which brought with it the threat of suspension and potential bankruptcy. Eventually, with the help of Potsdam mayor Jann Jakobs, they agreed to settle the penalty but only on the condition that half the money would go towards the club's fight against racism and extremism, with the other half to be used by the local football authorities for similar measures. 'If we can work against violence and racism in football, we have made a great step forward,' said Jakobs.

The campaign, which became known as *Nazis Raus Aus Den Stadien* (Nazis out of the Stadiums) attracted support from a host of Bundesliga and 2.Bundesliga clubs, among them Bayern Munich, RB Leipzig, Werder Bremen, Borussia Dortmund, Cologne, Stuttgart, Mainz, Freiburg and, of course, St Pauli. Many made donations or set up fundraising boxes to help Babelsberg's cause, as well as selling merchandise with the slogan on. It earned the club more than 200 new members and even garnered attention in the United States.

It was not the first time the club received publicity for their social initiatives. In the summer of 2014, Babelsberg launched Welcome United 03, a club for refugees in the area. The following season, they registered with the Brandenburg Football Association and became the first all-refugee team to officially compete in Germany, featuring players from Macedonia, Serbia, Syria, Somalia and more. Fans made donations and helped provide kits and balls for the team, while the refugees were given a free season ticket for first-team games. The project was initially a success on and off the pitch, the club receiving a prize for integration in Potsdam, as well as the team winning promotion to the top district league. It lasted four years but, for a myriad of reasons, eventually proved unsustainable. The number of refugees moving to the area decreased, while the success of integrating players into society was also the team's downfall. The more players integrated, found jobs and started families, the less they relied on football to fulfil that role for them.

Babelsberg's social core remains a strong part of the club's identity. Appeals to help others or raise money for fellow supporters can often be seen on message boards. The fans, particularly the ultras, are entwined in the fabric of the club and have been known to provide the stadium announcer, sit on advisory boards, organise childcare and produce the club's merchandise.

When Mike first started following the club, they were in the third division. 'I didn't realise at the time that was quite successful for them,' he laughs. He was also there to witness them get relegated. 'I was in the ultras section,' he adds. 'The players came over, stood in line and got lectured by the ultras. I had never seen that before, coming from watching English football, where they tend to run down the tunnel and disappear as quickly as possible!' He adds: 'The stadium, if you like that old type of stadium, is quite picturesque. It's close to the pitch. Even with a couple of thousand in there, the atmosphere is good because there's no running track and you're right up at the pitch. You find yourself being drawn to it more. You can stand with the ultras or there are plenty of other spaces to sit down, have a beer and watch the game, a bit more relaxed.'

In recent years, fans says they have noticed more English voices, as groundhoppers are drawn to the Karl-Liebknecht-Stadion for the unique atmosphere and cult status, rather than the quality of football. 'The ultras are what make the club,' adds Mike. 'Without them, it would kind of be a neighbourhood club – it might be quite dull. There are a lot of clubs around but the ultras bring the atmosphere and they are Antifa, very left-leaning, and do a lot of good work. There's a lot of choreography and pyro, when they're not getting fined for it! Their displays are very impressive; a lot of work goes into what they do. Without them, it's not really the same club anymore.'

Like many German clubs, it is the fans who make Babelsberg so enchanting and intriguing. And, in character with the rest of the city's football teams, they bear a strong and unique identity. So, while the wider Berlin region might not currently have a major football club capable of competing with the best from Europe's other major capital cities, in every corner there are ones at the heart of the community. Just like Babelsberg.

Chapter Seven

Tigers, Fat Cats and the Fenix

ALEX BĂCICA winces and checks his watch as the 14th goal goes in. The Kraków Dragoons founder has a flight to catch in a few hours but only after witnessing his side suffer a record hiding in the Fenix Trophy, the alternative invitation-only European Cup for non-league and amateur clubs. The competition is built on forging friendships, something Dragoons have done in abundance, but it can also be unforgiving when you come up against a vastly more experienced side.

Dragoons take their name from Poland's legendary Winged Hussars, the heavily armoured cavalry troops who struck fear into their enemies during the 1500s and 1600s. They would ride into battle on horses with huge, feathery wings strapped to their backs in an attempt to shock and scare the opposition. Dragoons' own shock and awe tactics, however, do not have quite the same effect on a tough afternoon at a drizzly Broadhurst Park, where a wintry chill still nips at any bare skin, despite March being well under way. That's north Manchester for you.

This is the home of FC United of Manchester, who prove to be as ruthlessly cold as the weather in emphatically putting away their visitors, buoyed by both an always vocal but welcoming home crowd. Just above a 'Hang the Glazers' flag flutters one reading 'FC United: Polish Fans', a nod of appreciation to both their guests from Poland and a Manchester-based Polish contingent who follow the side. Some fans have bought Dragoons shirts and merchandise from the stall the visitors set up inside the ground, while the club have asked young players from the local Polish youth football club to be mascots for the game. There is no tribalism here, no gloating about the scoreline. If anything, the home fans urge their visitors to get at least a glimpse of a goal.

Dragoons and FC United may rank similarly in terms of position in their respective countries' footballing pyramids but there is no doubt the latter sit among the competition's elite. Băcica, observing from the stands, is confident the semi-professional outfit would play in a much higher level than the seventh-tier Northern Premier League Premier Division if they were in Poland. In contrast, this is a different experience for Dragoons, an amateur club who found themselves travelling to Manchester without a number of key players. They had FC United pegged at 1-1 in the reverse fixture in Kraków before the visitors eventually ran out 4-1 winners. Availability and travel restrictions are just some of the logistical challenges that come with competing in continental competition at amateur level, especially for a squad who all have full-time jobs away from football and have seen some of their players' movements restricted further since Brexit.

'Dragoons started basically from nothing,' explains Băcica, who moved to Poland from Romania in 2012 and was effectively just looking for some mates to kick a ball around with. The IT specialist found a group of expats wanting the same thing in Poland's second-largest city and they sparked up a regular pick-up game. By 2015, the group were playing in a Sunday league run by an Irish bar in Kraków. Games started at 11am and ran back-to-back all day long at the same venue. 'It wasn't your typical English Sunday league,' laughs Băcica. They soon made the move to Saturday football and, after Băcica sought inspiration by meeting a sports lawyer who had previously worked for Wisla Kraków, drew up plans to join the league pyramid. In 2019, they entered the Polish eighth tier. 'We didn't really have a plan, we were thinking, "Just take it one day at a time and see where it leads us,"' he adds. 'I had this crazy idea … "What about joining the proper league system?" We had more and more people interested. We were the only international team, Kraków was growing on the expat scene and more and more people were going there for work.'

Dragoons' inaugural season was interrupted by the Covid pandemic; they were looking good for promotion when the campaign was curtailed. They have since climbed to the Klasa A Kraków I, the seventh tier of Polish football. But it has never been purely about the sport for a club who put a lot of work into being a social platform that helps migrants living in Kraków to integrate and embrace the local culture, making lifelong connections along the way. Of course, when you are a long way from home, the community aspect is often more important than the football itself. 'The team formed from a core group of guys,' says Băcica. 'So we were already playing together and they were our friends. We were seeing each other every week, at football and socially. Even if we were not playing football during Covid, we were still friends, right? We were talking every day, playing *Call of Duty* online and that sort of stuff. We had a small social media presence, so started doing clips, keepy-ups with toilet paper etc … trying to keep everyone engaged. I don't think we ever had a plan where we wanted to take the club. Everybody just wanted to play football and enjoy themselves.'

Yet, even with a large group of dedicated players, Băcica and Dragoons have felt the pinch in recent seasons. One of the considerations when opting to play in the Fenix Trophy was whether they could ask players to take on the extra financial burden of travelling around Europe. 'It is not easy at all, because the plague of modern football is, at any level, you need a lot of money,' he says. 'We are 90 per cent self-funded, so it is coming from our own pockets. Rent, training facilities, pitches, travelling have all got more expensive, so we are holding it together. The Fenix Trophy is a non-professional competition but you still need some finances to be able to travel and host the other teams.'

Ultimately, the lure of European football proved too enticing. After all, not every seventh-tier club is awarded that opportunity. Dragoons caught the eye of the Fenix Trophy organisers, not for their on-field performances or technical ability with a loo roll but for being a social bastion of inclusivity and equality. The club can boast of being a truly diverse community. More than 50 nationalities have represented the amateur side since they were founded, with players' backgrounds ranging from the Americas to Australia. The squad that travelled to Manchester featured players from seven different countries. 'We are arguably the smallest club in the competition but we are doing something right,' adds Băcica. 'The experience of playing in Europe is just amazing. For some of the youngsters, maybe it feels different. But, for me, who started playing in this organised fashion at 33, going away to Europe and having people watching you, learning your names and buying your shirts, it's crazy! People you have no relation or connection to, seeing you play and knowing your name? It is just amazing.'

It is the sort of experience that, for an amateur football club, is only possible because of the Fenix Trophy. And that is the epitome of what the organisers wanted when they created the tournament. The Covid pandemic and the lockdowns that accompanied it were incredibly tough for many different reasons. But sometimes out of adversity something beautiful is born. For Leonardo Aleotti and his father, Alessandro, the former journalist, publisher and founder of Brera FC – more on them later – the pandemic provided an opportunity to step back, take a moment and conjure up a truly unique proposition. What if, they thought, there was a tournament that allowed amateur and semi-professional clubs from around Europe to compete against one another? A novel idea, if it wasn't for the fact no one could leave their house at the time, let alone travel around Europe. 'We felt like amateur football didn't have a platform to express its most positive values and it was rather dragged to a pointless imitation of professional football,' explains Leonardo Aleotti.

The founders wanted to identify the most interesting experiences of being a non-professional club. They often came back to the idea of forging a community. From there, the intention was to create a continent-wide competition that showcased the best side of the non-professional game. 'This, and also we felt like we couldn't be a proper Milan club without some European football,' laughs Aleotti, an Inter fan at heart. 'We always try to lighten the mood, show that in professional football the result is important but there are so many more meaningful things attached to this kind of activity. It would be reductive to only consider football for football's sake. You have to find some different meanings, create a community around the club.'

The competition's name stems from its key values: Friendly, in that it creates a welcoming environment for clubs, players and fans; European, because it has created a network of clubs across the continent; Non-professional, in drawing attention to a different model of football; Innovative, as it has brought clubs together based on affinity rather than football rankings; and Xenial, with participants expected to be hospitable towards strangers and respect one another's cultural differences. Part of this is having the home side paying to help host their opposition. The name is also a play on/inspired by the idea of phoenix clubs, with several of its participants having sprung from professional outfits who either went bust or had a significant number of fans lose faith in their ownership.

Clubs are chosen to compete based on their 'exceptional social, historical and cultural distinctiveness', which, for the first edition in particular, took a lot of research. Aleotti Junior found himself scouring Europe for teams that fitted the bill. They also needed to be on board with the founders' vision and be able to imagine a world beyond lockdown in which this tournament could take place. 'Except a few unicorns that are famous worldwide, it's hard to find detailed information on non-professional outfits,' says Aleotti. 'Our idea was to have a multiplicity of models of how to run an amateur club, to sort of set an example for non-professional clubs in general. It could be fan-owned, expat clubs, artistic experiences, youth development – a valuable amateur football experience can come in many forms.'

Aleotti sent out correspondence to a number of what he believed, for one reason or another, were cult non-league clubs around Europe and was met with overwhelmingly enthusiastic responses, even if he does admit 'they all felt we were a bit crazy to suggest such an idea based on mobility in the midst, not even in the aftermath, of a global pandemic'.

FC United are one of Aleotti's 'unicorns' and the club's then-secretary Adrian Seddon was one of those to spot an intriguing email dropping into his inbox. 'I thought they were mad at first,' he confesses. 'We weren't allowed out of our house at the time and they were talking about going round Europe playing football!' There were countless meetings between interested clubs. Some dropped out during the process because they either felt it was too risky or they did not want to commit. 'Eventually, we had a big thing. Do we go for it or postpone for a year? Because Covid was still there,' adds Seddon. 'But we thought if we postponed, we would lose the momentum and enthusiasm, so we thought, "Let's just go with it!"'

Against all the odds, the competition launched for the 2021/22 season, not even a year since the idea was first mooted to clubs by the Aleottis. It comprised clubs from Italy, Spain, Germany, the Netherlands, Poland, United Kingdom and Czech Republic, all of whom enjoyed some aspect of cult non-professional status. 'There's a kind of transparent X-factor,' says Aleotti of the invitation process. 'Every club has a different story, so we didn't want to create some sort of benchmark. [They need] social awareness, community values, something extra. The tournament is managed very professionally, with clubs all over Europe, and it has the professional elements. But the F and X in the name are really the essence – clubs hosting and embracing each other's culture, which does not happen in Champions League games.'

Seddon remembers FC United's first away trip in the competition, to Warsaw's AKS Zly, a not-for-profit club whose work in their local district earned them the distinction of being named best amateur club in the UEFA Grassroots Awards in 2019. 'They had 1,000 fans in the ground,' he says. 'It was just amazing. After everything that had happened over the past two years, to be in a football ground with 1,000 people. Away from home, a big party afterwards, it was a brilliant occasion.'

To get a sense of the clubs Aleotti wanted to bring together, you can look at those who took part in the inaugural competition. As well as AKS Zly, there was: HFC Falke from Hamburg, founded by disgruntled Hamburger SV fans in 2014 after the club began selling shares to outside investment; Rome's AS Lodigiani Calcio 1972, a club with a famed youth academy and links to Marcello Lippi's son, Davide; CD Cuenca-Mestallistes 1925, an amateur club from Valencia with a rich history and who are now fan-owned; Amsterdam-based AFC DWS, who competed in the European Cup in the 1960s; Prague Raptors, a diverse and inclusive not-for-profit community club; organisers Brera; and, of course, FC United of Manchester, who were founded by Manchester United fans following the Glazer takeover of the Premier League club in 2005.

FC United's story is well known, if not always wholly understood. American tycoon Malcolm Glazer's arrival at Old Trafford was essentially the final straw for a group of fans who were already fed up with, among the other pitfalls of modern football, kick-off times being moved for television and overpriced tickets. The fans who broke away wanted something they could call *their* club again. One that was governed by *their* rules. Punk football rather than prawn sandwiches. Somewhere that felt like home and was accessible to the whole Greater Manchester community, providing affordable football for everyone. After all, 'making friends not millionaires' is one of their taglines. In 2025, they turned 20 years old.

'The first years, we bulldozed our way up the leagues. It was easy for us, we had the crowds, the gates, the budgets,' explains Seddon. The zenith was reaching the National League North, the sixth tier of English football, and at that point they were just two promotions away from joining the English Football League. But it was also at that stage that FC United ran into other teams with serious financial backing behind them, some of whom were fully professional. After four seasons, they dropped back into the seventh-tier Northern Premier League Premier Division. 'We went up the leagues really quickly but that was never our dream,' adds Seddon. 'For the first ten years, if you asked our fans what they wanted more than anything else, it was to build a ground in Manchester.'

It took a decade to get their own stadium in Moston, seven miles from Old Trafford. More than half the £6.5m cost was generated by fans, with the rest topped up by grants from Sport England, Manchester City Council and the Football Foundation. It was a collective effort, with fans chipping in and helping out in whatever way they could – building benches for the dressing rooms, painting the pitchside hoardings. The result is a stadium that still looks impressive ten years on and would meet the criteria for playing in the Football League, should they get there one day. That, however, may be a long way off. The club are still paying back a sizeable chunk of what they owe on the ground. It also means, despite attracting healthy gates of around 1,700 people for league games, not as much can be spent on the playing squad while repayments are being met. 'Our ambition for building our ground has hurt us a bit on the pitch,' explains Seddon. 'I think our fans understand that. Not to every extent but they do understand that we can't be as competitive on the pitch as we would like. We have to stabilise the club now for the next few years and then look to kick on again.'

FC United have more than 4,000 members, each of whom get a stake and a vote in club proceedings. It gives every fan a sense of ownership and the volunteer spirit remains strong. Supporters sell matchday programmes, make teas and coffees and help with groundskeeping when needed. They also serve up a ferocious, yet friendly, atmosphere for every game, with flags and banners hanging from the stands and almost non-stop chanting. For defender Curtis Jones, who started his career at Stockport County and had a spell in Scotland with Celtic, the club's ethos is something that helps attract players. 'There is no other club like it,' says Jones. 'The fanbase, the things they do in the community, they always try and arrange things with fans. That is massive, especially in non-league football. For the players to be really close to the fans, that's the difference.'

When he joined in 2018, manager Neil Reynolds was handed a book on the club's history and told to swot up. There has never been any doubt he is fully invested. 'To be here every week and share the experiences with fans and members, nothing else can touch it,' he beams. 'I am the proudest guy when I manage this football club.' And while things on the domestic front may have been more difficult for FC United recently, Reynolds and his team can now boast about being two-time European champions.

For the 2023/24 edition of the Fenix Trophy, the tournament grew to include 12 teams from ten different countries. Joining some of the initial participants were clubs from Belgium, Denmark, Norway, Romania and Finland. Helsinki's Gilla FC were of particular note. Their midfielder, the former Finland international Përparim Hetemaj, who played more than 200 times in Serie A, scored the last goal of his professional career for HJK Helsinki in the Europa Conference League at Greek side PAOK in December 2023. His next goal in European competition came in the Fenix Trophy. Gilla were also able to attract Finnish legend Jari Litmanen to manage the team – something tournament founder Aleotti jokes is 'completely anti-football'. 'They got a legend in for one day. He doesn't know the players!' he laughs. 'But it was a great stunt. I met Jari. He actually went and coached the team, spoke to the players and is a nice guy.'

Three English sides made the semi-finals that season. FC United, Enfield Town and Lewes were joined by Prague Raptors. FC United went on to win the final at Stadio Tre Stelle, perched on the edge of the beautiful Lake Garda, to reclaim the Fenix Trophy title they first clinched in 2021/22. It came as something of a consolation to Dragoons that at least their record defeat was against the most successful side in the competition's history.

While clubs are required to host each other in the group stages, it is the organisers who stage and pay for the finals at a neutral venue. In 2023, remarkably, Aleotti managed to arrange for the final four clubs to trot out at the iconic San Siro in Milan. It was an incredible day for all involved, even if there were some nervy moments on arrival when an overly suspicious security guard questioned the entourage's credentials and initially refused to let players, staff and fans into the stadium. Eventually, after the squads began getting changed in the car park, Aleotti managed to convince the guard their presence was legit. As beaten semi-finalists that year, FC United featured in the third-place play-off and ran out 1-0 winners against hosts Brera. 'It's probably the most amazing experience of my career, a pinch yourself moment,' explains FC United boss Reynolds. 'I was quite emotional, to be honest, thinking the likes of Pep Guardiola, José Mourinho and people like that had been in that dugout. It was just breathtaking. Every time you looked at a different place in the stadium, it seemed to get bigger and further away. It was just spectacular and to say you have managed there or you have played there or you've scored a goal there, that's an absolutely unbelievable experience and this is what the Fenix Trophy can do for you.'

Milan's historic, charm-filled yet crumbling cathedral is a venue that has hosted World Cup fixtures, European Cup and Champions League finals, the fiercely intense Derby della Madonnina and now, the Fenix Trophy. Goalscorer that sunny afternoon, adding his name to a long list of icons to have netted on the hallowed turf, was Matt Van Wyk, who missed his last college exam to make the trip. 'He said, "I can retake my exams but will never get the opportunity to play in the San Siro again,"' laughs Seddon. 'So he didn't take his exam and then he scored the winner!' Reynolds adds: 'Imagine telling stories about the best place you've ever scored and he says, "San Siro in

European competition playing for FC United to win 1-0." You cannot put it into words what it felt like. At the end of the game, they did the presentation and were trying to usher us out of the ground. We just didn't want to go because, the minute you stepped out, you weren't going back in there.'

The San Siro trip felt like a poignant moment in the story of FC United, too. Around 500 fans made the journey to support the team and, for many, this was the site of their last away game following Manchester United back in March 2005, when they were knocked out in the Champions League last 16 by AC Milan. Hernan Crespo grabbed the winner that day. 'When we started FC United, we were match-going Manchester United fans,' explains Seddon, who like many others had followed the Red Devils all over Europe. 'We missed the European trips and sort of demanded that we still wanted to go away in Europe, even though we couldn't support Manchester United away anymore. So, right from our first season with FC United, we went to Lok Leipzig, we played St Pauli for their centenary, we played Djurgårdens in the Olympic Stadium in Stockholm, we went to Detroit and South Korea and played there. It was really good but they weren't competitive games. For a lot of us, including myself, our last experience of competitive European football with Manchester United was at the San Siro. If you'd said to me then that we would one day be able to come back and watch FC United play there, I'd have thought you were mad. There are only a handful of Premier League teams who have played in the San Siro ... and little FC United!'

As a one-off experience, travelling to the San Siro was incredible for all involved. Yet, as Seddon says, one of the most rewarding aspects of being part of the competition is to meet and host other clubs, embrace other cultures and make friends with other fans. When FC United visited Valencia to face Cuenca-Mestallistes, for example, they discovered from supporters there that the fan-owned English club were the inspiration behind their Spanish counterparts adopting a one-member, one-vote policy of their own. 'It is just amazing. You go away to places and you get those sorts of experiences,' adds Seddon.

For 2024/25, the Fenix Trophy added another four teams, taking the number competing in the tournament to 16. Aleotti says he has also witnessed a noticeable increase in the reach of the competition's social media posts. Amid its growth and popularity, and bigger exposure for participants, it has even received the approval of European football's governing body, UEFA. But Aleotti remains passionate about the fact those clubs involved should stay true to the identities that earned them cult status in the first place. 'It all starts from the conviction that professional football and non-professional football are different environments,' he concludes. 'Professional football is a tiger and non-professional is a cat. They do belong to the same species, so they look the same, but they are very different animals. If you try to over-feed the cat, it doesn't become a tiger, it just becomes a fat cat! You spoil the experience by trying to be something you cannot be. The issue with non-professional football is it doesn't have a reference model. To become Real

Madrid, it doesn't just take a lot of money but a lot of time. You have this Icarus experience of pursuing resources without creating anything. It's not sustainable and they just land, with no trace.'

It was this philosophy that resonated with Kraków Dragoons founder Alex Băcica. When he spotted the email which had landed in his inbox from the Fenix Trophy organisers, he knew, despite any financial implications, the club had to accept. More than that, Băcica, who was already aware of the fledgling competition at the time, saw it as a privilege. 'It is all about making these connections, right?' he says. 'Getting to know people, getting to know how other clubs work and maybe borrowing some of the ideas. This network of amateur and semi-professional clubs are mostly about the sport, about playing football and giving back to grassroots, not worrying about big-money competitions.'

As for Aleotti, working for Brera and organising the Fenix Trophy has become a full-time gig. He has been involved with the club his father founded for more than a decade, starting off at the age of 18 by running the line and coaching the junior teams, having been an avid fan who was regaled long before that with his father's stories. 'It's great because I love football and working in football with something I created, something that is mine,' he beams. 'I wouldn't reject a job at Inter but, at the end of the day, you are part of the system. Imagine my team in Europe? It is really a childhood dream and very rewarding. I have fond memories of both the good times and the bad times, to be fair. While the home games have always been tough to manage, the away matches were absolutely wonderful. From the crowds in Warsaw and Manchester, to the enthusiasm in Copenhagen and an amazing venue in Belgrade. I do remember very well the stressful moments at San Siro as well! But all in all, it has been great. I've been travelling a lot, meeting some great people and seeing some great places. The Fenix Trophy experience is something unique and truly unforgettable.'

Chapter Eight

Made in Milan

GOSSIPING OVER a coffee and brunch in central Manchester, Leonardo Aleotti casually drops something into conversation that makes me look up from an overpriced plate of avocado on toast. 'Have you seen *The Pursuit of Happyness*?' Like most people, my response to this question is, 'The one with Will Smith?' Indeed. So far, this has little to do with football or the Fenix Trophy. 'Well …' he continues, explaining how Chris Gardner is the guy whose real-life story the 2006 hit is based on.

Gardner is a remarkable person. After all, Will Smith doesn't just ring up anyone and ask if he can play them in a Hollywood movie. That film showed the real-life struggles Gardner faced as a homeless single father in 1980s San Francisco. He and young son, Chris Jr, would sleep in subway station toilets, in parks, at church shelters or under the desk where he worked as an intern at a stock brokerage, eating at soup kitchens and using the little money he made to put his son through daycare. Eventually, because of his perseverance, resilience and talent for selling stocks and shares, Gardner made it as a full-time employee and could afford to give his son the life they yearned for. By 1987, he had opened his own investment firm, Gardner Rich. Now, he is thought to be worth $60m.

Gardner, it turns out, is also part of a group of investors who, in 2022, purchased Brera Calcio, the club founded by Aleotti's father in Milan and the ones who organise the Fenix Trophy. Aleotti rattles off some of the other names involved, including former Manchester United, Villarreal and Italy striker Giuseppe Rossi, who was born in New Jersey, and ex-Inter, Lazio, Genoa and North Macedonia forward Goran Pandev. Across the company's board and advisory board, there are also finance moguls Pierre Galoppi and Daniel McClory, as well as Alan Rothenberg, dubbed the 'father of US football' for his role in helping launch Major League Soccer and bringing the 1994 and 2026 men's World Cups and the 1999 women's World Cup to American shores, and Massimo Ferragamo, the son of famous luxury Italian shoe designer Salvatore. But why Brera, the lowly underdogs pining to be the third club in Milan? For that, we need to go back to the beginning.

Like all good stories, it begins in the pub. Back at the turn of the century, Alessandro Aleotti was having a few drinks with some friends and threw out the idea of starting a football club, a prospective third team in Milan. He wanted to name them Brera, a district at the heart of Milan that is often considered the most beautiful and charming neighbourhood in the city. Brera is known for its art and culture and is a destination for creatives and designers. It's very chic. The fact former Italy international Marco Borriello lives there and has previously looked into purchasing the Brera brand name to start his own club gives you an idea of the area's upmarket elegance.

Anyway, Aleotti Senior went ahead and founded the club in 2000. They began life in Serie D, under the tutelage of Algerian coach Noureddine Zekri, a former professional in his homeland who came to Italy during the 1990s. Aleotti Sr met him during a previous venture the young journalist set up, called Milano Mondo, which was a World Cup that brought together 24 communities of non-European Union immigrants living in Milan. At the time, as well as the immigration situation being very different in Europe to today's climate, Italian regulations meant foreigners were unable to join a club in the football pyramid at amateur level. In fact, during Brera's second season, Aleotti Sr fielded an under-19s team of players of African, South American and Eastern European descent in protest at the current laws. 'At the end of the season, the federation changed the rules in non-professional football,' explains Aleotti Jr. 'That debate [about immigration] is less progressive than it used to be. To do something then was really trailblazing.' It also gives you an idea of how the Aleottis see football, which is with a social conscience.

Zekri was sacked, although it would not be his last spell as Brera boss, and he was replaced by a big name. Goalkeeper Walter Zenga won 58 caps for Italy, set a record run without conceding a goal during World Cup 1990 on home soil, played more than 300 times for Inter, winning a Scudetto and two UEFA Cups, and enjoyed a distinguished 20-year career that also took him to the

United States. In 1999, he hung up his gloves after a spell as player-manager with New England Revolution and was doing a stint on reality television when Aleotti Sr reached out to offer the man once named UEFA's goalkeeper of the year a job in the dugout at the Arena Civica. Perhaps it was the attraction of managing at Brera's grand and historic home ground that convinced Zenga to join. The Arena Civica played host to both Inter and AC Milan before they moved to the San Siro. Opened in 1807 under the watchful eye of Napoleon Bonaparte, then King of Italy, it is thought to be the oldest stadium in mainland Europe. Zenga, despite being sent to the stands on his managerial debut, lasted most of the season before being encouraged to resign by Aleotti Sr as relegation loomed. The Italian has gone on to have a varied coaching career that includes a league title in Romania, a domestic double with Red Star Belgrade in Serbia and spells with Sampdoria and Wolverhampton Wanderers, among many others.

Meanwhile, Brera's dream of becoming 'the third team in Milan' has never really come to fruition, at least in a footballing sense. Instead, the club have become renowned for their social and cultural projects in the north of Italy and beyond. 'We always try to think outside the box and use the tools football has given us to create something unprecedented and very noticeable,' explains Aleotti Jr. It helped that Aleotti Sr was a journalist, so he always knew his way around communications and had contacts in the press. 'Because he had so many ideas, so many unborn ideas, the ones that saw the light of day were the best ones,' adds Aleotti Jr. 'It was always something very innovative. There are so many divisions above you in football, without coming from a presumptuous point of view, they might know football better than you, in purely technical terms. So, we have always tried to do things that are not *just* football. That's what caught the attention of the American investors and the general public. That's what made us the third team of Milan, not results. Walter Zenga on the bench, the Arena Civica, some of these things were like out of a movie.'

Among the more ambitious ideas to not come off was buying a local Italian club and filling it with South American players. It is said 20 players were ready to sign up and that Mario Kempes, the Argentine World Cup winner, was lined up as coach. He spent a couple of months waiting for the project to take off before instead accepting a job with Casarano in Lecce, in the south-east of Italy. Kempes then had a short spell with Club Deportivo San Fernando in Spain before he retired from coaching. Who knows how things would have played out for both parties had he got the gig with Brera's South American imports XI?

The idea that really put Brera on the map, however, did not involve World Cup winners or Serie A legends. Quite the opposite. The Carcere di Opera on the outskirts of Milan is one of Italy's largest prisons and regarded by many as one of its toughest, too. In 2003, wishing to shed light on the living conditions faced in jail, Aleotti Sr made the decision to create a team of prisoners, called FreeOpera Brera. It took a lot of negotiating with the prison, Italy's ministry of justice and the Italian football authorities but eventually Aleotti Sr was able to convince respective stakeholders of the benefits of such a project and a team was entered into the local ninth-tier amateur league. 'What matters is having something to believe in and to compare ourselves with the people who come from outside,' Mario, a player doing a 17-year stretch, told *Corriere Milano* at the time. There was one catch, of course, and that was, for security reasons, the prison team could only play home games.

'That was the most important project we have ever done,' confesses Aleotti Jr. It garnered huge coverage at home and abroad. Journalists came to write about the prison games and national broadcaster RAI visited twice a week to film a documentary. It captured the imagination of the public and even professional players. Gennaro Gattuso, the tough-tackling AC Milan midfielder, was one of those reportedly spotted watching from beneath the safety of his hoodie. The legendary José Altafini was another. 'It was opening prison to people from outside,' adds Aleotti Jr. 'They weren't playing friendly games – they were actually playing in the proper league where students, workers, people who play football in the official rankings every Sunday, play.'

They were also playing against the prison wardens and guards who watched over them in their cells every day. Aleotti Sr insisted that for the project to work, it must reflect the entire prison society. If they did something only for the prisoners, the 'bad guys', he stressed, then the 'good guys' would feel left out, excluded, and the project would not realise anything. So Brera also funded the registration of a guards team, Frecce Azzurre Opera, and entered them into the same league. 'It was a nice social experiment,' explains Aleotti Jr. 'Because the first time they played, after a month or so, the inmates were very scared. They were scared of the repercussions. They drew in a tight game and generally were intimidated by playing against the wardens.' By the time they played again in the reverse fixture, the inmates were a lot more confident and had become comfortable with the notion they were allowed to compete properly. 'They won 4-0,' says Aleotti Jr. 'No fear whatsoever. They knew they were better. At the end of the season, the team got promoted in the play-offs. It was very much like movie night!'

The team almost didn't get off the ground at all, though. Understandably, talk of the project reverberated around the wings of the penitentiary, as did the impact it would have on the lives of those prisoners involved. Not only would they be able to leave their cells to play and train three or four times a week, any positive involvement and good behaviour might be reflected when it came to reviewing their sentences. The first trial the organisers held when looking for players to represent the team was like a *Goodfellas* spoof. From 1,400 inmates, Aleotti Jr says only 50 turned up. They were all aged over 40 and overweight. Basically, it was those sitting at the top of the prison social structure. 'My father understood that these people were the bosses, the Mafia-type guys, and they wanted to be in on the discounts,' he adds. 'So, he said "Listen, guys, the project is nice and it has got everybody's attention but if we don't do something that also has value on the football side – we don't have to win the league – but if we don't show this is properly managed, it will fade away and nobody will care anymore.'" Aleotti Sr told the 'bosses' they could be involved in the organisational and management side of the team but that he needed them to find the best players in the prison to make up an XI who would take to the field under the guidance of Marco Nichetti, the former Inter youth prospect who had been appointed head coach. 'My father was very aware of the environment of prison,' adds Aleotti Jr. 'The next day, out of nowhere, all these South American, Moroccan, southern European guys started to appear.'

To keep everyone engaged in the project, for each game, 500 inmates who were not playing or involved in running the squad would be given permission to come down and spectate. Carcere di Opera might just have made for one of the most intimidating away days in all of Italy. 'It was a very intense crowd,' laughs Aleotti Jr. But the prison environment, at least when it came to football, was at peace. So impressed with what Aleotti Sr had done for the inmates was notorious mobster Salvatore 'Toto' Riina, known as the 'boss of bosses' for Sicily's Cosa Nostra and serving 26 life sentences in isolation at Opera before his own death in 2017, that one Christmas he gifted the Brera president a Mafia-style hat. 'The inmates came to him and said, "This is from Toto,"' explains Aleotti Jr. 'It was pretty tough, because my father was working with the top-ranking people of organised crime.'

What happened next also belongs in a movie. Having watched the inmates team win promotion in their debut season, the prison director got 'football fever', as Aleotti Jr puts it. He took control of the prisoners' side himself and disbanded the team of guards and wardens. Nichetti, the former coach, has since said sponsors such as Benetton were willing to invest up to €1m in the project but pulled the plug after the changes. 'The director started sending telegrams to other prisons to send their best players to his prison, so he could make an even stronger team,' adds Aleotti Jr. 'A transfer market version of inmates! He created a huge imbalance between the prisoners playing and the ones who were not playing.' The players threatened to go on strike or start a revolution, calling for Aleotti Sr and his partners to stay on, but he talked them down. 'He told me he had this Al Pacino moment,' explains Aleotti Jr. 'He was saying "Guys, calm down, you are here. The difference between me and you is tonight, you are going to sleep in this shithole and I am going to bed in my house, with my son. I appreciate you doing this for me but you have to think about your wellbeing, you have to listen to what the prison director says. He is our chief and don't go against him for the sake of having me here!"' Under the guidance of the director, the team lasted another season before being discontinued. Overall, though, the experiment was a success. 'The project opened the path for other prisons to do the same,' explains Aleotti Jr.

Plenty more social projects have followed since. One saw Brera create and manage a team for boys from the Martinitt orphanage in Milan. A few seasons later, in 2011, they entered a team of young Gabonese footballers into the Torneo di Viareggio, one of the most prestigious youth tournaments in Europe and which is played every year in Tuscany, featuring all the top Italian clubs. The team were named Brera Emergence Gabon and, despite going out in the group stages, they got to play against Palermo, who were then a Serie A side. Several of the Brera Emergence players, now in their 30s, are still playing top-flight football in Gabon. It fed into Aleotti Sr's ambitions to one day start a club abroad. He managed a team in the Maltese second division and went to Lithuania to meet with Vladimir Romanov, the former owner of Hearts in Scotland, but that ultimately came to nothing.

Instead, in 2016, in a bid to change the perception of the Romani population in Italy, Brera partnered with the Romani People Football Team with the intention of competing in the CONIFA World Cup, a global tournament for associations from unrecognised states, regions, minorities, micronations, stateless peoples or generally any group not allowed to have a FIFA membership. After a match in Milan against Padania, a proposed independent state in northern Italy, they were due to join the likes of the Chagos Islands, Kurdistan, Somaliland and Western Armenia for the tournament in Abkhazia, the subtropical, separatist region of Georgia in the Caucasus. Visa and travel issues meant the team had to withdraw but a spotlight had been cast on some of the issues and prejudice faced by the Romani community.

With the Brera district being Milan's art hub, there has also been no shortage of cultural projects, celebrating the area's heritage. Brera have staged action painting performances with students from the local art school during half-time of matches, which naturally raised eyebrows from their opponents in amateur football. One season, their jersey boldly displayed a 'more art, less fashion' statement amid protests from artists who were campaigning about the gentrification of Brera and the district's rebranding as more of a fashion neighbourhood.

'Every season has its own various projects,' says Aleotti Jr. 'What my father has always done and has always believed in, is non-professional football has to offer ideas outside of football. You have all these coaches in non-professional football trying to imitate the ideas of Roberto De Zerbi and Pep Guardiola – one guy has Manchester City or Barcelona, top-notch players, and the other is trying to do it in the fifth or sixth division in Italy. The players are not going to be the same, they don't do it as a job. The value comes from the fact we don't have to show off our results and say we were founded in 1930, etc. Who gives a shit about that, because it is non-professional football anyway? It was always something different, never "Let's spend a lot of money and we can win the league." That was never the case. He was always very aware of money and never wanted to waste it!'

For the past few years, things have been a little different for Brera. Aleotti Sr stepped away from the club as a group of US-based investors moved in, listing a company called Brera Holdings PLC on the Nasdaq Stock Exchange in January 2023. They wanted to build on the club's history of ESG-themed projects by expanding the Brera portfolio in other countries. The message the investment group took to the market was a new category called 'social impact soccer'. They like to use the tagline 'making friends not millionaires', tapping into an ethos espoused by FC United and Brera's own European competition, the Fenix Trophy. The idea was, and remains, to take Brera global while also staying true to the club's roots and philosophy. It is multi-club ownership with a difference, one with a keen eye on social impact. It is also a model that aims to allow any investors, big or small, who believe in the project to claim some level of ownership by buying shares.

Both those concepts resonate with Chris Gardner, who, when we chat, has just returned from a week-long trip doing motivational speaking on a cruise around the south of Italy, which is incidentally where Brera have just made an investment. 'Anybody who wears two watches should never be late!' he laughs, a timepiece on each wrist, after arriving a few minutes behind schedule for our chat. It's not just any laugh, it's a wise and weathered roar that rumbles from deep down and bearhugs your soul until you cannot help but chuckle along, too. Gardner says it was his first time on a cruise, visiting Palermo, Sicily, the Amalfi Coast, Corsica and Salerno. 'I love Italy,' he beams. In that sense, Brera were an easy sell. Gardner is open, honest, engaging, pumped full of charisma and modest, too. He's spent time with Nelson Mandela and met a million magical people himself but makes you feel like an old friend. He sadly lost his wife, Holly, to brain cancer in 2012, and candidly explains how he fell in love with her many times over as they explored Lake Como, Lake Bracciano, Milan, Rome, Florence and more together. 'When I walk through any place in Italy, if the wind blows a certain way and the clouds and the sun shine a certain way, you can feel it,' he smiles.

Gardner never knew his dad. He was brought up in poverty by a mother who made him believe he could achieve anything, despite the presence of an alcoholic and physically abusive stepfather. Gardner fulfilled his dreams and went on to make his fortune. But when Holly was ill, she taught him to re-evaluate his life, to do what he was passionate about. Now in his 70s, the American puts his effort into what he feels can make a tangible difference. That is why he got involved with Brera. As he puts it: 'To build your own table.'

'You see that piece of furniture that sits behind me?' he asks, pointing to a wooden desk with family photographs on it. 'That's the desk I started my own firm on, 36 or 37 years ago. If this place was on fire and I could only grab one thing and run out the door, I would grab that table. Because that's where a dream was born. But, more importantly than that, my mom was still alive when I was trying to start my own company. When she would come to visit, all the stuff that was on the table, all the notes and the business cards and the phone, that was all removed and that table became where I had dinner with my mom. So, when I talk about building a table, that's what I am talking about. I hope that makes sense?'

Even before Brera, Gardner was passionate about making a social difference in Italy. He visited several schools in the country and found it most rewarding working with those children from less privileged backgrounds. 'I found a school for working people's children, called Galdus, in Milan,' he explains. 'These young people are not trying to go to college, they are trying to learn a skill-set that will allow them to take care of themselves and their families. They're starting from the bottom. I know a little something about that. These are my kids!' He was also handed an important lesson of his own when he had the chance to attend his first Derby della Madonnina between the Milan giants. 'When you put your feet on the pitch, you can feel that it's not just a soccer match. It is something more,' Stefano Rellandini, the photographer who captured an iconic image of Marco Materazzi leaning on Rui Costa's shoulder as flares lit up the 2005 Champions League meeting, once told me. For Gardner, the experience was incomparable. 'Dude, I have been to Super Bowls, heavyweight professional fights, NBA Championship games. I have never seen anything that matches that level of intensity,' he says.

The calcio-crazed city of Milan will always be Brera's home but the investors have been keen to export the brand to other countries and regions. After the takeover, Brera created a club in Matola, a suburb of the Mozambique capital Maputo. Brera Tchumene began life in the second division but won promotion to the top-flight Moçambola league in their inaugural season. They also launched an initiative with an orphanage in Maputo, with players from the men's and women's teams paying regular visits to play football and games with the children, as well as helping with the delivery of basic goods and food.

In Asia, they purchased Mongolian Premier League outfit Ilch FC, based in Ulaanbaatar (also known as the coldest capital city in the world) and rebranded them

Brera Ilch. They forged a partnership with local youth football clubs to help support young children from disadvantaged backgrounds pursue healthy lifestyles, as well as tackle substance abuse.

The most notable of the initial flurry of purchases, though, came in North Macedonia. Goran Pandev was only 18 years old when he left Macedonian football to join Inter Milan. Bar a very brief spell in Turkey with Galatasaray, the forward spent his entire career in Italy, winning a Champions League, Serie A and Coppa Italia treble under José Mourinho in 2010, as well as the FIFA Club World Cup later that year after the Portuguese boss had departed for Real Madrid. With further successful spells at Lazio, Napoli and Genoa, he is regarded as a Serie A cult hero. Back home in North Macedonia, however, where he won 122 national team caps and guided his nation to a first ever major tournament at Euro 2020, Pandev is a bona fide legend. 'It is such a powerful story,' explains Maria Xing, Brera's head of investments and corporate development, who wrote her business school thesis on how football can change societies. 'Goran Pandev changed the country's hopes for the future, both from a sporting perspective but also from a societal perspective.'

Helping Inter to an historic treble was not the only thing ticked off Pandev's 2010 to-do list, mind. That year, he launched his own football club, Akademija Pandev, in Strumica, a short hop from the borders with Bulgaria and Greece and the city where he was born. They quickly climbed the ranks and now play in the top-tier Macedonian First League, reaching the Europa League and Conference League qualifiers in recent seasons. In 2023, they were taken under the Brera umbrella and renamed FC AP Brera Strumica. The company paid Pandev $600,000 for 90 per cent of the club, while keeping him on as president and making him a member of the Brera board. 'He could do anything with his post-playing career but, instead, he has chosen to go back to Macedonia and start up an infrastructure to provide for people and kids who wouldn't have had the opportunities he did when he was a kid,' adds Xing, who held roles at Liverpool and 777 Partners before joining Brera.

Xing is just as excited by another acquisition in the city. When word got out about Brera's deal with Pandev, the player-manager at local club ZFK Tiverija Strumica, Aleksandra Terziski, reached out to Brera's chief executive officer Pierre Galoppi to see if the company would be interested in investing in women's football in the area. Galoppi, Xing and co. were more than happy to oblige, bringing the club under the AP Brera Strumica banner as Brera Tiverija and making Terziski the general director. In doing so, Brera became the first foreign investor in a women's football club in North Macedonia. 'Our players will have more opportunities,' said Terziski. '[It] will bring us a connection to the global football ecosystem and provide players with the chance to play abroad.' Xing, a champion of women's sport and inclusivity, believes it can be a powerful and impactful union. 'It is definitely a story worth telling,' adds Xing, who was attracted by the prospect of working for Brera to use football as a tool to do 'something good and enhance society'. 'I believe in it a lot,' she says of the women's team in

Strumica. 'It is not going to be the most profitable thing in the next couple of years but it is a really good way to support a marginalised group.'

Investment in women's sport is one of Brera's commitments. They own a majority stake in professional volleyball club UYBA Volley, who are based in Busto Arsizio, north of Milan, and plan to widen the brand the same way they have done with the football side of the business. 'Women's sport globally is a huge growth opportunity,' explains Gardner.

Following an initial wave of what McClory calls 'modest' acquisitions, those in places and countries Brera felt they could have the most impact, the company made a splash in Italian football by signalling their intent to purchase a Serie B club. They initially spoke to 12 teams and engaged in further conversations with eight of those, finding that the interested clubs were keen to pitch to Brera about why they should be considered because of what they were doing to have a social impact in their respective areas. For many of the prospective clubs, it was one of the first things they opened with when meeting the investors, who were delighted those clubs recognised its importance to Brera. 'They know that is part of our DNA and our criteria. They know it was a key part of our history,' says McClory. In many ways, the social aspect has gone from being an interesting angle that sets Brera apart to becoming a key part of their fabric, something that is recognised as a core value.

They were close to purchasing Spezia, in the port city nestled down the Ligurian coast from Genoa. Instead, they eventually concluded a deal for Juve

Stabia, from the town of Castellammare di Stabia on the outskirts of Naples. It positions Brera in an area with wide and varied cultural interest, close to Sorrento and the Amalfi Coast, as well as Pompeii and Mount Vesuvius. 'Juve Stabia shares the social impact mission of Brera and will extend their reach into the greater Naples area, starting with Castellammare di Stabia,' said club president Andrea Langella when the deal went through.

At the same time, Brera have gone back to their roots with the original football club. Brera Calcio's on-field performances have often played out in the background to their social and cultural projects, at least to the outside world. Leonardo Aleotti says it is a stretch to call themselves, from a footballing perspective, the third team in Milan anymore. 'But we have so many positive sides,' he adds. 'What we have done in the past and what we are doing in the present.' After all, the club's focus has always been on what they call 'the innovative use of football as a social, sporting, cultural and communicative experiment'. They decided to relaunch the football aspect of things from the lowest division, with men's and women's teams that tap into the local student population in the Brera district.

Aleotti Jr has been involved with the club as long as he can remember, from watching his father hire World Cup stars, mix with Mafia bosses and attract global attention, to running the line and coaching the youth teams. Now he gets to be president of the new, amateur venture. 'My father started from the top,' laughs Aleotti Jr. 'I will start from the bottom!'

Chapter Nine

The Record Breaker

ILDEFONS LIMA scans the walls of his office, where around 800 carefully bagged match-worn shirts hang like trophies. He has collected more than 1,300 in total, many as swaps with other players during a career that spanned Andorra, Spain, Mexico, Greece, Italy and Switzerland. But the collection has only continued to grow since his retirement in 2023. 'If there was a fire and I had to keep one shirt,' Lima ponders, contemplating the question for a second before laughing and shaking his head. 'Pfft! ... maybe I prefer to die!'

Lima is a special character. He holds a Guinness world record for the longest career in men's international football, one that began with Andorra when he was 17 and ended at the age of 43. He has played against some of the greatest players of several generations. Ronaldo Nazário, Zinedine Zidane, Cristiano Ronaldo, Gareth Bale, Kylian Mbappé. Once, he was a plucky young defender with the youthful courage to venture into every opposition changing room and ask for a shirt swap, whether that was against Brazil or Latvia. Now, he sees every jersey in his collection as telling a story from a long and distinguished, if not widely known, professional football career.

'I am really mad,' he laughs. 'I have space problems now because I have all the Andorra shirts in national history, from the first game until the last game. When I was a pro, I swapped every game. I have some big names in my collections. I was very lucky to play for Andorra, because I have some shirts here that, if you don't play for a national team, it is probably impossible to take. I have Mbappé, Robert Lewandowski, Cristiano Ronaldo. If you don't play against those players, how do you take those shirts? It's impossible, unless you spend a lot of money and people are crazy about that, so you cannot do it.'

Lima has always loved football shirts. When he was a kid, growing up in the 1980s, it was not easy to pick up exotic kits from abroad like it is nowadays. So, on family holidays, he would go with his father to the local club stadiums to try and get his hands on one. When his brother, Antoni, who is nine years older, began playing professional football, first at Barcelona C and then Real Madrid B, before featuring for a host of lower league Spanish sides, he fuelled Ildefons' thirst by bringing back jerseys of his own. That only intensified when the younger brother's own club career began at FC Andorra and, soon after, with the national team. He scans the room once more: 'I can see the Belarus shirt when we won our first game. Macedonia, a Las Palmas shirt, Barcelona. I like to collect shirts because it is a good way to explain the history. I say "This shirt I played against Lewandowski" or "This was the first

Andorra game." This is the thing I like to collect – history. In that context, I have one Yugoslavia shirt that was a gift from Bruno Conti, the Italian player who won the World Cup. I played with one of his sons in Switzerland for two years. One day we went to Rome. He knew that I collected shirts and said he would give me one and it was Yugoslavia. It will never exist anymore! It is a match-worn shirt from 1981 against Italy in Belgrade and is a piece of history.'

It's not just the big hitters that Lima holds dear: 'I have Ronaldo and Shevchenko, but I love Andy Selva from San Marino, Liam Walker from Gibraltar, Mario Frick from Liechtenstein, because we have something between us, you know? He feels like me when we play against big teams, he's suffered like me, he's next to me and I love to have these shirts, too.'

The Principality of Andorra sits to the east of the Pyrenees on the border of France and Spain, about a three-hour drive from both Perpignan and Barcelona, where Lima was born. By population, it is the 11th-smallest nation in the world, with just over 85,000 inhabitants by the end of 2023, around the same as the Isle of Man. In footballing terms, that makes Andorra the fifth-least-populated nation to be registered with UEFA, though only around 40 per cent of the population living there have Andorran passports, making the pool of players the national team can choose from even smaller. Naturally, with its rugged, mountainous terrain, an average elevation of 6,549ft and a capital, Andorra la Vella, that is the highest in Europe, it is a nation renowned for winter sports, cycling and hiking. It was only in 1994 that

Andorra formed its own football federation, with a domestic league coming the following year and, finally, a national team that was recognised by the sport's governing bodies in 1996.

Lima was 16 at the time and watched that first game from the stands, a 6-1 home defeat by Estonia. By the time Andorra's second-ever international fixture came around seven months later, this time an away trip to Estonia, both he and his brother were part of the travelling squad. 'It was our first game outside Andorra,' he remembers. 'They called me and I was very surprised but I played that game. I scored, too!' He chuckles thinking about it. There is no footage of the goal, so Lima has the artistic licence to tell people whatever he wants – overhead kick, rabona … only the players, coaches and 1,100 fans in attendance know how it really went in. Nevertheless, it was the first of 11 for his country, making Lima Andorra's record goalscorer. Not bad for a defender.

But, for all his 137 caps and 26 years in international football, those early days remain some of the most treasured. He has watched football change over the past three decades, even in Andorra, and senses the innocence they enjoyed on those fledgling international trips has been lost: 'We were friends, we played together here in Andorra and it was like a college trip. Representing your country, playing international games. Now, it is normal but we didn't know anything about that. The memories of that period are amazing. We played because we loved that. They didn't pay us anything, we travelled for free, spent our holidays travelling with the national team and playing friendly games versus Estonia, Lithuania. In 1997, they were very rare games. We created some feelings with this group of people that, 26 years later, if I find one of my team-mates in the street, it is something special. Now, that is impossible, because it is another era.'

For Lima, his debut lacked just one thing. Three days after the defeat by Estonia in Kuressaare, Andorra were set to face Latvia in Riga. The players had to hold on to their shirts to use for the second game, so Lima was unable to swap his with an opposition player. Now, he is talking with players from that Estonia side to try and track one down. They suffered another 4-1 reverse in Latvia but there was a bonus after the game when someone from the federation told the players they were free to do as they wished with their jerseys. Lima headed straight for the away dressing room: 'I said "Change? Change?!" There was a player called [Mihails] Zemļinskis and I swapped the shirt.'

The next summer, as the footballing elite were gearing up for the 1998 World Cup in France, Lima and his Andorra team-mates suddenly found they, too, had a role to play in preparing the stars for the game's most prestigious competition. Andorra's head coach at the time was Miluir Macedo, a Brazilian whose previous job was at Happy Valley Athletic in Hong Kong. But Macedo had contacts at the Confederation of Brazilian Football and, to the surprise of everyone inside and out of Andorra, in just their fourth-ever international fixture, the tiny, mountainous microstate were sent in to play reigning world champions Brazil in Paris. The game took place at Red Star's historic Stade Bauer, just seven days before the Seleção's tournament opener against Scotland. 'We were playing against Estonia, Lithuania, Azerbaijan, these rare games,' grins Lima. 'And one day, they say, "Oh guys, we are going to play against Brazil, the week before the World Cup." We thought "You are crazy!"'

Lima was 18 and playing his football with FC Andorra, while his brother Toni was at Portuguese third-tier side União da Madeira. A report in British newspaper *The Independent* that year suggested almost all registered footballers in Andorra had moved there from other countries, meaning there were only 50 adult males eligible to play for the national team at the time and, the report said, 'just 32 regarded as proficient in the basic football skills'. Yet they were going up against a team that included Roberto Carlos, Cafu, Dunga, Rivaldo, Bebeto and Ronaldo. Brazil were ranked the world's No.1 team, while Andorra were 182nd, with a starting XI who had accumulated just 22 international caps between them heading into the fixture and had a total of zero victories. Brazil, meanwhile, boasted more than 500 caps, World Cup winners and the world's most expensive player. It was just up to the Lima brothers to stop him.

'It was the first big player I played against,' explains Lima. 'That day, I had a lot of feelings. You are very young, you don't have football experience, you don't have international experience and you are playing against Brazil, you are playing against Ronaldo! Before that game, you just think of Ronaldo when playing with the PlayStation, you know? And one day, in June, you are going to go to the pitch and the players next to you are Ronaldo, Rivaldo, Cláudio Taffarel, Dunga.

The old and the new; Athletic Club's iconic San Mamés stands on the banks of the Nervión.

Athletic's stadium has stood on this site since 1913, with the new San Mamés opened a century later.

The Mr Pentland Club is an international Athletic supporters' club; members meet at the Txoko in Bilbao on special occasions.

Once the residence of Ramón de la Sota, Ibaigane Palace is Athletic Club's impressive headquarters in the centre of Bilbao.

Allan Cockram, founder of the Brentford Penguins, meets legendary Athletic Club goalkeeper José Ángel Iribar at the Thinking Football Film Festival. Credit: Athletic Club

Allan Cockram and 'Bilbao Al' lead the Penguins and Athletic Genuine teams out at Lezama. Credit: Athletic Club

L'Olympic has become the regular meeting spot for Red Star fans before games at Stade Bauer across the road.

Redevelopment is under way on a new-look Stade Bauer, with a capacity of 10,000 expected.

The Dutch fan walk has become an iconic part of Netherlands supporters' pre-match routine; up to 40,000 followed the Oranje Bus in Berlin during Euro 2024.

Despite playing in Germany's second tier, Hertha Berlin average crowds of more than 50,000 at the Olympiastadion. Credit: Joseph Corlett

'The Bench' is a significant spot for the Hertha Inters fan club; it's where they meet for every home game. Credit: Joseph Corlett

Named after the German revolutionary socialist, the Karl Liebknecht Stadion plays home to SV Babelsberg 03.

St Pauli stickers can be spotted at Babelsberg, with the two clubs sharing a friendship.

FC United's Broadhurst Park home is kitted out in flags; with messages ranging from anti-Glazers to support for their Polish opponents in the Fenix Trophy.

A lemonade stand in Naples is awash with nods to Diego Maradona and other Napoli heroes.

Naples is dotted with murals to the legendary Diego Maradona, with some of the most iconic found in the Quartieri Spagnoli neighbourhood.

Fans have also laid scarves and trinkets beneath a Maradona mural in Quartieri Spagnoli in honour of their former hero.

Players, staff and directors all have to pass the famed fan wall after arriving at Cambridge United's charming Abbey Stadium.

Cambridge United legend Dion Dublin has a bar named after him at the Abbey Stadium and is one of the club's board members.

Ruben Jongkind was the man tasked with writing and implementing Netherlands legend Johan Cruyff's plan for the future of Ajax.

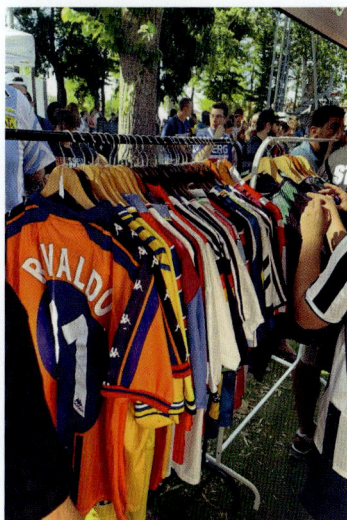

More than 8,000 Serie A supporters visited the fan village at Operazione Nostalgia, browsing vintage shirts and enjoying the pre-match entertainment.

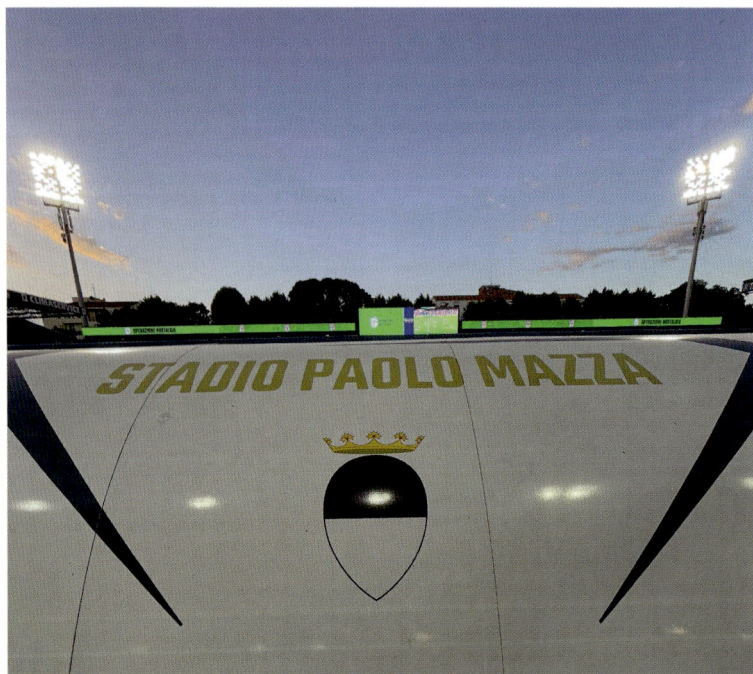

Home to third-tier SPAL, once of Serie A, the Stadio Paolo Mazza has a capacity of 16,134.

Francesco Totti and Alessandro 'Alex' Del Piero captained the sides at Operazione Nostalgia.

Where it all began. Kyoto Sanga fans prepare for the second-division clash with Machida Zelvia in Japan.

The memories are amazing. Ronaldo was in fantastic condition. He was not happy at the end of the game because he did not score against Andorra. For us, it was a positive thing, because Ronaldo played against Andorra and he didn't score! I remember my brother touched him on the arm and Ronaldo looked like "Oh, you are touching me? You know I am Ronaldo?"'

Ronaldo may not have scored but Cafu, Rivaldo and Giovanni did as Brazil won 3-0, a very respectable scoreline for the Andorrans. Once marking the world's greatest striker was over, Lima set off on another quest. As he remembers it, only Cafu and Leonardo had swapped shirts at the end of the game and the defender had not been able to get his hands on what would have undoubtedly been the most prestigious piece of his collection yet. 'I was young,' he says. 'I went to the Brazil dressing room, like I did a lot of times during my career, but in front of the door there were two bodyguards, big boys! I tried to go inside and they told me I could not. They opened the door and I saw a lot of shirts on the ground and I said, "Just one of these shirts for me?"' He was met with another firm rejection. Giving up hope, Lima decided to cut his losses and head back. 'I was walking to my dressing room,' he continues. 'And César Sampaio from Brazil was going to his. He had probably been with the press or something like that. So, I said "Oh Cesar, please, swap me the shirt?" Probably because I was young and he saw my face, he swapped the shirt!'

Remarkably, Brazil were not the last world champions Andorra faced that year. France defeated Brazil in the World Cup Final to swipe their crown and, a few months later in Euro 2000 qualifying, took on their tiny neighbours in front of 75,000 people at the Stade de France. Bixente Lizarazu, Frank Leboeuf, Laurent Blanc, Didier Deschamps, Zinedine Zidane and David Trezeguet all started, while Robert Pires and Nicolas Anelka came off the bench. But, again, Andorra acquitted themselves well against the footballing big boys. France won 2-0, with Vincent Candela and Youri Djorkaeff scoring. In fact, in the reverse game, played in Barcelona, Andorra almost snatched a remarkable 0-0 draw, only for Leboeuf to break their hearts with a penalty in the final five minutes.

'We played against Brazil and a few months later we played against France, the past two world champions,' recalls Lima, shaking his head in disbelief. 'I said at the end of the game, "Okay, this is a masterclass of football, nothing will be better than this. Play against any opponent you want in any stadium you want but to be better than this? It's going to be impossible." Paris Saint-Denis was full of people, the World Cup trophy was there, it was an amazing atmosphere and we just lost 2-0. Brazil lost 3-0 in the final a few months before! This experience was something – before and after. Before, you have no experience and then you play the best players in the world and your mentality changes. "Okay, who wants to play against Andorra?!"'

Still, it took until April 2000, almost four years after making their international bow, for Lima and Andorra to taste victory for the first time. It came at home, too, in a 2-0 friendly win against Belarus in front of 500 people at the Comunal d'Andorra la Vella. 'It was special because we didn't expect to win,' recalls Lima, fondly. Though, for him, the real 'miracle' took place 17 years later. Andorra were on a run of 66 matches without a competitive victory, a streak that stretched back 13 years, when they met Hungary in 2017. Lima, however, had missed an historic 1-0 win over Macedonia in 2004, so had, in fact, never won a competitive game for his country. 'You don't expect to win,' he says. 'Obviously, all the games you go on to the pitch thinking you have chances to win. If you have one chance and score, and they have a bad day, you can win. But if you think with your head and your brain, it will be very difficult.' Yet, against Hungary, it was Andorra who took the lead in the 26th minute and, for once, it was the home side who managed to hold on. 'At the end of the game when the referee blew the whistle, it was one of the best moments in my career,' adds Lima. 'We started crying, smiling, hugging all the people, kissing people. Your feelings, emotions are crazy because it was something new for us. A lot of players on the pitch had never won a game before with the national team. It was one of the best moments of my life.'

The wait, the struggle, the years of hurt made such moments even more poignant for Lima and his Andorra team-mates. Football is about glory, yes, but it is also about sacrifice, togetherness, embracing the hard times, as well as the good. Lima has many triumphant moments to reflect upon. He has scored in qualification games against the Republic of Ireland, Wales and Belgium but those games ultimately ended in defeat. In fact, in his 137 caps, Andorra managed just five victories. When you accept that, realistically, almost every team you face is better than you, there is an alternate sense of enjoyment or satisfaction to be achieved from such fixtures. 'We are just 30,000 people playing against countries that are millions of people,' explains Lima. 'When you play against big teams – Spain, England, Portugal, Brazil – you don't need motivation. You run, run, run like a crazy person. For me, during my international career, it was very difficult to play against small teams like San Marino or Liechtenstein, because there you cannot make a mistake. You have to win – or you cannot lose – because it is your level. But to play against France or England, you have to enjoy it. I told my team-mates, "Enjoy it, take nice pictures, swap shirts; you will remember that game all your career." I remember games against Russia, Belgium, Portugal and you suffer a lot. The maximum score I took was six, not a lot of goals if you see the difference between both teams. The difference should be more like 60 goals! If you play against France or England, you think I'm going to enjoy the people, the pitch, everything. If we lose, it is the normal thing.'

Lima also strongly rejects the idea that the big nations should not have to play against sides like Andorra in qualifying, as well as the notion that he and his team-mates were any less professional. They may not have been on eye-watering salaries, like some of their opponents, but they possessed the same hard work and dedication to their craft. In many ways, they were a lot more resilient. 'You can imagine what you go through with your friends playing big games,' he stresses. 'We do miracles with our results, fighting as we fight. Sometimes, when people see your reality they say, "These guys from Andorra are amazing." You have to see the other view, no? It's a good way for small countries to keep growing. Iceland, 20 years ago, it was impossible they won a game at Wembley. Now, a lot of people respect Iceland.'

Lima also appreciates he got to live out the dream of many young kids by going on this journey with his brother. They played against the world's best players together at iconic stadiums, none more so than Wembley, where Antoni marked his international retirement.

'I learned a lot because he is nine years older than me,' says Lima. 'He was like my dad. He told me what I had to do, gave me a lot of good words in bad moments to continue working. And he was very important in my career. Playing with your brother for your national team is amazing. He played his last game at Wembley against England in 2009. I started to play in 1997 and we played for 12 or 13 years together. We played about 60 games together and had very good feelings.'

The brothers were recently at home together discussing that fixture against England. They played together in the middle of a back five as Andorra lost 6-0, with Wayne Rooney and Jermain Defoe both scoring twice and Peter Crouch and Frank Lampard also on the scoresheet. It was Lima's joint-record defeat but that does not dampen the memories. 'The midfielders in that game were Lampard, Steven Gerrard and David Beckham,' laughs Lima. 'When you think about that you say "Oh my God!" For me, England and France, playing in Paris and Wembley, or the Luzhniki in Russia, you remember that forever.'

Lima's own retirement came in 2023, his international career prolonged by a row that saw him miss more than a year with the national team. Lima, if you hadn't already reached this conclusion, is strong-willed. During the pandemic, he suggested players should be Covid-tested before training with Andorra. Instead of being heard, he found himself ostracised from the national set-up. 'There was a person who tried to fuck me in every way,' he groans. Such is fate, it meant Lima returned to the squad at the age of 43, 26 years after making his debut, something that earned him a world record. If he had not had that break, then he would likely have retired earlier. 'I have no more power, I have nothing,' he recalls. 'But I wanted to leave against a big name.'

Lima spent two years of his club career playing in Switzerland, featuring against the likes of Granit Xhaka and Xherdan Shaqiri when they were young. When he spotted on the calendar a European Championship qualifier against Switzerland in Sion, he knew that was the moment to bow out. 'When you play in Andorra, it's a very small stadium, not full, you don't smell football, you know? So, I decided to leave football outside Andorra,' he explains. Lima, sporting the captain's armband, was given a rousing reception by the home crowd when he was substituted midway through the first half. 'Everything stopped, the stadium did a standing ovation. Xhaka, Shaqiri, they came to hug me. It was amazing. Goosebumps. It was in front of all my family – daughters, wife, brother, dad. I really did the right thing.'

But what fills the void when you have spent your whole adult life playing football for a living? Before he retired, Lima took on the role of president of Andorra's national player union, the Associació de Futbolistes Andorrans. It was in this role that he voiced concerns over Andorra's Covid protocol and was then excluded from the national set-up. Now, he uses his position to try and help Andorran players at home and abroad, making sure they are paid on time and helping to sort any problems that may arise. Lima is keen to keep developing the game in Andorra but has his frustrations. 'I want to see football growing,' he says. 'Here, they want to be quite relaxed.' He has found other ways to keep in touch with football and has taken his UEFA 'A' coaching licence, while running half-marathons keeps him fit these days; Andorra's mountainous terrain makes for some gruelling training runs.

But what really fuels Lima's passion now is shirts. He has turned this obsession into something beneficial, forming a not-for-profit charitable association that aims to help the most disadvantaged children in Andorra. Lima runs the Gol Solidari association alongside ex-Andorra international Juli Sànchez and former Argentina, Barcelona, Real Madrid and Benfica striker Javier Saviola, who lives in the principality. The former footballers raise money by auctioning off shirts and other memorabilia and then use those sales to make donations to a number of local projects for children. 'A lot of people ask for shirts and we decided this was a nice way to make money for charity,' explains Lima. 'We started with Andorran team shirts, national team shirts.'

Once Lima and Sànchez reached out to Saviola, who was happy to come aboard, getting hold of the big names became a little easier. 'We have had shirts from Luka Modrić, Lionel Messi, Vinícius Júnior, all big names,' adds Lima. 'We auction the shirts, take money and help children here in Andorra. And when Javier goes to Argentina, he always does some charity movements there. Andorra is a small village; we know everyone and we know the job they do. Sometimes, I have to buy a shirt from the auction but it is a good way to buy it!'

Yet, for all his years on the pitch and for all his work off it, Lima believes he has not been shown the respect his career deserves by those he served at the football federation. 'I am so sad because of that,' he confesses, his usual profoundly positive exterior breached for a moment. That has nothing to do with ego. Far from it. In fact, Lima enjoys engaging with people on social media who are keen to find out more about one of the world's smallest footballing nations. In that sense, Lima has become a kind of digital footballing ambassador for Andorra. 'I always try to explain what Andorra is, to know our reality,' he says. 'We are normal people. We have to continue being normal people – we are not stars. Now, the big names are untouchable. We are lucky to play against big teams and represent our country. So, maybe it is better to admire a player like us than a big name? Obviously, they have qualities we don't have, that is why they are in that position, but we are normal people.'

'Normal' is subjective and typically understated. Lima may not boast the luxury lifestyle of football's multi-millionaire stars or enjoy the same global profile some former players do. But he has competed against the very best, shared a pitch with generational legends and swapped shirts with icons. He has captained his country, represented Andorra alongside his brother and earned a Guinness world record. He's kept arguably the greatest striker of all time off the scoresheet. The journey so far has been unique, fulfilling and, like tackling the Andorran terrain, challenging and exciting. Wherever Lima's story takes him next, you can guarantee it will be anything but 'normal'.

Chapter Ten

Hot and Crazy Naples

LUIGI DI Nunzio flicks an errant strand of slick brown hair behind his ear and cracks a joke about having a sibling named Mario. He is all in on this one. 'My brother, hey, he's a plumber. He goes around catching mushrooms. I think he has a problem!' You sense he's told it before, delivered in perfect, flowing English and flourished with a Neapolitan twang. In many ways, Di Nunzio epitomises the warm, welcoming nature of most people in Naples. They're proud, generous and boast a good sense of humour. They treat you like an old friend.

Dig a little deeper with Di Nunzio, though, and there is a soul so pure he has devoted much of his adult life to helping others who have found themselves in less privileged situations. With boats bobbing on the waves and the lunchtime sun sparkling off the water in the background as we first meet, Di Nunzio is also refreshingly humble and pragmatic about his role in a project that has changed the lives of many people to have embarked on these shores.

The quaint marina at Borgo Marinari is a magnificent blend of Naples' most ancient past and its modern-day status as one of Europe's fastest-growing tourist destinations. Between 2010 and 2017, according to the Florence-based Centre of Tourism Studies, the city experienced a 91 per cent rise in tourism as the region continued to shake off its association with organised crime clans of the Camorra and the historic problems it faced with waste disposal and pollution.

At the same time, Naples has become more accessible by air, rail and sea and is no longer merely a landing point for visiting destinations such as Pompeii, Mount Vesuvius and the Amalfi Coast. A decade ago, there was little tourist pressure on the city centre. That has changed significantly. By the summer of 2023, for example, there were more Airbnb properties in Naples than Venice.

It is easy to see why Naples, with its coastal location, is so popular and, no doubt, tourist numbers will continue to grow. The harbour is a pleasant mix of wooden fishing boats and fancier-looking day-trippers primed for a ride to the islands of Capri and Ischia or a jaunt further down the Sorrentine Peninsula. Yet it is also the scene for a discovery of huge archaeological importance. The marina is now connected to the shore by a short stone walkway that leads to the foot of Castel dell'Ovo, the oldest castle in Naples and one whose name translates as 'Castle of the Egg' because, the story goes, Roman poet Virgil buried an egg here. Should it break, he proclaimed, the castle will fall.

When merchant travellers first settled in the area almost 3,000 years ago, this land was cut off as an islet known as Megaris. It is here that legend says a heartbroken Parthenope, one of the three Greek sirens whose seductive voices would lure sailors to their death, washed up after throwing herself into the sea and drowning, having failed to entice the legendary Greek king Odysseus. The original settlement on the nearby hill became known after her. Parthenope, you *Football Manager* anoraks will know, is also the name given to Napoli in the game. Indeed, one of their nicknames is 'I Partenopei', the Parthenopeans.

It was here in the picturesque marina in 2018 that underwater archaeologists discovered what they believe to be traces of an historic port, predating the newer city of Neapolis that was founded by the Greeks in 470 BC. It makes Naples, with its historic centre deemed of 'outstanding universal value' by UNESCO's World Heritage Convention, one of the most ancient cities in Europe. And, in short, a city founded on migration and the movement of people. A melting pot of different cultures. Greek, Roman, Arabic, German, Hungarian, Spanish and French conquerors are among those to have all laid claim to the land at some point (though it should be noted Neapolitans are also resilient and principled and Naples was the first Italian city to stage a rebellion against Nazi occupation during World War Two).

Today, in an Italy purporting to take a hard line on immigration under prime minister Giorgia Meloni, holidaymakers are welcome but the message is that refugees and asylum seekers are not. At the height of the migration crisis in 2016, more than 180,000 people arrived in Italy, via the Mediterranean, from North Africa. Then, in April 2023, Italian ministers declared a state of emergency in response to the rising number of crossings. The government has tried to stop non-governmental organisations from bringing stranded migrant boats to shore, while drawing up plans to build migrant holding centres in Albania. Alongside the European Union, it has also put money into training coastguards in Tunisia and Libya, where many crossings depart.

While the government continues to try and find ways to discourage people from making the dangerous journey, Di Nunzio is one of those fighting to help migrants who do land in Naples try to build a better life for themselves. 'The government is not very keen, at least not officially, because that is the ideology,' he says. 'The official line is that we don't welcome anyone but we are actually doing it. The government has to respect the deal we have and, secondly, we really need them. Italy is old. We don't have children, our pension system is in collapse and the market demands workers.'

Yet, Di Nunzio's way of connecting with the arrivals is via a medium we can all appreciate: football. 'We are from Naples, we are the centre of the Mediterranean, we get in touch with people all over the world and we are the first or second approach port in Italy for migrants,' he explains. 'So, for us, it was easy to say "Okay, let's address the issue. This is what we must do now."' Such is Di Nunzio's affable nature that it is impossible not to get drawn into conversation when mooching Borgo Marinari's cute, narrow streets in the shadow of the castle. The mini peninsula is scattered with intriguing restaurants, many with tables decked in blue and white, approaching the water's edge. Perched on the steps outside 'O Tabaccaro, Di Nunzio opens up about a project that is dear to him. 'Have you heard of Afro Napoli United?' he beams. 'We're Naples' second club.'

It all began in 2008, when Di Nunzio and his colleagues were struggling to make up the numbers for their weekly pick-up games after work. In Naples, after all, *everyone* is passionate about football. It is more than just a sport. 'We grew up playing in the street, so it is a way of life,' says Di Nunzio. 'It is our teacher, it is the way you learn how to get in touch with other people, how to share a place, how to respect each other.' To keep their regular game going, they decided to invite some of the migrants they often passed on their way to the office, who would hang around outside Naples' central station. Once they got chatting, the original group realised many of their new team-mates had arrived in the city after travelling from Africa in search of work and the opportunity to build a new life. It became a two-way relationship. Any members of the group who held prejudices about the migrants soon shed those when they got to know one another. Meanwhile, the migrants found the football games an effective way of helping them integrate in the city and wider society.

'Usually, they form a close community in the place they establish,' says Di Nunzio, explaining how many migrants struggle to forge bonds with local people or have a social life outside of their immediate community. 'Football helped them do this,' he adds. 'We made a lot of friends.' It helped that Di Nunzio and some of his acquaintances, including club president Antonio Gargiulo and co-founder Francesco Fasano, already worked in areas of human rights and social activism, meaning they spotted the opportunity to do something powerful and meaningful and had the nous to overcome the many obstacles that followed.

A year after their casual kickabouts began, Afro Napoli United were formed. 'Antonio is the father,' smiles Di Nunzio. 'He is the real one who made Afro Napoli.' The club brought together refugees who had travelled from all over Africa, starting their journeys in Cape Verde, Ghana, Niger, Senegal, Sierra Leone and beyond. They were pitted together alongside native Neapolitans to create a formidable team in the amateur leagues. The name was important to the club's mission, too. Rather than just wanting to be a team for refugees and immigrants, which the founders feared would invite outside discrimination, the aim was to help them integrate with local players and provide an inclusive environment. Afro Napoli United became that in a nutshell. 'We are very present in the territory because we have lots of organisations working and trying to address issues, so, as people, we were already known in the city,' adds Di Nunzio. Word spread quickly and Afro Napoli United were able to gather plenty of interest from other organisations and individuals who wanted to get involved.

The team were also very talented, winning several competitions in those early years. 'We were powerful,' Di Nunzio continues. 'We were a mix of culture, physicality and technique.' But when it came to wanting to enter the official Italian Football Federation (FIGC) pyramid, effectively joining the league ladder that leads all the way up to Serie A, Afro Napoli United found they would be unable to register many of their players. 'Surprise,' says Di Nunzio. 'The law did not allow us because we had a lot of migrants. We faced a lot of difficulties.'

Part of this was because of regulations put in place by FIFA, world football's governing body, over the registration of non-European players. Di Nunzio says those laws were created to prevent opportunists posing as agents from poaching talented young players in Africa and trying to smuggle them into Europe. 'They make them promises: "I will let you become a great player, blah, blah,"' he says. 'And then they don't give a shit about them.' There were similar problems to overcome with Italian governing bodies but, after starting a national campaign, Afro Napoli United managed to successfully lobby both FIFA and the FIGC to modify their laws and allow migrants and refugees to represent the club.

Another potential hurdle lay not in the shape of bureaucratic red tape but with the deep-rooted problem of racism within Italian football. Despite historical issues in Serie A and leagues higher up the Italian pyramid, Di Nunzio says Afro Napoli United were welcomed by the majority of clubs, players and fans in the regional Campania divisions. 'At least in the first years in the low series,' he adds. 'Naples is not a racist city at all, so we have been welcomed everywhere we have been.'

Entering at the bottom of the FIGC's league system, Afro Napoli United blazed their way through those lower divisions to become the first club to win four successive promotions and reach the fifth-tier Eccellenza, one level below Serie D. Such is the structure of the Italian football system, the Eccellenza is made up of 28 regional leagues and comprises some 464 teams. Football at this level is a huge movement. 'We are talking about teams with more than 100 years of history, more than Napoli itself,' adds Di Nunzio. 'Football is a very serious question here.'

The club dropped the 'Afro' from their name when they began to welcome players from other countries, too. Wanting to appear inclusive to all, they became known as simply Napoli United. As well as the sub-Saharan African nations mentioned earlier and the local Italians, the club have been represented by players from as far afield as Tunisia, Portugal, France, El Salvador, Ecuador, Brazil, Chile and Argentina. 'You can see the connection with Naples in Africa and South America, where people literally grow up in the street playing football,' says Di Nunzio. 'It is everything we do. We exit school and we go play. We have lunch and then our mother threatens to kill us if we don't go home! And then we go back to playing football.'

Representing the club may present a happy, positive ending for some players but many people suffer on their journey to reach Naples, bidding to escape persecution in their own countries, only to face months-long voyages through deserts and across seas to reach their destination. One player, Sarjo Conteh, was smuggled through six countries. Another, Omar Gaye, spent nine months travelling with his uncle from Gambia through Senegal, Mali, Burkina Faso, Niger and Libya, only to be held in Tripoli for four months. He eventually found his way on to a small boat carrying 175 people but it broke down out at sea. Omar made it to Italy but he does not know what happened to his uncle.

Many don't even make it across the desert and, of those that do, there is a cruel proportion who become victims of the overcrowded smuggler boats. Data from the International Organization for Migration's Missing Migrants Project suggests that, in 2022 alone, at least 2,406 people who set off from North Africa lost their lives in the Mediterranean Sea, while it is estimated that the number of deaths on the central Mediterranean route stands at more than 22,000 over the past decade. Di Nunzio says people's journeys follow a similar pattern. They cross the desert and get arrested in Libya. There, they must either pay their way out or offer some sort of work or other service. 'Most of the people I get in touch with have suffered. They have signs and scars on their body,' he says. 'It is not easy at all. That is why, when you give them a chance, they will take it.'

For all their sporting success, the thing Napoli United remain most proud of is their social project. Achieving on the pitch just happens to be a by-product of the work that goes into their main objective, namely fighting racism and discrimination and promoting social inclusion. As well as migrants and asylum seekers, it means also looking out for young people in Naples who are at risk of exclusion and helping them to find housing and get a job. The project has since evolved to include a women's team, an amateur side, a youth sector and an academy with two affiliated football schools, as well as a futsal team. In those seasons they were powering their way up the Italian football pyramid;

the whole community would often come together on Sundays to watch the first XI play.

It is the grassroots amateur team, though, where many players begin their life at the club while waiting to obtain the correct documentation. Part of the problem players face when wanting to register is having no permanent address. In this regard, the club help provide them with housing, which has seen groups of young men from different backgrounds and cultures all living together. Di Nunzio was even known during the Coronavirus pandemic as the guy who would deliver food and supplies to the various accommodations on his motorcycle. Di Nunzio talks of players entering the 'United family', a network of people who try their best to help new arrivals integrate in society. That means helping them with the bureaucracy of arriving in a new country and administrative procedures, as well as helping them find work. That is the real aim of the project. 'Football is a tool for us, not the target,' adds Di Nunzio.

After our initial chat on the charming, weather-beaten steps of the marina, Di Nunzio promises to introduce me to players who have progressed through the club so that I can get their perspective on Napoli United and the work they do helping migrants to settle. 'It is a family. It is a club that welcomes everybody. It's something I can call a second home,' says Abu Sheriff, who was only a teenager when he left Sierra Leone during the Ebola crisis, which hit West Africa between 2013 and 2016, and arrived in Italy by boat from Libya. 'Football is somewhere where you find peace, a place where you make friends. Now, most of my friends are in Naples, even my girlfriend! Even Luigi!' Sheriff says Di Nunzio is like a brother to him. 'He showed me a lot of love and helped me,' he adds.

Sheriff was living in a refugee camp after first arriving in Campania when he caught the eye of the club. He explains: 'When I was in the refugee camp, we used to play a football match with the white people. Afro Napoli United contacted us and said they wanted a friendly match. We did a competition, three teams. We played against them and we won! So Afro Napoli saw me and took me. Now Naples is a home for us, for everybody. It is welcoming. This is a place of hope. You see a black community. We are like brothers now. Just like family, we take care of each other. It is football but they care about us.'

A powerful, left-footed striker, Sheriff was 19 when he began playing for Napoli United on a semi-professional basis, something he didn't imagine was possible as a kid growing up in Sierra Leone. 'In Africa, we have the talent,' he explains. 'We play because we love football. We don't play because we want to be professional, we just play for joy. After school, we go with friends, we play, we don't have positions. No, we play three versus three. If you defend, you defend, if you are a striker, you score and then you come back and defend. But in Italy they said "Abu, you have to play striker." So, for two months, I found it difficult. I had to study, I had to watch them play. That's why sometimes we Africans find it difficult to play in Europe, because we don't have one position. You have to play defender, midfielder, striker. You have to have the energy to work. And you have to go to school in

Africa, because you can't make money playing football. Our father used to flog us to go to school!' That is until one day Sheriff's father realised how talented his kid was. He let him play football, as long as he was keeping up with his studies. 'When you play football and don't go to school, the opportunities are slim,' adds the striker. 'That's why many of us came to Italy, for our families, for opportunities, because there is nothing. I have a family, so I have to work and I have to play. You have to be serious on the field and serious with your life.'

After his initial foray into the lower reaches of Italian football with Napoli United, Sheriff's career has continued elsewhere. There have been spells with AC Ottaviano in the Eccellenza and at Serie D club New Sondrio. But his bond with Di Nunzio and the Neapolitan club remains strong. 'The day I left my family, I was not sad because I knew I was coming to make money for them to send back home,' confesses Sheriff. 'But the day I went on loan from Afro Napoli, I saw Luigi write a note on Facebook and it made me feel sad. It was a nice thing that he wrote about me. It made me want to go back to Napoli.'

Sheriff is not the only player to have been given a foundation on which to launch a prospective football career. For some, the opportunities awarded at Napoli United have led to becoming fully fledged professionals. Maissa Ndiaye, a young Senegalese centre-back, was one of the many migrants to pass through the island of Lampedusa. It was in the waters off Lampedusa, situated halfway between northern Africa and the southernmost tip of Italy, that more than 600 people drowned in a matter of days in 2013 when, first, a fishing trawler capsized and then a boat carrying mostly Syrian refugees, including many medical professionals and their families fleeing the conflict, became shipwrecked. Ndiaye made it to Naples, however, and joined the club in 2018. He was only allowed to feature in non-competitive and youth matches because of laws around under-aged non-EU players but still attracted the attention of scouts from Roma. After a trial, he joined the Serie A club's youth academy the following year.

In 2021/22, Ndiaye trained with the first-team squad under manager José Mourinho and came agonisingly close to getting a taste of top-flight football. As *Il Romanista*, the Roma-dedicated daily newspaper, put it: 'He inevitably started further back than the others [in the youth team] but he had physique, running and the desire to improve. In three years of Primavera, the progress was evident, so much so that, in December [2021], Mourinho called him up to the first team.' In a match against Inter, with Roma 3-0 down, Mourinho had the defender prepped and ready to come on for the final moments of the Serie A game. *Il Romanista*'s report added: 'Ndiaye placed himself on the sideline, next to the fourth official, waiting for the ball to come out to make his debut. Sometimes, in these cases, his team-mates notice it and throw the ball out on purpose but it didn't happen to him. Perhaps they didn't notice. The game didn't stop and the referee blew the whistle for the end.'

Ndiaye joined Cremonese the following summer and was part of the matchday squad for the visit to the Stadio Olimpico but, again, did not get a chance to make his Serie A debut against his old club. It was one of five games that season that Cremonese named him on the bench in the competition but in all of them the defender was an unused substitute, instead joining Vicenza on loan in Serie C after Christmas. As of yet, the youngster is still to make his bow in the Italian first division. Following Cremonese's relegation to Serie B, the Lombardy club have sent him out on a succession of loan deals, first to Serbian SuperLiga outfit FK Železničar Pančevo and then to Serie C side Turris. Hopefully, Ndiaye's time will soon come.

Another player to have passed through the Napoli United ranks and carved out a professional career in the game is Ailton Jorge Dos Santos Soares, better known as simply Dodo. His footballing dream began with Batuque in his native Cape Verde. The club would occasionally take players to France or Portugal for tournaments and trials with professional clubs. On one such trip to the French mainland, Dodo saw an opportunity and took it. At the age of 19 and having not found a club in Europe to take him on, Dodo escaped the travelling party and made his way to Naples, where his mother was already stationed. 'I spoke with the president to say that I need to stay in Europe because Cape Verde is very, very difficult,' he tells me. 'He said "No". So, after this, in France, I took my passport and stayed in refuge on the French border for maybe ten days. Then, when my visa was validated, I went to Naples. My mum, my uncle and my cousin lived there.'

Seeking asylum and facing a wait that ended up taking five years to receive his official documents,

Dodo worked as a plumber during the day and then showcased his undeniable talent by night in various football tournaments in the Neapolitan suburbs to earn a bit of extra cash. The skilful forward was playing 11-a-side twice a week, on top of eight-a-side and five-a-side competitions, but his status meant he was unable to officially register for a team in the FIGC structure because of rules regarding refugees. 'There are a lot of Cape Verdean people in Naples,' he explains. 'Naples is very crazy, positive, hot; they live football. It's like in my country. You play football beside the street, you know? For me, it was easy to play football.'

Dodo found a home at Afro Napoli United, who were then still an amateur side, and repaid his new management and team-mates by scoring more than 100 goals for the club. Not that he can remember the exact figure, just that he earned an award for passing his century. 'This team is my life, my family,' he adds. 'I was so happy to play with this team and stay with these people, you know? Antonio, Luigi. It is one family for me. They possibly gave me *too* much. Antonio is like my dad. Antonio started to give us support about the documents, some opportunities like jobs, clothes, a house, food, everything.'

Eventually, his citizenship papers were processed and the forward was able to enjoy a stint in the Eccellenza with Procida, the club representing a tiny island in the Bay of Naples that was Italy's Capital of Culture in 2022 and is known for its pastel-coloured buildings, extra-large lemons and providing a beautiful backdrop in *The Talented Mr Ripley*. Dodo returned for two seasons with Napoli United once they earned promotion into the official league set-up but was always destined for bigger things. He signed his first professional deal in 2019 with Hamrun Spartans of the Maltese Premier League, ten years after he first fled to Italy. His goals and assists helped Hamrun to two league titles and a place in the Europa Conference League qualifying stages before, at the age of 30, Dodo earned a call-up to the Cape Verde national team.

The journey has continued for Dodo in Saudi Arabia, first at Al-Ain and then with Arar FC. But however far he travels from Naples, there is always one club that remains closest to his soul. 'It's in my heart and I have a tattoo here,' he says, proudly gesturing towards his bicep and a drawing of the lion represented on the club's badge, with their name inked underneath. 'In 2009 I left my country to come to Europe to play football. It was a dream. I saw the difficulty in Europe, about the documents, everything was difficult, and I tried. After five years, I got the documents, I played in Italy and saw my opportunity to go to Malta. They are professional. I don't know this country but I go; I don't care, this is my dream, no? We stayed four years in this club and Malta is like home – first my country, second Naples, third Malta. The dream is not full. We won the league but I didn't play in the Champions League. But to play in the Europa Conference League and win, win, win, I was so happy. It was a good experience. Now, I am old in football. Here, in Saudi, I come for the money, to open a door for the future.'

Dodo will go down in Afro Napoli United folklore. But, despite his success, he cannot claim to be the club's most famous former player. That honour falls to a man with a name that resonates around the globe, in football and beyond.

It's April 2023 when I visit Naples and the city is throbbing with anticipation and excitement. Neapolitans are usually superstitious but even they cannot help getting a little carried away. Napoli are on the brink of a first Serie A title in 33 years and the party is ready to break out at any moment. Flags and shirts bearing the names of current stars and those from the past line the alleyways of the historic Quartieri Spagnoli, blue and white banners and bunting hang from the balconies overhead, shirts are pegged to washing lines between buildings and crumbling walls have been freshly painted with a shield proudly sporting the number three in the middle, symbolising Napoli's incoming third Scudetto. Stairways are also coated in the colours of the Italian flag and outside a bar in one quaint piazza there are life-size cardboard cutouts of the whole team, plus coach Luciano Spalletti. Fans and tourists queue for selfies with masked striker Victor Osimhen. A Georgian flag has been wrapped around the shoulders of fabulous throwback winger Khvicha Kvaratskhelia. Faces of the soon-to-be title heroes can be seen on posters in the windows of almost every bar and shop, while market stalls flog knock-off shirts bearing their names. But wherever you look in Naples, there is one player who burns brighter than all others. One whose cherubic face and knitted curls appear on every window, door, wall or bumper sticker in the city. Here, he is worshipped as a demigod.

Perhaps fate brought Diego Maradona to Naples. He embodies the charm and chaos of a gloriously edgy and alluring city like they were made for each other. In many ways he *is* Naples. On one fruit and veg stall, a picture hangs from the shutters with Maradona rising above Mount Vesuvius, peering over Spalletti and members of the current squad. At a lemonade stand, a cardboard cutout has been knocked up with the Argentine holding a fresh jug of the stuff, next to the words 'La Bomba di Maradona'. Famously, at Bar Nilo, there is a lock of his hair constantly rotating in a small glass box as part of a shrine to the legendary forward. Since his death in 2020, Napoli's home ground has been renamed Stadio Diego Armando Maradona in his honour. And there are murals everywhere. A ten-storey portrait flanks the entire length of a block of flats in one suburb but the most famous overlooks a small square in the Quartieri Spagnoli, painted in 1990 and portraying Maradona in his Napoli heyday, the iconic Mars logo emblazoned across an unmistakable sky blue shirt.

The shabby courtyard below is overflowing with hundreds of items of Maradona memorabilia that have been gathered by the thousands of fans who make a pilgrimage to pay their respects, laying Napoli and Argentina scarves, as well as those from other clubs he represented. The narrow connecting streets nearby are a whirring thrum of chatter and a stop-start churn of scooter engines as locals try to navigate near-impossible gaps in the crowd.

Maradona identified with the people of Naples before he even arrived. His own poverty-stricken upbringing in the Buenos Aires neighbourhood of Villa Fiorito was not dissimilar to the ones lived by many

Neapolitans in the wake of the Irpinia earthquake in Campania that killed almost 2,500 people in 1980. Away fans in the north still taunted Napoli supporters about an outbreak of cholera in the city in 1973, unemployment was high and the Camorra – who cashed in on the billions sent in aid to the region following the earthquake – had a huge influence on the city, while feuding clans brought violence to the streets. Naples was as dysfunctional as the man about to move there, the world's best player, who had never settled in Barcelona. When it looked like a world record move for the Argentine was on the rocks, residents came together to help make up the difference and even the mayor chipped in to make sure the deal was completed. All this at a time when the Bank of Naples was facing bankruptcy. Maradona later talked about how fans had gone on hunger strike and chained themselves to fences at the club's San Paolo stadium until he arrived. 'Naples was a crazy city,' he said. 'They were as crazy as me.'

The hysteria when Napoli finally got their man was wild. But Maradona duly delivered. In seven seasons in the Italian south, he guided a team that finished narrowly above the relegation zone before he joined, and one who had never won the Scudetto, to two Serie A titles, first in 1987 and then 1990, as well as a Coppa Italia in 1987 and the UEFA Cup in 1989. Maradona added a World Cup, and one of the all-time iconic individual tournament performances, to the mix with Argentina in 1986 for good measure, making him the most revered and talked-about player on the planet. But it was not just his on-field magic that was of intrigue. A colourful private life of drug binges, Mafia parties and all-night romps often impacted on his football, seeing the star miss training or turn up late for games.

Maradona confessed, having first tried cocaine in 1982 while at Barcelona, to being an addict and, according to John Ludden's *Once Upon a Time in Naples*, even snorted a line in the bathroom during a private audience with Pope John Paul II in Rome in 1985. 'Maradona is part of the people,' Napoli fan Paolo Cimmino told me. 'He is a common man but he is the best of us. He had many problems in his life but, in Naples, we only remember him for the joy.'

Part of Maradona's legacy, however, is a son who he at first refused to acknowledge, born to a woman who was not Maradona's childhood sweetheart, future wife and mother of his two daughters, Claudia Villafañe. Diego Armando Maradona Jr was born and raised in Naples following his father's infamous affair with local woman Cristiana Sinagra. Diego Jr was thrust into the public consciousness immediately, with his mother announcing his birth and the name of his father to a news-thirsty TV crew who visited her at her hospital bed. Arriving in September 1986, just two months after Maradona Sr guided Argentina to World Cup success in Mexico, the boy was only legally declared a Maradona in 1993. Despite a court ruling that Maradona Sr owed child support for his son, the world's most iconic footballer continued to not recognise the child as his own.

Nevertheless, Maradona Jr says he enjoyed a happy childhood in which his mother always told him the truth and his grandfather filled the void as a father figure. As a seven-year-old, he watched his dad on television at the 1994 World Cup and witnessed the fallout as he failed a doping test when weight-loss drug ephedrine was found in the Argentine star's system. It was almost another decade before Maradona Jr finally met his father, sneaking into a golf tournament in Fiuggi, near Rome, in 2003 to approach him. And it was longer still until Maradona Sr was finally at ease calling the young man his son.

By the time Diego Sr passed away in November 2020, the pair had come to enjoy a happy and positive relationship. 'He was kind,' Maradona Jr told *Il Riformista* about the initial 2003 meeting. 'He said some nice things to me but there was no follow-up. At that moment, he wasn't ready, he wasn't well, for drugs. The second time, however, when we met in Argentina, I found a different man, a changed man who no longer used drugs. He is my football idol, like all of us Neapolitans and all football lovers. He wasn't just any person, he was the "chosen one" and that celebrity was the price he had to pay. Together we watched football, drank maté [a South American herbal tea]. I had a good time with dad.'

At 5ft 6in, the dark-haired and barrel-chested Maradona Jr bears a striking resemblance to his father. Unlike his father, though, he is predominantly right-footed and, before hanging up his boots to pursue a coaching career, tended to play in a deeper midfield role than Maradona Sr.

There was a time the footballing gods looked to be leading them down similar paths. The younger Maradona was on the youth team books at Napoli from the age of 11 and represented Italy at under-

17s level, moving north for a brief spell in Genoa's academy when Napoli went bust in 2004 and were plunged into the third division. Maradona Jr's beach football career turned out to be more successful than his more conventional one, finishing as a World Cup runner-up with the national team in 2008, while his 11-a-side days saw him journey around Serie D and the regional leagues before he was led back to Naples and Napoli United.

Interestingly, and perhaps this is most telling about the heavy burden of carrying the Maradona name, Maradona Jr hopes his son – also named Diego, like his father, grandfather and great-grandfather – does not follow in the family line of work. 'I hope he doesn't play football,' he added in that *Il Riformista* interview in 2021. 'A part of me wants it because every father hopes to share a passion with his children. On the other hand, however, this is no longer the sport I loved when I was a child. Observers look more at how physically structured you are and not if you know how to play football. Parents are often unbearable. And I hope that my son doesn't have to feel all the bad things that I have endured, all the shit they threw at me over the years.'

Unlike the most famous of Maradonas, however, it is in the dugout rather than on the pitch that Diego Jr has so far had his biggest impact. In his first senior coaching role after earning his UEFA 'B' badge, he returned to Napoli United as first-team manager. The young coach guided the club to within a play-off defeat of Serie D during the 2021/22 campaign, playing a brand of what local media dubbed 'clean and modern' football and implementing a philosophy that was underpinned by keeping the ball on the ground and maintaining possession. Naturally, Maradona Jr liked to field what he calls a classic No.10, whose job it was to find space and link play in the hole behind the strikers.

Unfortunately, that tenure came to an unsatisfactory end for both parties in March 2023, towards the end of his second season in charge at the club. 'We gave him the chance to gain experience and prove himself as a coach,' explains Di Nunzio. 'And we were right, because he is pretty good. He is a good man, he lives our values. That is why it was so natural to get him in the project and he joined us very happily.'

Being part of the Napoli United family means standing for something beyond just football. Amid the drugs, alcohol and unhealthy lifestyle choices, Diego Maradona Sr was also outspoken on issues away from the game. 'El Pibe de Oro' was, after all, a man of the people, an anti-establishment rogue. It is what endeared him to Naples and Naples to him. He was a more political figure than some might think, meeting many heads of state across a wide range of countries during his lifetime and enjoying a close relationship with several left-wing Latin American leaders, most prominently the Cuban revolutionary Fidel Castro. Maradona described Castro as a 'second father' and Castro is credited with helping the footballing legend battle drug abuse, offering the use of Cuban rehabilitation clinics. The Argentina star even had an image of Castro tattooed on his leg, as well as having a depiction of Che Guevara, the man he called an 'idol', on his right bicep. Maradona was a socialist, visiting Lenin's Mausoleum in Red Square before a European

Cup last-16 tie against Spartak Moscow, and a social activist, never forgetting his poor childhood in Villa Fiorito. Following a later visit to Pope John Paul II, he criticised the Vatican for what he believed was a focus on opulence, rather than a desire to help the poor, and told the Pope to sell the gold ceilings.

Maradona had a brief foray into football politics, too. In September 1995, while serving his doping ban following the World Cup the previous year, the forward came up with the idea of launching a new union to promote and protect players' rights across the world, with policies to include free transfers, a fairer share of television money and an opposition to midday World Cup matches. He also objected to players having an overcrowded schedule in which they faced too many games. Three decades on, it's hard to argue that Maradona did not have a point. He was joined in his ultimately unsuccessful crusade by 14 other high-profile footballers including Manchester United's Eric Cantona, also serving a suspension at the time for his attack on a Crystal Palace fan, AC Milan forward George Weah, Juventus striker Gianluca Vialli and Brazilian World Cup-winning midfielder Raí.

To fiercely defend your principles is something, it seems, which is in the Maradona blood and it was Maradona Jr's principles that ultimately saw him step down as Napoli United boss. 'From rags to riches,' he wrote on Instagram after handing in his resignation. 'I could summarise my experience at Napoli United like this. A club that I have respected and loved since it was born, way back in 2009. The stars, in my stomach, of that phone call in June 2021 in which president Antonio

Gargiulo asked me to become first-team coach. Thank you, thank you ten times, for the opportunity he gave me. The first, a fantastic year, everything in its place, everyone pushing in the same direction. Some defeats, many victories. The ride to the play-off semi-final, the highest goal ever achieved by Napoli United.'

However, life became tough for the club in Maradona Jr's second season. His Instagram post continued: 'The second year, the one in which I resisted until today. That of unpaid salaries to staff and players. Four months, over 100 days without receiving money. Work and personal relationships were affected. There are boys in the team who are thousands of kilometres from home and Napoli United left them without a cent for shopping, without food, in one case even without hot water for several days. I couldn't resist, I was no longer able to stand still in the face of such injustices. Integrating, welcoming and leaving people without food is a bit out of place.'

It was a controversial and loaded goodbye and one that came at a difficult time for the club, who were facing an uncertain future away from the pitch. Few could have predicted it, even then, but a few months later Napoli United would no longer be competing in the Italian football pyramid in their current guise. Change was, perhaps, inevitable.

President Antonio Gargiulo was measured in his response to Maradona Jr's farewell post: 'In December we were in first place, then we collapsed. We had a difficult season from the beginning. We had bet on the field [new stadium] which then boomed, with no stands, and it only made us waste time, commitments, jobs and money. Some historic partners turned their backs on us and the season went like this. Diego's sentences are heavy but I understand the outburst. I won't comment, because those who know us know we have been doing these activities for almost 15 years now: football, social and integration. It's a bad year for us. I repeat, I understand the outburst. Affection and esteem for Diego remain the same.'

As referenced in the president's statement, for a long time Napoli United had been banking on moving to a new stadium of their own towards the centre of Naples. They began life upon entering the FIGC pyramid in 2013 at Dietro la Vigna on the northern outskirts of the city, a base that at the time allowed the club to work closely with local people in what was a disadvantaged area. But their prolific rise through the divisions meant the ground was soon insufficient and they found a new temporary home at the Stadio Comunale Alberto Vallefuoco, further out of town in Mugnano.

The goal was always to have a ground of their own, however, and Napoli United looked to be building towards that with the acquisition and renovation of San Gennaro dei Poveri Stadium in Sanita, a neighbourhood on the edge of the city centre that has suffered from marginalisation and poverty but is now enjoying significant redevelopment. The club felt that not only could the stadium be a focal point for sporting projects aimed at generating opportunities in the area, but that having a home nearer the city in an area with a large migrant presence would help cultivate a culture of belonging. They hoped to grow and maintain a fanbase who shared the same values.

Unfortunately, after years working with local institutions, stakeholders and authorities, the project fell through at the last minute. 'We had a lot of economic problems and issues,' explains Di Nunzio. 'We were ready for the brand new stadium in the heart of the city, which would have brought lots of interest in the team and, hopefully, lots of sponsors but we never had the permission to open the stands for the supporters.'

It was a bitter blow for Di Nunzio and the other directors, who have put a lot of their own personal money into the upkeep of the club over the years. Playing in the fifth tier, they were up against clubs well established in the system and with bigger budgets. Di Nunzio says these clubs could spend 'five or six times' what Napoli United could afford. 'We have a model,' he adds. 'We try to do the same with less money. This is possible thanks to our network, where everyone tries to put their effort into reaching the target, but it is pretty hard. The huge economic issues affected the results on the field, the first team. But our club boasts an amateur team, in which all people without the legal requirement play, the youth sector, a female team and futsal team. We managed to build a lot. It is very important for us to not just have a team and discover talent and win. Winning is a way to let people know we exist and to promote our project but it is not our target. To spread our values, we strongly believe we need to start from the grassroots level, start with the youngsters and make them grow with a view of football which is our view. Our model is not only about the value you profess but the value you live with.'

What Di Nunzio and the other founders continue to strive for is 'solidarity' through football but within a sustainable development model. And so, in their moment of need, Napoli United found solidarity in the form of another Neapolitan club who share similar principles and targets. ASD Quartograd, based on the outskirts of the city, position themselves as a staunch anti-racist and anti-fascist team. They put a focus on development, social inclusion and educational projects. Before the start of the 2023/24 campaign, the clubs came together to announce a merger that would allow them to continue to support their respective projects while playing in the fifth-tier Eccellenza Campania under a new name: CSDS Quarto Afrograd. 'We have tried to bring together the subjects who in recent years, on both sides, have always imagined football as a tool to convey values and passion at the same time,' the new-look club said in a press release.

'Things are going quite well,' reflects Di Nunzio. 'We have another target and made this merger based on our values, so I guess we lost something on the sports aspect but gained something about the community and the force we are able to put on the field to work with the youngsters. The core of the project is still doing what we started 15 years ago. Our head is always Antonio and this really matters because this is the consistency line of the project. He is the father of the project but also a little bit of a father to all of us. He gave a lot, something special to each one of us. We still try, we don't give up, we push stronger every year!'

In the decade and a half since those initial casual after-work kickabouts, Afro Napoli United blossomed and evolved into something far more powerful than Di Nunzio could have ever imagined. On the pitch, winning championships, gaining promotions and coming within a whisker of Serie D, they outstripped any of the expectations the founders had when the idea of creating a football club was first mooted. In truth, there was always a fear that, should the club become too successful on the pitch, climb too far up the Italian pyramid, they may lose sight of the meaning of the project and risk betraying their values. It has always been away from the field where the most important work takes place.

In accepting that a merger is the best way forward, the club have practised what they preach in terms of integration being a powerful tool. As a unified force, the club hope they can continue to battle racism and discrimination and provide opportunities for those who need them most. However, going forward, they have decided to leave the football aspect in the hands of Quatro and concentrate on exporting their social projects on an international stage. 'We gave everything we had,' concludes Di Nunzio. 'We achieved way more than we expected at the beginning. We will keep pushing our values stronger than before to spread them around the world.'

Chapter 11

The Birthplace of Modern Football

IT'S 4.30PM, five days before Christmas, and, as tyres crunch across the gravel to park outside Cambridge United's Abbey Stadium, late afternoon is already meandering into night. The Abbey is looking festive and, with just over three hours to go until kick-off against Huddersfield Town in League One, there's a twinkling of anticipation in the air you feel at this time of year. Places are set in the boardroom for dinner, each complemented with a Christmas cracker, and in the Dion Dublin Bar across the hall, staff are preparing for service. Alex Tunbridge, the Cambridge United chief executive, steps in from the cold to greet me with a familiar smile and a handshake. Three decades ago, he was in the year above me at Knebworth Primary School. Now, he's running a Football League club, his third such role since first taking on the challenge at the tender age of 28.

Beneath the terraces, narrow corridors filter like a rat run towards the changing rooms. One wall is plastered with a floor to ceiling image of the 'Amber

Army', showing fans decked in resplendent shirts and sunglasses on a visibly brighter day than this one. Jason Euell, the former Wimbledon, Charlton and Jamaica forward, who is now Cambridge's assistant coach, wanders by and smiles as players and staff begin to arrive. Garry Monk, who a decade ago led Swansea City into the Europa League knockout stages, is in his office, otherwise known as 'The Bunker'. It's recently had a new carpet, he explains, because a fox got in and peed on the last one.

Outside, strolling the side of the pitch, the floodlights begin to flicker on but all is quiet. There's something magical about an empty football stadium. So still, for now. Soon, studs will churn up the carefully pruned grass and footballs will fizz across the dewy surface as the players come out to warm up. Thousands of supporters will flood through the turnstiles and pack out the creaking wooden stands after picking up their Friday evening food and drink from the stalls outside. Such is the ageing nature of The Abbey, a charming and romantic old stadium but one built for a bygone era, there is no concourse to house any refreshments.

The club have played on this site since 1932, when they were known as Abbey United. Fans have watched them reach the brink of the Premier League, losing the play-off semi-final to Leicester City in 1992, but also plummet to the depths of the fifth tier. In 2004, they had to sell the stadium to keep afloat. Eighteen years later, they finally bought it back. Now, after also investing £3.5m in the training ground, a redevelopment worth between £20m and £30m is planned to improve the stadium and grow the capacity from 8,000 to around 12,000, the club having ruled out relocating. It is about striking a balance between modernising the ground, making it more accessible for families and enhancing the current matchday experience, while also maintaining the club's history and heritage. But, when you're scrapping it out at the bottom of League One, the immediate future is of more concern to some supporters. 'Initially, some of the decisions we've had to make have been difficult for fans to digest,' says Tunbridge. 'Because we are reaching such high capacities, the only way for us to grow as a club is to improve our facilities.'

That was the case at the training ground before it was redeveloped, where players were having to change in portacabins at one of the university sites and food was sometimes served cold after being ferried across town from the stadium. The new complex has helped with the recruitment and retention of staff and players, as well as with integrating youngsters into the first-team squad, as they're now all training at the same place. 'We have been able to slowly educate and show people this is the journey we're on,' adds Tunbridge. 'We're not just going to put it all into the playing budget. As great as that would be, you're not guaranteed success. Particularly in this league, there are some big budgets. And even then, let's say we got success, it is probably unsustainable. Being a custodian of the club, ownership, CEO, whoever, nobody wants to be guiding the club and walk out the door and it's gone into administration and is in non-league. Sustainable growth is the thing and I think fans get that now.'

In co-owner Paul Barry, they have a lifelong fan right at the heart of the club. Barry, who made his fortune in the travel business, lives in Seattle and is usually up early to follow live streams of Cambridge games. He has been on the club's board since 2005, when the U's dropped into the Conference, and took full control of the club in 2019. Despite that, on his regular visits to the UK, he takes up a spot in the stands alongside his 87-year-old mum, a season ticket holder at The Abbey. Back in Cambridge for Christmas, tonight's game is no different for the unassuming and understated owner. 'Paul is immensely valuable because he cares about the club in the long term, he is making decisions for that next generation,' explains Tunbridge. 'His background is travel, he has great business acumen and cares about the club, but he is letting people with the expertise and experience within the game run the club for him. He is giving us the space to go and do that within the parameters and values and culture he sets. It is such a different way of doing it.' Tunbridge usually has a catch-up with the owner once a week. 'A lot of the time, it is excitement and interest from him, because he cares about what's going on and there are some great projects,' he explains. 'And we have a really good board that sits underneath that. When Paul can't be around, he's got a fantastic group of people that are safeguarding the club.'

Getting the right people is key in maintaining the values and culture at Cambridge United and the board is a mix of heavy hitters in the world of business and academics, as well as former players such as Dion Dublin and Graham Daniels. 'Because the owner is a long-term fan, his vision is about making sure we all leave the club in a better position for that next generation,' adds Tunbridge. 'We are very much custodians. No one is bigger than the club, there are no egos. The three values are teamwork, hard work but then humility. In some clubs, that humility piece doesn't exist. Everybody at the club is on the same page. Everybody is treated well. There's a whole piece about staff welfare and wellbeing. Football is all-consuming, it is literally every day, and I think it's a really nice balance here that they understand everyone is a person. There are ups and downs, feelings, emotions, families and it is almost not a job; it is kind of, like, a way of life.'

There is also a commitment to engaging with the local community. The club gave up non-matchday conferencing and banqueting packages to, instead, gift the rooms to the Cambridge United Foundation, which welcomes hundreds of local residents each week for education and social interaction programmes. Another project saw one supporter and his daughter team up with a local primary school to release a Christmas song, 'United at Christmas', to raise money for the club's foundation. Very much Union Berlin-style, the club also host their own Christmas market at The Abbey, complete with brass band and carol singing for fans in the South Stand. And then there was a successful world record attempt, which saw a Cambridge shirt tour the city for six weeks and rack up 2,146 signatures, breaking the previous Guinness world record for the greatest number of signatures on a piece of sports merchandise set by Kawasaki Frontale in Japan. 'You get lots of clubs who say they are a community club,' says Tunbridge. 'This is what I would call a *proper* community club. Players going out into the community is non-negotiable, that is part of the culture and we're very clear about it in our recruitment as well: "This is what it's about. If this isn't for you, that's fine." We're really strong on it.'

Cambridge is a picturesque city rich in culture and heritage, renowned for its stunning architecture, famed university and colleges and, of course, its punting. Lesser known, perhaps, is the city's claim to being the birthplace of modern football. Around one mile from The Abbey stadium is Parker's Piece, a large, flat common near the city centre that is ideal for sport and recreation. It is said to be here where Cambridge University students came up with the rules of the game in 1848. A large proportion of those were later adopted as the official laws by the Football Association. Now, a sculpture marking the 'birth' of the modern game sits where the students once played. An early proposal for the sculpture to feature a Subbuteo-style referee didn't come to fruition (unfortunately). Instead, the monument features four granite pillars with the 11 original 'Cambridge Rules' inscribed in seven different languages. Five other pillars were sent to locations around the world as part of a cultural football exchange. One was installed at Shanghai Shenhua's training complex, linking the birthplace of the rules with the birthplace of the game – the ancient Chinese military sport of Cuju is widely recognised as the first form of football. Another was unveiled at the Maracanã in Rio de Janeiro, while others went to Mombasa, Cairo and Chennai.

Cambridge United have tapped into that history through their shirts. The moss green 2024/25 third jersey took inspiration from Parker's Piece, with its flower and leaf motifs, as well as sporting the coordinates of Reality Checkpoint, the city's first electrical lamppost, that sits in the middle of the common. The away shirt design, meanwhile, was inspired by water lilies on the River Cam and has outsold the home shirt. 'With Umbro, our kits are different,' admits Tunbridge, who has been part of delivering a rebrand of the club crest and identity, which were voted on by fans. 'I think the kits are a great way in which you can bring your community, your city, into the club.'

There is also a feeling the club can use the global recognition of the city to tap into an overseas market. Especially the United States, where interest in League One has been higher because of North American owners at Wrexham and Birmingham City. 'If you survey people around the world, a vast majority know the first part of the club's name,' explains Tunbridge. 'So how do we change the perception of the club locally, to make it more professional and more attractive to families? Then, on a commercial level, how do we tap into what's going on in the city? The so-called Fen Valley is the fastest-growing economic hub in the country. Everyone is saying it is a bit of a bubble. Around the country, we're looking at a reduction in houses being built, whereas here it is the complete opposite.

'There is lots to tap into and there is also this incredible landscape and backdrop of education, the university, the city. What we are trying to do is look at how do we bring the two things together without losing our own identity?'

Tunbridge has become something of a specialist in modernising clubs and maximising resources. After studying a sport and business degree at the University of Southampton, he wrote physical letters to every Football League club looking for opportunities. Only two responded and only one had an opening. That was Bournemouth, who were in danger of dropping out of League Two at the time after being handed a 17-point deduction following administration. A youth coach named Eddie Howe would take the reins in January 2009 and steer them to safety. Tunbridge, meanwhile, took on a mixed role that included coaching, helping to develop the young supporter base and working with the club's foundation.

As a boyhood Stevenage fan, however, when he spotted an impassioned message from the Boro chairman, Phil Wallace, calling on the town to support their local team, he felt he could help. He sent a speculative letter, along with a piece about him in the Bournemouth matchday programme, to the National League club. 'It was just before Christmas. I was going to go to the game with my dad and I just got a call from the chairman at like 12pm,' explains Tunbridge. 'He said, "Right. I've got your letter here. We should have a chat. Can you get here in 15 minutes?" I got in the car, got into this office and sat down and he said, "This is what I want you to do, this is how much I am going to pay you and this is when I want you to start." So, I was like "Okay, fine."'

Tunbridge spent seven years at Stevenage, watching them rise from the National League to the League One play-offs. He set up the club's foundation and then worked in the academy, before suggesting he might leave. 'I was just bored,' he says. 'I was 26 and needed something.' He was persuaded to stay and help rebrand a nursery school the chairman had bought that was going into liquidation, growing the number of kids from 30 to 100 in six months. Then it was time to move on. 'I want to work in football, I don't want to work in childcare,' he recalls. The States beckoned, moving to Florida with his now-wife and working at an indoor soccer centre for a year. Until he took a call from former Stevenage boss Graham Westley, who took charge at struggling Newport County in October 2016. Westley told Tunbridge he wanted to bring him in as chief executive.

At 28, it was an incredible opportunity to run a Football League club. Even if they got relegated from League Two, Tunbridge thought, it would still be an unbelievable experience. 'In your wildest dreams, you wouldn't think you'd be running a National League club under the age of 30,' he says. In his first January at Rodney Parade, Newport released 15 players and signed the same amount. 'We stayed with my partner's grandparents in the valleys for the first six weeks,' he laughs. 'I had never done a transfer window before, didn't know what I was doing and I didn't have any phone signal! I used to have to go and sit in my car down the road from her grandparents' house to be on the phone to Graham. He would sign all the players and then I'd do all the paperwork. When I went there,

there was an accountant and a commercial manager, and that was it. It was nuts. They didn't have any money. They didn't have anything.'

Westley was sacked by the board in March, with the club 11 points adrift at the bottom of League Two. Michael Flynn was appointed and, remarkably, won seven of the remaining 12 games, including a 2-1 victory on the final day of the season, sealed with an 89th-minute winner, to keep them up. The following season, they beat Leeds United in the FA Cup and took Tottenham Hotspur to a replay staged at Wembley while the London club's new stadium was being built. 'Everything we touched just turned to gold, it was ridiculous,' beams Tunbridge. 'I loved Wales. Such a great community ... industrial.'

But then the chance arose to go back to Stevenage as chief executive. It was the club he grew up within walking distance of and where his dad remains a season ticket holder. 'I didn't want to leave Newport,' he adds. 'I felt like there was more to come and there was. They got to two play-off finals, played Manchester City in the FA Cup. But I couldn't turn down the opportunity to run my boyhood club. That's not going to come up again.'

Tunbridge was involved in building Stevenage's new North Stand and plenty of other innovative projects. One saw former Chelsea, Juventus, Sampdoria and Italy striker Gianluca Vialli, who sadly passed away in 2023, become an investor in Stevenage. None was more eye-catching, though, than the club's deal with Burger King. The fast food giant was announced as Stevenage's shirt sponsor for the 2019/20 season – but with a twist. They created the 'Stevenage Challenge' on the popular video game *FIFA*, calling on players to complete challenges with Stevenage in the game in return for free food prizes. It went viral during the Covid lockdown, when Stevenage had furloughed the majority of staff apart from Tunbridge and an accountant. He ended up shipping shirts to more than 100 countries as Stevenage became the most-played club in *FIFA 20* career mode, garnering a whole new set of fans in the process. The campaign racked up more than a billion impressions online. 'It created that niche of this new community who are now communicating with the club – they are gamers. They are not coming to games but they are buying merchandise and replying,' explains Tunbridge. It also created a legacy for the club's shirt sponsorship, with Burger King followed by Amazon Prime Gaming on the front of their jerseys. 'That's probably gone under the radar a little bit,' adds Tunbridge. 'The biggest company in the world and we've got them on a League Two football shirt! Which, in a way, is probably more incredible.'

The dream of running his own boyhood club came with mixed emotions, though. 'People ask me whether I enjoyed running my club,' says Tunbridge. 'When I was at Newport, one of my motivations was to go and run Stevenage. I didn't think it would happen as quickly as it did. When I got to Stevenage, I thought, "What's my motivation?" And it was really weird, because my motivation was to be able to not mess it up and be able to go and stand back on the terrace with my dad. That was almost the most valuable piece. I was thinking "Shit, if I mess this up, I can't go and stand back there with my dad." And it was tough, because you couldn't leave it. You're living close to it. You go to your family's house for dinner and they just want to talk to you about football. And then you go for a beer with your mates and they just want to talk to you about work.'

That was especially hard when Stevenage found themselves fighting for survival in League Two in successive seasons. 'When I was at Newport, it was fan-owned and they were very much leading with their heart not their head, where I was probably head over heart,' he adds. 'When I went to Stevenage, I was trying all the time to be head over heart, because that was the job, but it was always really difficult. And then, even when you did lead head over heart, even though it was the best decision for the club, maybe the fans didn't see that. And then your friends don't see that and all of a sudden it's, "You're not a real fan." Whereas I think at Cambridge, it's allowed me to flick it back. Yes, you care immensely about every result, about the whole thing, but you can look at it with a bit more of a clear head.'

Ultimately, especially during Covid, it proved tiring running the club he loved. 'We got through Covid and I was kind of thinking I'm not sure how much more I can affect things here,' adds Tunbridge. 'If I want to work at a higher level, I need to go into an environment where nobody knows me.' Stevenage is only 30 miles from Cambridge and Tunbridge stills lives closer to the Lamex Stadium than he does The Abbey but the nature of being chief executive at a League One club means there is little time to follow your own. 'In a way, I have become disconnected from it,' he explains.

'The love I had for the club pre being CEO was a lot stronger than it maybe is now. It's funny, the club you end up working in becomes the most important thing because you get to know everybody, particularly here and in terms of relegation and the impact that can have on people. People might lose their jobs and you've built relationships with them.' He has managed a couple of visits to the Lamex Stadium with his dad, as well as through work when Cambridge have faced Stevenage in League One. 'People talk to you and say "hello" but it's very different and it's almost a very strange feeling,' says Tunbridge. 'I've been back twice in my role at Cambridge and it is a very surreal experience. It's great to see people. But, ultimately, you're thinking "We have to win, three points is really important." Only in football, I think, could you have that sort of dynamic and emotions.'

Back at The Abbey, it is a tough evening for Cambridge United. The home fans clap as it is announced more than 1,000 away supporters have made the trip from Yorkshire on a cold night in late December, showing appreciation even though the visitors have taunted their hosts with chants of 'You should've gone Christmas shopping' during a convincing 4-0 victory. The U's were ultimately up against a superior Huddersfield Town side, one who were playing Premier League football six seasons earlier. The result leaves them in danger towards the bottom of League One and with potentially difficult decisions to be made.

But if you had told Tunbridge all those years ago, when he was fresh out of university and sending hopeful letters to Football League clubs, that he would be running one of his own, he would no doubt have been surprised. 'As a 21-year-old, you're probably thinking, "Get me to the Premier League! Get me to Spurs!"' he smiles. 'But, actually, the best place to learn is the Football League, particularly League One and League Two. They have a great connection to their communities and are very challenging environments at times. And the more you do it, the more you fall in love with that connection and the realism. The Premier League is now, I would say, a completely different industry. Having had the background of working in your club, running your club and coming to one here that is very community-driven, there becomes a bit of a moral piece and I'm not sure I could give that up. That's probably what gets me out of bed every day and makes me want to come to work: improving the lives of everybody around the club and the community. I think in a League One or League Two club you can effect change really quickly and you can grow. The challenge is how do you protect your history and heritage while at the same time driving forwards?'

In the birthplace of modern football, Cambridge United will always have history and heritage on their side. But their future also appears to be in safe hands.

Chapter 12

Johan and the Plan

RUBEN JONGKIND is talking about the impact of positive childhood experiences. 'There are imprints that never leave your system,' he explains. 'Things that make an impression on you and shape your life.' He is also talking with the hindsight of having worked closely with Johan Cruyff and having helped develop some of the finest footballers in the world. I, meanwhile, am confessing how getting to grips with coaching four-year-olds is both a heart-warmingly satisfying, yet humbling, experience. Essentially, however, when speaking to young players, the same principles apply. 'On the other side, if you do something out of your own emotional instability or urges at that moment,' adds Jongkind, 'you might also damage somebody and have no idea. It was not your intention, but you did it.'

The notion of having an impact you didn't necessarily realise at the time on a child particularly hit home for Jongkind when hearing one of his former players talk about a conversation they had shared years earlier. It was 2018 and Noussair Mazraoui was a guest on Andy van der Meyde's YouTube show, in which the former Ajax, Inter Milan and Everton winger takes players for a drive in his car, sharing a chat and a laugh with them. In the show, Van der Meyde asks the young defender why he was overlooked by the Dutch youth teams, instead choosing to represent Morocco, despite being born and raised in the Netherlands. Mazraoui explains he was not seen as having enough potential during his time in Ajax's academy and that Morocco were the ones who offered him a chance at national level. But there was also a coach who gave him the belief to succeed. 'There's one person who said I was going to reach Ajax [first team],' explains Mazraoui. 'His name was Ruben Jongkind. It turned out he was right about me.' After watching the YouTube clip, Jongkind remembered the chat Mazraoui was referring to. 'It was maybe 15 minutes in the coffee corner,' he recalls. 'He must've been 13 or something. Those principles of psychological security are so important for children.'

Mazraoui was part of a talented Ajax generation but, despite being technically good, he was small and skinny and on the verge of being let go by the club. Jongkind was able to instil confidence in the youngster by mapping out how he believed his development would progress. He told Mazraoui he would grow taller, like his father, that he was born in November and, therefore, one of the youngest in his age group, so would mature later than others. 'In a few years, you will grow, become stronger and your technique is very good,' Jongkind remembers telling him. 'You will move very well, very efficiently, so it is just a matter of keep going, get stronger, focus on the things you can focus on – sleep, nutrition, strength training – and you will make it, you will become a pro player, without any doubt.'

With his future at the club undecided, Jongkind was also among the coaches who pushed for Mazraoui to be retained. He was but he was also held back an age group. Then, among boys of a similar stature, he began to flourish. Mazraoui went on to spend five years in the Ajax first team before moving to Bayern Munich and then Manchester United, as well as helping Morocco to a first-ever World Cup semi-final in 2022. 'I don't believe you should tell anybody "Yeah, you can become a pro player,"' adds Jongkind. 'Realistically, it is more about "Okay, this is what you're good at, this is what might happen, this is what probably will happen," and just bringing them back from fear to being grounded more. That is very important in professional football, because of the pressure. There is so much pressure for boys and girls nowadays, it is detrimental. Too much pressure causes psychological insecurity.' It was part of a way of thinking inspired by Ajax and Netherlands legend Cruyff and one that helped restore the club to their role as Europe's great talent factory.

It began in December 2010, at a secret location in the south of Amsterdam, where some of Ajax's most iconic former stars were gathering to plot a revolution they hoped would restore the Dutch giants to their past glories. Just two years earlier, Johan Cruyff, the most iconic of all those to ever pull on the famous white and red jersey, looked set to be heading back to his boyhood club in his first official role in Amsterdam since 1988, when he was manager. Cruyff, however, pulled out because of a difference of opinion with incoming boss

Marco van Basten, the man he had recommended for the job, over how quickly the club needed to revamp the youth academy. Cruyff wanted to immediately get rid of coaching staff he felt were not the right fit, while Van Basten urged a little less haste. Instead, Cruyff continued advising his other footballing love, Barcelona, until his close friend and ally Joan Laporta's term as president ended in 2010. Cruyff had, by then, been made honorary president but previously it was a more casual arrangement. Cruyff recommended fellow Dutchman Frank Rijkaard for the head coach's job in 2003 and would occasionally meet with the manager and Laporta for lunch to discuss all things Barcelona. Laporta later said he suggested to Cruyff, who won four league titles and a European Cup with his Barcelona 'Dream Team' in the early 1990s, that he should succeed Rijkaard in the dugout in 2008, with young coach Pep Guardiola as his assistant. Cruyff had other ideas. Guardiola, he thought, was ready to go it alone. Guardiola, as we know, proved the perfect match for sporting director Txiki Begiristain, who had been another Cruyff recommendation five years earlier and someone he initially signed as a player when taking over as head coach in 1988.

Back in Amsterdam, with Ajax his focus once more, Cruyff was mobilising the troops. Wim Jonk, a UEFA Cup winner with Ajax in 1992, was one of those to be personally invited by the Netherlands' most famous star to the covert meeting. Van Basten, who resigned at the end of his one season in charge of Ajax, was among the other legends present. Jonk was an outlier among the guests in that he, along with Dennis Bergkamp, was currently coaching at Ajax. But it was not the Ajax Cruyff knew and loved. The club had just split with boss Martin Jol, were without a title in six years and the future looked bleak. Jonk and another academy coach, Ruben Jongkind, were already in the process of trying to change things from the inside. They wanted to implement an approach they felt would benefit the talented youngsters at the club's disposal, one based on giving youth players individual programmes to follow.

Cruyff was keen for Jonk to show his plans at the meeting, to which the former Inter and Sheffield Wednesday midfielder said he was happy to come but would be bringing Jongkind with him. 'Fine,' said Cruyff. 'You take whoever you want.' As the day of the meeting arrived, Jonk and Jongkind turned up early. Nervous about introducing the plans they had been stewing over for the academy, they popped into a bar down the street to go through them one more time. They laid the A3 printouts on the table, grabbed a coffee and talked through how best to present their ideas to a cast of legends. Soon, it was time to settle the bill and go. 'I paid,' smiles Jongkind. 'We walked out of the bar but, after 200m, I looked at Wim and Wim looked at me and said, "Did you take the drawings with you?!" We'd forgotten them! I sprinted back. Luckily, they were still there.'

Reaching the location, plans safely in hand, they climbed the steep, narrow staircase of an old Amsterdam house to the fourth storey. 'We got up there sweating and panting,' adds Jongkind, who strolled in to see a host of former stars. Rijkaard, Van Basten, Bergkamp, Bryan Roy, John van 't Schip, Peter Boeve and even Piet Keizer, a legend of the dominant Ajax team in the 1960s and early 70s, were all in attendance. It was a who's who of Ajax through the eras. 'Of course, I worked in Ajax but I was just an individual coach without a big reputation,' explains Jongkind. 'As a boy, I always looked up to these players. I thought I was dreaming. Is this real? I pinched myself!'

The special committee sat for about an hour, talking and analysing what was going wrong at a club who, as well as stagnating on the pitch and not displaying the style of football many felt was befitting of the Amsterdam institution, were also not producing the kind of young talent they had long been renowned for and, instead, appeared to be overpaying for average first-team players. As Cruyff wrote in his famous *De Telegraaf* column after a 2-0 defeat by Real Madrid that should have been a lot worse: 'I honestly admit that I feel a lot of sorrow. Because this is no longer Ajax.' In fact, Cruyff argued, the club were in a worse state than before legendary coach Rinus Michels arrived in 1965 and turned Ajax from relegation candidates to the best club side in Europe with his brand of Total Football. The article was the culmination of a long battle of words and opinions between Cruyff and those inside the club about what Ajax should really stand for – and for whom. Cruyff insisted he only wanted to fix the club, rather than stage a coup. He despised the complex and confusing leadership structure, especially the fact there were no former players on the commissioners' council or among the club's administrators. Among the legends gathered in that fourth-storey apartment in Amsterdam, Cruyff believed he had the answers to Ajax's problems.

'They analysed it pretty well, I think,' says Jongkind of those present at the meeting. 'Then there was a little bit of silence. Wim and I hadn't said anything and, of course, I was silent. Then Cruyff said, "And Wim, what do you want to say?"' At Ajax, Jonk and Jongkind had, so far, been introducing their personalised plans to certain individual talents within the academy. Largely left to get on with things on their own, they had not been given any real structure or guidance from the club hierarchy and they wanted to broaden their approach to work with all the youngsters, not just the best in each age group. At the meeting, they started handing out the A3 drawings to the legends in the room and offered what they believed to be some solutions to the issues the others had been discussing. 'After a while, Johan says "I didn't bring my glasses!"' laughs Jongkind. 'But he said, "I think it sounds good; we're going to do this!" He was very intuitive.'

Rijkaard, the former Netherlands and Barcelona boss, was also impressed. He appreciated how their vision would come to fruition. 'Rijkaard was very smart,' adds Jongkind. 'He gave some very good feedback right on the spot.' The former Ajax and AC Milan midfielder pinpointed a part of the plan that suggested the academy should be subdivided by the development phases of the children, with a technical manager appointed for each area. 'Rijkaard said we have to stress those technical managers more, those are very important,' recalls Jongkind. 'In hindsight, he was really accurate about that.'

Pleased with the positive response to their ideas, as the secret meeting began to wind down, Jonk and

Jongkind were casually chatting with others when Cruyff approached the pair and told them to book their flight. 'I was like, "What flight?!"' smiles Jongkind. 'And he said, "You're going to Barcelona next week. Give me your number. I don't have a phone but I'll reach you!"' So off they went, to Barcelona, where those Cruyff trusted most within his inner circle analysed the ideas. 'He had some people basically scrutinising the plan,' remembers Jongkind. 'I had to present it and they had to evaluate if everything was okay, a second opinion. That all went fine.' Cruyff was satisfied with the proposals and beefed up the initial plans with some more of his own ideas, some of which Jongkind had to jot down on the back of a roll of flowered wallpaper after the Dutch legend caught him off guard with an impromptu phone call. He was ringing on wife Danny's phone, of course, because Johan didn't have one of his own. 'I put it straight away into the computer, in a PowerPoint presentation!' says Jongkind, although he has kept hold of the original notes sketched out on that wallpaper. The Cruyff Plan was born; all that was left to do was implement it. But to do that, Cruyff needed to get back in at Ajax. What would become known as the 'Velvet Revolution' was about to take hold.

Cruyff's philosophy on football as a means, not an end, is endlessly fascinating. His ideas and beliefs as a player and coach changed and shaped the modern game, most obviously through Guardiola and the 'Pepification' of football. Guardiola recalls how he would often visit Cruyff to seek guidance during his first season as Barcelona boss. 'Cruyff built the cathedral; our job is to maintain it,' he famously said.

As former Ajax goalkeeping coach Frans Hoek told Adam Bate at Sky Sports: 'Cruyff taught me more in a week than I had learned in 12 years as a player.' The Dutchman revolutionised talent development and, to some extent, the running of a football club. To Cruyff, football was a microcosm for everything else in the world. 'He was a family man, absolutely,' explains Jongkind. 'But I would describe him as really obsessed with the content of the game. The game itself, players and also extrapolating the views he had on football to other fields, all the time. Whatever it could be, traffic jams, politics, health care, whatever, always with the growth mindset, this idea that nothing is impossible, we can change things. He was a problem solver.'

With age and wisdom, the stubbornness Cruyff was renowned for also seemed to mellow. His relationship with Rijkaard was a good case in point. At the beginning of his third season at Ajax as a player under Cruyff, Rijkaard stormed out of training. According to Jonathan Wilson's brilliant book *The Barcelona Legacy*, he shouted at the boss, 'Fuck you and your eternal whining!' and only returned to the club six years later when Louis van Gaal was at the helm. But by 1998, the pair had put aside their differences to the point Cruyff lobbied for Rijkaard to get the Netherlands job and then, five years later, for him to take the helm at Barcelona. 'Although people would say he is very direct, I would consider him in the last stages of his life, as I got to know him, more indirect, diplomatic,' explains Jongkind. 'He had learned about the past and he said we need to find broader acceptance within a group, we need to find people who can do it. "It is better if a third person tells X than I tell them" … setting aside his ego very much, giving other people the space. "It is now your time, you can do it."'

Jongkind remembers visiting Barcelona with Cruyff around the time they were looking to implement the plan at Ajax and experiencing the impact merely his presence had on those at the club. 'We went a few times to Barcelona,' he says. 'We never presented our plans, really, we just went in and listened and he said, "Look what is happening here."' Cruyff felt Barcelona had moved away from the guiding principles that brought them so much success, both in terms of developing young players and winning titles. He insisted that within five to ten years, things would not be going well for the club. 'We have to change this, people here, the board,' he told Jongkind, who adds: 'It was very strange because, when you walk there in the grounds at La Masia, on one hand people are really admiring him but, on the other hand, you feel people don't like him. I could really sense that. It was the same at Ajax. "Oh shit, what is going to happen now?" Cruyff stepped in and said, "We have to change back to the things we are famous for and our core values." Funnily enough, you see the same things happening now in Barcelona. Their football vision is derived from the ideas of Johan. They are creating value and are on an upwards trend with very young guys.'

In Amsterdam, by March 2011, a pathway for Cruyff to return to Ajax had emerged. It was something fans were calling for in the stands at Amsterdam ArenA. 'Johan already had the idea that we have to go in and basically reform everything,' explains Jongkind. 'But he was smart, because he was thinking about the political energy you needed for that. That's why he got all those former players.' They had to sell the philosophy to the members' council and club leadership, too, as some were still to be convinced there was a plan behind more than just 'Johan's ideas'. That job fell to Jongkind, as hundreds gathered for a special shareholders' meeting. 'It was funny,' he says. 'Out of the blue, I was this individual performance coach with Wim and then, suddenly, I had to be in this special shareholders' meeting to present the plan, in the Arena, in a big hall. I said "Wim, Dennis Bergkamp, you guys do it," and they said "No, you have to go!" So, I was standing there, defending the plan. Then, the same evening, there was another meeting with the supervisory board, who are basically in charge of the company Ajax. There I saw another face of Johan. "Okay, you guys are standing in the way of Ajax." He didn't tell them to get out [specifically] but he was very hard on the subject matter, the content. One of the CEOs attacked me and Johan jumped on him. "You should be ashamed of yourself, you coward," and stuff like that.'

Cruyff officially rejoined the club on an advisory basis, named on one of three sounding board groups with a focus on technical issues. The other two, he was told, were to look after financial and association matters. Change, naturally, brought turmoil and, after that meeting in March, Ajax's board of directors stepped down because they did not agree with Cruyff's vision. Where Cruyff saw creativity, others saw chaos. In Cruyff's world, nothing was written down – it all lived within his head. Cruyff also wasn't impressed by the rigidity of his new role; he wanted to give his opinions as he saw fit. 'According to the rules, I had to keep my mouth shut where the outside world was concerned,' he wrote in his autobiography, *My Turn*. 'Was it in the interests of Ajax for me to stick to the rules or should I speak out? For me, it was very simple – whatever the rules and regulations, the interests of my club outweighed everything else.'

Despite the changes, politics and powerplays continued behind the scenes in the boardrooms and offices but also on the training field. Some within the coaching set-up left because of changes in the hierarchy. Jongkind, for example, went from an individual coach to head of talent development. There were times when Ajax were light on staff as the changes took hold and for the man tasked with writing and implementing the Cruyff Plan, that meant mucking in with pretty much everything. Dennis Bergkamp was sent to the first team to help as part of manager Frank de Boer's staff, while Jonk and Jongkind were given the responsibility of transforming the structure and strategy at Ajax. 'I ended up picking up phones. "Good morning, welcome to Ajax!"' laughs Jongkind. 'At the same time, we had to do under-18s training because we didn't have a coach and we had to run the whole thing and change the whole thing all at the same time.'

If Cruyff had his way, there would have been a second part of the plan, too. Ajax were floated on the stock market in 1998 and the move to becoming a public limited company had made the club far more complex. Cruyff insisted there was a reason he was able to help reorganise Barcelona and create a winning machine that played beautiful football, while at Ajax he kept running into bureaucratic walls and disputes. 'One big difference is that Ajax is a business whose shares are traded on the stock market,' he wrote. 'And Barcelona is still a club in private hands. In Amsterdam, you're dealing with directors and commissioners and in Barcelona with a president.' The next stage of Cruyff's plan was to take Ajax off the stock market. (Ironically, following his death, some fans paid tribute to Cruyff by buying up 14 shares each in the club.) He eventually met too much resistance to pull it off but he had begun making plans. He confided in Jongkind, who said he knew a little bit about stocks and shares but was by no means a specialist. Instead, Cruyff gave Jongkind an English phone number and asked him to call it. 'Who is it?' asked Jongkind. Never mind, he was told, just call the number. 'I called him in the evening,' remembers Jongkind. 'He said "Hello, this is Marc." I said "Okay, this is Ruben from Holland. Cruyff asked me to call you."' Jongkind continues: 'He said "Yeah, Johan said someone would call me but what is it about?" He didn't know either!' Trying to figure out why Cruyff had brought the two together, Jongkind asked the voice on the other end to explain who he was and what he did. 'He said, "I'm Marc Bolland, I'm the CEO of Marks and Spencer!" We started talking and he gave some advice. That was typically Johan!'

The squabbles continued behind the scenes, most notably when Louis van Gaal was appointed chief executive during a board meeting Cruyff was unable to attend. Cruyff insisted he wanted a younger generation of former Ajax players to take control of the club, having brought in the likes of Edwin van der Sar and Marc Overmars. Others, outside Cruyff's circle of influence, felt the legendary figure was out of touch with the reality of running a football club and saw Van Gaal's appointment as a way of edging him out. 'It was a clash,' says Jongkind. 'There is an ego thing, both want to be seen as the king of Ajax, of course.' Their feud was long-running and can be traced back to Van Gaal's time in Ajax's second team in the early 1970s, where he was never likely to oust the Ballon d'Or-winning Cruyff from his position. Later, as a coach, Van Gaal followed in Cruyff's footsteps as he took charge at Ajax, leading a young, largely homegrown side to Champions League success in 1995 and then moved to Barcelona.

There is also a story about the pair falling out over a Christmas dinner at Cruyff's house in Barcelona in 1989. Van Gaal spent several evenings with the family while taking a coaching course in the city but then got a call to say his sister was ill and he had to leave suddenly. Cruyff later insisted there were never any hard feelings about that. But, despite being similar in many ways, the pair believed they were fundamentally different when it came to footballing philosophy. So, when it came to Van Gaal's appointment at Ajax, the Cruyff camp took legal action. They eventually won their case on appeal after the court said other board members had 'deliberately put Cruyff offside' by making the appointment without consulting him.

Despite the in-fighting, Jonk and Jongkind were able to implement their plan. It stated Ajax should be a team who play attractive and attacking football, with the aim of having homegrown players making up at least half the starting XI. They began by thinking about what it meant to play attractive football and how they would achieve such a philosophy and playing style. This would define the Ajax DNA. It was based around select principles: positional interplay, with players able to swap positions; creating one-v-ones and an extra man in midfield; using depth and third-man runs to play forward; defending from the front, compacting the pitch when out of possession and counter-pressing. Then, they set about convincing coaches the focus should be on individual development, rather than putting too much emphasis on winning or losing games. To help with this, coaches changed the teams they were working with every eight weeks. It meant they were less driven by the results of matches, willing to give players a chance to grow and develop. It also exposed those young players to different trainers. Experts from other sports were brought in, with specialists from judo, gymnastics, basketball, American football, athletics and triathlon sharing their knowledge.

They created a methodology department, where each player was drawn up a bespoke individual plan to help them realise their potential. This was something that resonated with Cruyff, who, as a skinny 15-year-old, had been sent to track and field sessions to work on his strength and endurance. Jongkind says it created 'a top-sport, elite environment that drove a lot of players into professionalism from a very early age'. They worked on nutrition and refined the catering at their De Toekomst (meaning The Future) academy, improved the medical department and built a school on site, mixing up the age groups so younger kids could learn from their older peers. They wanted less structure and more of a 'street atmosphere', the way Cruyff had learned to hone his unmatchable craft all those years ago. In essence, that was the difference between Cruyff and Van Gaal. Both had similar philosophies on how the game should be played but Van Gaal liked structure and Cruyff thrived on chaos.

Cruyff, Jonk and Jongkind believed Ajax's academy could be a breeding ground for Champions League winners but this notion was laughed off in the boardroom. When Cruyff wanted to put posters up around the club suggesting such, he was told to do so in the privacy of the academy. And when Jonk became frustrated with a reluctance to invest an extra €200,000 in the academy, he insisted to those in charge they would see a return of €200m in five years. He was proved right. Across the summers of 2019 and 2020 alone, the sales of Frenkie de Jong, Matthijs de Ligt and Donny van de Beek, to Barcelona, Juventus and Manchester United respectively, brought in just shy of that figure between them.

The implementation of Cruyff's plan can be seen in the individual development of those players, which in turn had a huge influence on Ajax's first team. De Jong was one of the big beneficiaries of the programme, despite only joining as an 18-year-old. Growing up in Arkel, where Ajax didn't have a youth scout at the time, he had gone under the radar. He was not even named on a list that Ajax's recruitment department compiled and which, featuring hundreds of the country's most promising talents, was handed to Cruyff and co. when they arrived in 2011. Not that he hadn't enjoyed Cruyffian influences. The football-obsessed kid would roam the village streets with a small ball, honing his touch and dribbling skills, just like the grand master did generations earlier. De Jong, instead, progressed through Willem II's academy and was awarded his first-team debut aged 17, albeit sometimes frustrating coaches with his high-risk, vertical passing approach. Ajax quickly snapped up the midfielder and loaned him back for a couple of months. Despite having had a taste of senior football, when De Jong returned, he spent time developing in Ajax's academy and was used sporadically in the first-team squad before being fully exposed to the rigours of representing the Dutch giants.

Jongkind, with his background in athletics, was blown away when he met the youngster by his physical attributes and explosiveness, especially considering he was still just a skinny teenager at the time. Those attributes, he felt, provided the talented technician and keen dribbler with the time and space to control games and go on progressive runs, the way we have seen him do at Ajax and Barcelona. Sometimes, in keeping with Ajax's development of many young talents, he was played out of his natural position, in central defence. De Jong's intuitive nature was at odds with some involved in Dutch football, which had become more conservative and full of sideways passes, but made him the archetypal Cruyff player.

Donny van de Beek was another midfielder to thrive in the Ajax system and one touted for the top from the age of 11 by his future father-in-law, Dennis

Bergkamp (he has two children with the former Arsenal star's daughter, Estelle). Jongkind met Van de Beek aged nine. They came from a similar area of the Netherlands, so struck up a rapport and would work together on individual aspects of the youngster's game, such as his running and movement. He was still raw, yet what Bergkamp appreciated was the way Van de Beek could recognise and utilise space on the pitch at such a tender age. His passing was superb but the coaches felt he had a slightly defensive mindset and was, therefore, being used generally as a defensive midfielder. Jonk worked individually and in small group settings with Van de Beek on arriving in the penalty box, being a little more dynamic and creating spaces for others in those attacking situations, as well as his finishing. They started to play him in more attacking positions, with the ultimate goal of developing as a No.8, and saw huge progress in his final years in the academy. Aged 18, he delivered on Bergkamp's premonition by breaking into the Ajax first team.

The jewel in the crown, especially in terms of seeing how the Cruyff Plan accelerated his development, is Matthijs de Ligt. He joined Ajax aged nine after being recommended to the club by his boyhood side in Abcoude, on the outskirts of Amsterdam. Ajax had reservations about his pace and body composition but took a punt on a kid who was already starting to show a maturity in his game intelligence. A few years into his Ajax journey, he was deemed good, rather than one of the exceptional talents in his age group, but the environment created by the Cruyff Plan helped get the best out of the young defender. His running style was not as efficient as it could be. 'He was a bit clumsy before,' explains Jongkind. So De Ligt worked hard with performance coaches to change that, including with Dutch 800m specialist Bram Som. By under-15s level, he had physically matured and was stronger than most of his peers. A colossus at centre-back, he had good technique and an impressive mindset. The Ajax coaches, however, felt he could improve in the speed of his decision-making, that he was slow when receiving the ball and in moving it forward. They shifted him into central midfield, where he had to think fast, quickly spot the correct pass and further hone his touch. Not only that, they wanted him to play up several age groups. That was met by resistance from both the coach who was losing the best defender in his age group and the coach who felt he had to feature a younger player out of position in midfield. But this was the epitome of the plan not being results-driven and, instead, focusing on the development of the individual. A short-term loss to the youth team was a long-term gain for the senior side. The rise was meteoric. De Ligt made his first-team debut as a 17-year-old and captained the club from the age of 18.

Three years into the cycle, Jonk, Jongkind and Cruyff felt the project was beginning to bear fruit. There is one game, in particular, that sticks in Jongkind's mind. Ajax's under-19s side were garnering a lot of attention for their attractive, attacking football. Many fans were getting excited about some of the young prospects they hoped would soon break into the first team. When Ajax drew Barcelona in the UEFA

Youth League in 2014, hordes of them packed into the Sportpark De Toekomst for a glimpse. The official attendance was 3,482 but Jongkind reckons almost double that number were actually present. 'The first fruits we saw in the under-19s, when we had this Champions League Youth League campaign,' explains Jongkind. 'It was really incredible. Not the results but the football itself was really good. There were no seats available. The people in the first team started to feel a threat from the academy.' Václav Černý, now a Czech international, scored past future Ajax goalkeeper André Onana in a 1-0 win. The assist was provided by Abdelhak Nouri, the supremely talented playmaker whose career came to a tragic end at the age of 22 when he suffered a cardiac arrest that left him with permanent brain damage. Also in that side was Van de Beek, while 17-year-old Jaïro Riedewald had already joined up with the first team. Justin Kluivert, Mazraoui and De Ligt, from the age groups below, were also pushing for inclusion. 'A lot of them got through to international football,' says Jongkind, proudly.

Just three years later, Riedewald, De Ligt, Kluivert and Van de Beek were all part of Ajax's matchday squad in their Europa League Final defeat by Manchester United. As was the majestic Frenkie de Jong and homegrown talents Kenny Tete, Joël Veltman and Davy Klaassen. Danish forward Kasper Dolberg, meanwhile, had been there since the age of 17, discovered by the same scout who brought Zlatan Ibrahimović and Christian Eriksen to Amsterdam years earlier. It felt like the beginning of a return to Cruyff's Total Football heyday coupled with Van Gaal's successful homegrown

Ajax sides of the mid-1990s, when Ajax boasted Patrick Kluivert, Edgar Davids, Clarence Seedorf, Edwin van der Sar and more.

Then, in 2019, that core of talented Ajax youngsters took the club to the brink of a first Champions League final in 23 years. The Dutch giants were 3-0 up on aggregate against Tottenham Hotspur with 35 minutes to go at the ArenA, only for Lucas Moura's scarcely believable hat-trick, including a 96th-minute winner, to deny them in the most agonising fashion. Ajax had already beaten Juventus and Real Madrid in the knockouts, clubs with far bigger budgets, but taking a group of homegrown youngsters to the pinnacle of European football would have been the ultimate vindication of Cruyff's plan. After all, part of his vision, the one written on Jongkind's roll of wallpaper, was to build a team under the age of 23 who could compete for the Champions League.

Cruyff, sadly, was not able to witness either of those European runs, having passed away in 2016 following his battle with lung cancer. Jonk, Jongkind and the many disciples of the Cruyff Plan were no longer at the club, either. Despite the future success the plan would bring, there were constant, ongoing boardroom battles and disagreements over how the club should be run, as well as between Jonk and the 'technical heart' of Marc Overmars, Frank de Boer and Edwin van der Sar. 'There was some difference of opinion in the path to follow in regard to Plan Cruyff,' explains Jongkind. 'Wim said at some point it doesn't make any sense to keep getting into these meetings because the club needs to decide are we really going to follow the plan or are we doing it a little bit?' Jonk, feeling forced out, stepped down in December 2015 and Cruyff, Jongkind and a host of others decided to join him. 'When Wim left, Johan immediately said "I am leaving" and around 20 people also said "We don't want to continue here,"' adds Jongkind. 'It is hardly ever shown, things like this in football.'

Cruyff suggested they take the plan abroad. In fact, one of his ideas for Ajax was to create a multi-club ownership model and he even identified Brentford, then playing in League One, as a suitable partner. 'We went to the United States, to different clubs there, to federations, to the Middle East, to China, Malaysia,' explains Jongkind. 'He also had his foundation, Cruyff Courts, for children. We worked for that until the people in Volendam asked Wim Jonk to help them. Seven or eight of us said "Okay, let's jump into this project."'

Volendam were Jonk's boyhood club, the one he'd made his debut with in 1986 and helped win promotion to the Eredivisie the following season, before joining Ajax. When Jonk was asked to return as manager in April 2019, however, they had spent a decade outside the top flight. Worse than that, the supporters were just bored. 'They were sitting at the bar and watching the beer tap instead of watching the game,' Jonk told me. The fishing town to the north of Amsterdam was popular with tourists but the football club presented a whole different spectacle to the relative riches those leading the project had enjoyed at Ajax. For Jonk, there was also the emotional draw of wanting to save and re-establish his old club. And, albeit on a smaller scale, the problems they faced were not dissimilar to the ones they had encountered in Amsterdam. The quality in the first team and academy was lacking, fans and sponsors were disgruntled and the club needed to find a more sustainable future.

The principles of the Cruyff Plan remained the same. Jonk was quickly able to instil the virtues of the attacking football he wanted – playing forward, defending forward, playing the three-second rule and offering third-man options. The fans started to leave the bar and enjoy the football again at Kras Stadion. Behind the scenes, they set about focusing on high-potential transfer targets, prospects who had been missed or prematurely cast off by other teams, and unearthing those young gems already inside the club. At Ajax, it was almost a guarantee there would be top-quality talents within the academy but Volendam's scouting net was not cast as wide; in fact, they didn't even have a scouting department at first. They had to find and train scouts and academy coaches who bought into the philosophy.

It meant drawing the best out of what they had available to them and this is where the Cruyff Plan came to fruition. The group audited and revamped the academy accordingly, creating a performance culture like they had at Ajax and developing individual programmes for players based on their characteristics. They found that giving youngsters a platform to develop, alongside minutes in the first team, made them more confident and, in turn, they produced better performances. They built a network with Inter Milan, one of Jonk's former clubs, that saw several of the Serie A side's players arrive on loan and also had a Tottenham contingent visit to look into creating a similar pathway for their young stars.

Micky van de Ven, the now Tottenham and Netherlands defender, was arguably the biggest beneficiary of the revamp. He joined the club aged 12 as a striker, before being moved to central defence. At the age of 17, playing in the under-19s, he was told he was surplus to requirements and was free to look for another club. When Jonk and Jongkind arrived, they were blown away by the youngster and immediately offered him a new contract. 'We came in and saw him playing in the under-19s and thought, "Oh my God, this guy is a raw diamond, incredible!",' explains Jongkind. They saw the youngster as a 'Cruyffian' defender and within about six weeks, he had moved to the first team. Van de Ven had incredible pace and could run 60m in seven seconds flat from a standing start. He could dribble past defenders like a winger. There were areas to work on, too, of course. Volendam's new management team put Van de Ven on a plan to improve his agility, heading and one-on-one defending, as well as his tactical awareness and technical ability. He worked with a nutritionist, gained muscle and learned to adopt what Jongkind calls a 'top-sport mindset', training hard on the pitch and taking care of himself off it. But he was already mentally strong. That is perhaps no surprise when you learn that his father, Marcel, had been an undercover agent fighting serious crime. Now he's one of the lead detectives on the Dutch version of TV show *Hunted*. Like De Ligt at Ajax, Van de Ven was also sometimes used in midfield to help challenge and develop him. A year into their time at the club, Jonk and Jongkind were already tipping the teenager to be a future national team centre-back.

Van de Ven became a regular in the Volendam side and was handed the captain's armband at the age of 19. Naturally, playing in the Dutch second tier, bigger clubs began circling. Volendam initially held off the advances of AZ Alkmaar, Marseille and Wolfsburg. But Van de Ven's agent at the time, Mino Raiola, felt they were demanding too much money for his client. Raiola took the club to court, only for the Dutch football association to rule in favour of Volendam, who eventually sold the defender to Wolfsburg for €3.15m, almost three times what they initially offered. Volendam pocketed a sizeable sell-on percentage when he then moved to Tottenham for £43m in the summer of 2023, just four years after he was plucked from obscurity by Jonk and Jongkind. 'We fought so hard to get what is good for development clubs,' says Jongkind about holding out for an appropriate fee for Van de Ven. 'Big predators must also think about this. They can take and grab what they want but football is an ecosystem. You have to give a little bit to others, sell-ons, [otherwise] for what purpose would we still develop players?'

Volendam finished third in Jonk's first Covid-curtailed season in charge, a vast improvement on the 16th place they had managed a year earlier. 'The Other Oranje', as Volendam are known for their resplendent shirts that mimic the national side, followed that up with a sixth-placed finish in which they fielded a squad with an average age under 22, before sealing promotion as runners-up the following term. Jonk, just as he had as a player in 1987, had guided Volendam back to the Eredivisie for the first time in 13 years. They consolidated that season by finishing 14th in the top tier, before Jonk stepped out of the dugout to become technical manager. In December 2023, however, Team Jonk again found themselves leaving a club where they had seemingly done so much to add value and improve.

A row between chairman Jan Smit, the Volendam-born singer and television host, and the supervisory board over the club's finances led to Smit leaving the club. That made national news, with Smit one of the most famous singers in the Netherlands. Jonk, Jongkind, head coach Matthias Kohler and others among the Cruyff Plan entourage showed their solidarity with the celebrity chairman, who was the one to bring them into the club more than four years earlier. They were also eked out but eventually won a dismissal case for their departure against the board of directors. At the end of the season, Volendam were relegated back to the second division. 'That is also football,' says Jongkind. 'We were there for almost five years and built a club but you have to stay with your moral principles. It is interesting to see what Cruyff had in his past. He got into conflicts in the end, always with people from business, bookkeepers. You build something up and then people think in these power terms. We are just focusing on players and football but when you have success, they see it as power.'

Jonk, who is now coaching in the Netherlands set-up, Jongkind and their colleagues will continue to push the Cruyff Plan. They believe the principles inspired by the Dutch legend that have given Barcelona, Ajax and, on a smaller scale, Volendam a platform for success remain as pertinent as ever. Now, they are evaluating and planning for the future, using Cruyff's wisdom but also looking at how advances in technology and data can be best utilised. 'We are collecting all our knowledge and experience over the past one and a half decades and seeing what the lessons are we have learned,' explains Jongkind. 'What we showed in Ajax, is we created an environment where the players can grow, get the most out of themselves, with a relatively good budget. But we also saw this kind of approach can work when you don't have any pennies, like in Volendam, a very small club. If you can get both sportive success and create financial value, that is interesting. Maybe we can help people who want to invest in football? They love football, they have money but they don't want, after ten years, to lose half of their assets because of wrong decisions. I believe the Cruyff ideas and things we developed after that, if you packaged that well in a very simple-to-understand tool, taking into account technology and data and combining it with the laws of the street, then we have some interesting proposals for owners or potential owners to create value. Or to repair and increase value for them and for players. Always with the side notion that we believe in the academy and we believe in talent. That is our speciality, I think.'

Chapter 13

The Pilgrimage

WITH ITS narrow, cobblestone streets, charming old buildings and picturesque spot on the River Nive, it may seem hard to pull yourself away from Saint-Jean-Pied-de-Port but that is exactly what thousands of people who arrive in the idyllic Basque town do every year when they use it as a base to set off on a 500-mile trek. Nestled in the foothills of the Pyrenees, deep in the countryside of south-western France, the town is best known for being one of the starting points for pilgrims walking the Camino de Santiago. This version of the route is known as the Camino Francés, or the French Way, and has been trekked by those making the holy pilgrimage to the tomb of St James in Santiago de Compostela on the opposite coast of Spain since around the tenth century. And by Martin Sheen in 2010 movie *The Way*, of course. Some find it a spiritual or enlightening experience, others a gruelling test of resilience and perseverance. Maybe those things are intertwined.

Setting out in mid-September, hoping to find the weather a little cooler and the paths a littler quieter, it wasn't the climate or the physical challenge that

Chris Pidgeon found tough. 'Your feet ache but you would expect nothing less,' he explains. 'Mentally, at times, it's draining. The middle section, you are going through plains, they're quite flat. Quite samey.' Pidgeon began his quest alone but it was the people he met along the way that kept him going, such as the Australian girl who was following the summer for a year by continuously moving west. 'You meet all kinds of different nationalities,' he adds. 'You bump into people three or four days later and you have had completely different stories from the last time you saw each other. There are people walking it barefoot, people doing it for whatever reasons, and it is just fascinating. Everyone who does it has their own story and you get a glimpse of a person's life, a little snapshot.'

Pidgeon's own story from the Camino, a moment that changed his life, is truly unique. Many people talk about the beauty of crossing the Pyrenees, medieval villages, picturesque vineyards or idyllic towns bursting with culture but, for Pidgeon, the defining moment of his journey was discovering the football stadium of a little-known club he previously did not know existed. It was a footballing epiphany for a man who was already not short on experiences of following foreign football teams. Pidgeon, a Newcastle United fan when he was growing up, spent two years teaching English in Barcelona between 2004 and 2006 when a side managed by Frank Rijkaard beat Arsenal to win the Champions League. He enjoyed watching Samuel Eto'o, Ronaldinho, Carles Puyol and an emerging young talent named Lionel Messi. At the same time, city rivals Espanyol won the Copa del Rey. 'The whole city was abuzz,' he remembers. Then he moved to Italy, following third-tier side Pro Patria, who sit north of Milan and within striking distance of both Lake Como and the Swiss Alps. That was before taking teaching jobs in Serbia and Bosnia, where his lust for the game continued.

However, after checking into his €10-a-night hostel, having finished up a leg of the Camino in Ponferrada, the last major town before pilgrims reach Santiago de Compostela, it was while taking an evening stroll in his new surroundings that the football obsessive found a club that would come to mean more to him than all others. 'All I wanted to do was go and walk and explore, see the city while the sun was setting,' he explains. 'I saw the Templar Castle, walked over a bridge and saw the football ground just as darkness was approaching. It just had an effect on me, almost unexplained. A lot of people have spiritual experiences doing the Camino walk; perhaps mine was a calling to El Toralín?' El Toralín is the 8,400-capacity home ground of third-tier club SD Ponferradina. 'Something about it appealed to me,' adds Pidgeon. 'I don't know if it was the shadowing, the time, maybe exhaustion? But it just started nagging at me; who was this club? I hadn't really heard of them; I didn't know anything about them. I learned what standard of football they played at but unfortunately there wasn't a game when I was there and I moved on and left.'

Pidgeon completed the Camino but couldn't shrug the itch to learn more about Ponferradina. He started following their games as best he could back in the UK and then, remarkably, they drew Real Madrid in the two-legged Copa del Rey fourth round. 'I watched the first game on TV and I remember hearing the fans sing this folk song, famous for the region,' recalls Pidgeon. 'There was a picture of Yuri, our famous forward, with Cristiano Ronaldo in the same shot and, for me, it was just, "I have to go and see this live."' The hosts lost 2-0, Ronaldo and José Callejón with the goals. Two weeks later, Pidgeon found himself in the Santiago Bernabéu with the travelling Ponferradina fans, celebrating wildly as Acorán Barrera netted for the underdogs, although José Mourinho's Real Madrid ultimately ran away with the tie. 'We lost 5-1 but I was hooked!' beams Pidgeon.

By the time Pidgeon made it to his first home game, having got completely engaged in the club's online and social media community, he had become something of a legend among Ponferradina fans. They dubbed him 'The Englishman'. When he thinks back to that first game at El Toralín, and perhaps this comes with having followed Newcastle as a kid – after all, the Camino is known in English as the Way of St James – Pidgeon recalls the famous Sir Bobby Robson quote about the small boy clambering up stadium steps for the very first time and falling in love. It certainly wasn't the match itself – which was a 'rather boring 1-0 victory' – but, instead, everything around it. Particularly the welcome and warmth of the home fans. 'I was interviewed by someone who reached out to me on social media from Ponferrada,' he remembers. 'He was a 16-year-old kid, doing it as part of his college course. He couldn't have been more friendly. I met his family, stood with them at the game and there was a lot of interest in me because "El Ingles" had finally come to a game. There was a certain level of expectation when I got there and everyone wanted a photo. The welcome was fantastic.'

Perhaps 'The Englishman' was lucky, too. Later that season, Ponferradina won promotion to the second tier.

So charmed by the town and the football team was Pidgeon that, in 2014, he made the decision to up sticks and move to Ponferrada with his wife at the time and their daughter. Not simply satisfied with the adventure of moving to a new country, he also decided to cycle to every one of Ponferradina's away games that season. He covered 12,000 miles on his bike in total, with Cartagena, in the south-east of the country, a quad-burning ride of more than 500 miles. 'The obsession for the football team by that point had gone into complete overdrive,' he laughs. It was some feat, especially for someone nicknamed 'Non-homing Pidgeon' by his mates as a youngster for his propensity to get lost. 'The only game I missed was a cup game,' he explains. 'I was up in Catalunya and we got Huelva in the Copa del Rey on a Wednesday. Huelva is near the Portuguese border, the opposite end of the country, and I couldn't do that in four or five days.' There were also away games in Gran Canaria, for which Pidgeon cycled as far as Madrid, to the airport. And then, towards the end of the season, there was a trip to Santander. While he was there, Pidgeon's wife went into labour with their youngest daughter and he had to rush back to Ponferrada to attend the birth.

The following weekend, Ponferradina, with a young goalkeeper on loan from Athletic Club called Kepa Arrizabalaga, had the chance to reach the promotion play-offs, putting a potential place in La Liga within their grasp for the first time ever. A 1-1 draw with Alcorcón in front of a packed house at El Toralín saw them finish seventh and come up narrowly short. But it was a dream few days for Pidgeon.

Curious friends back home would often ask why the family had moved to Spain. Was it to have that year-round sunshine? Days on the beach? Strolls by the sea? It left Pidgeon to explain that, actually, the region of El Bierzo is cold and mountainous. But he loved the food, the warmth of the people, meeting pilgrims who passed through the city, just as he had done years earlier, and hearing their stories. 'It is just a fairytale place,' he says. 'I saw beauty in every corner.' After two years living in Spain, however, the Pidgeon family returned to the north-east of England so their eldest daughter could begin her education in the UK system. If anything, the absence and longing for Ponferradina made Pidgeon's desire to watch the club even stronger. He would return whenever he could for home and away games, sometimes up to 14 times a season. Then, in 2019, he finally got his chance to enjoy a promotion party.

The year after their flirtation with the top flight, La Ponfe were relegated back to the third tier. They spent three seasons there but, in 2019, went soaring back up, finishing second and winning the play-offs. Pidgeon, who admits he will go to any length to see his beloved Ponferradina, had to fly via Copenhagen to make the second leg of the play-off final against Hércules. But it was worthwhile. The hosts won 1-0, sealing a 4-1 aggregate victory. Perhaps the closest thing the club

have to a celebrity fan, he was asked to go on the radio
and give his predictions before the game. Afterwards,
the club invited him into the changing rooms to join
the celebrations with the players and manager Bolo,
the former Athletic Club striker. The fun didn't stop
there. At the promotion party in the city, Pidgeon was
invited to meet the mayor and then found himself on
the balcony of Ponferrada Town Hall celebrating with
the players, after one of the squad spotted him and ran
over to give him a big hug. He ended up speaking to a
crowd of 6,000 euphoric fans. The players responded
by chanting 'Chris is on Fire!' That night, he joined
them in the VIP section of a local nightclub as the
party carried on into the next morning. Other than
the birth of his children, Pidgeon says, it was the best
weekend of his life.

The following season, just before Covid hit, in
March 2020, Pidgeon flew out to Tenerife to watch
a 1-0 defeat in the second division's Saturday evening
kick-off slot. With an early flight back to the UK
booked for the following morning, he decided to head
straight to the airport rather than book a hotel on the
island for the night. Only it turned out the airport
isn't a 24-hour operation, leaving the Ponfe fan stuck
outside until 4am, waiting to use the toilet. Half-awake
and slouched over a cold coffee, he thought he must
be dreaming. 'A mirage of blue passed me through my
bleary eyes,' he remembers. 'The Ponferradina squad
were flying back home at about 6am.' Pablo Valcarce,
one of the twins playing for Ponfe at the time, bought
Pidgeon a coffee and offered him a sandwich from
his packed lunch. 'A lot of the players knew me,'

he explains, normalising the idea that professional footballers would recognise one of their fans in the airport, let alone offer to share food with them.

Unfortunately, lockdown meant it would be his last face-to-face interaction with them for some time. Pidgeon, however, had ways of showing his continued support. Back in York, he created a dedicated Ponferradina museum in his home and gathered almost 3,000 items. There were souvenirs, pin badges, scarves, match statistics going back years, photos of him in different stadiums with a Ponfe scarf 'spreading the good name of the club throughout the world'. People would even submit things for him to display. And it is still being added to. There are handmade individual tea coasters for each game of Ponferradina's centenary year in 2022, key rings with team photos on and Pidgeon's own paintings of team logos throughout the Spanish football pyramid.

Of course, Pidgeon is still a regular at Ponferradina matches, home and especially away, ticking off new grounds and discovering new anecdotes. 'Pablo Infante,' he begins. 'A winger we signed from Mirandés. He was a bank manager. He didn't really want to be a footballer; he was just very good at it. He played on the wing and was nicknamed "The Magician", *El Mago*. He was fantastic and we got so close to promotion the season I followed them by bicycle. I remember he high-fived me on the last home game of the season and my friend, who he also high-fived, said he wouldn't wash his hands because "The Magician" had touched him.' The reason Pidgeon is telling this story is because he is recently back from a game at Real Unión, the club owned by Unai Emery, where 'The Englishman' was one of just seven Ponferradina away fans. Bringing the endearing tale full circle, he adds: 'I met the father of Nacho Castillo, who is a current Ponfe player. His dad played on the opposite wing to Pablo Infante in the Mirandés team who had an amazing cup run. It was lovely.'

Pidgeon says he left a piece of his heart in Ponferrada and will forever be going back to find it. And he will continue to champion SD Ponferradina. In fact, he probably gets more publicity for his unique story than the club do themselves. He'll forever be passionate about the Camino, too. The 'Non-homing Pidgeon' completed another section of it on his bike without a map, just keeping the sun on his left so he knew he was heading in the right direction. Friends have been convinced to walk it after hearing his stories, as well as his parents. Naturally, there was a welcome party from the locals waiting for them in Ponferrada. 'I would recommend doing the Camino to anyone, if you are lucky enough to have that sort of time,' says Pidgeon. 'I am still passionate about it and I would love to do it again. It's a lovely country and the enthusiasm of a Spanish teacher when I was 14 has given me a love of Spain that burns as brightly as ever.'

Next time you happen to be passing through Ponferrada, then, or paying a visit to El Toralín, just mention you know 'The Englishman' and you will be granted a warm welcome. Who knows? Maybe part of you will never leave.

Chapter 14

Dinner With Totti

ONE THING that always astonishes me, and perhaps this is part of why it is so attractive, is how cheap it is to fly to mainland Europe. A lot cheaper than a train ticket from Manchester to London, for example. I have flown to Milan and bought a ticket to watch Champions League football at the San Siro for a combined price that is less than some Premier League matchday tickets alone. Flying is not the most sustainable method of transport, admittedly, but it is cheap and it is quick and, for the most part, probably more reliable than UK trains. On this occasion, the flight from Manchester to Venice's Marco Polo Airport needed to be punctual if I was going to make dinner with Francesco Totti that evening. Luckily, it was.

Most people flying on a Friday afternoon are kitted up with sightseeing gear and flashy carry-on bags ready for a weekend exploring the City of Canals, yet I was arriving with a notepad and a vintage Tottenham Hotspur shirt hastily crammed into a backpack. The little I see of Venice comes mostly from the air as the plane circles before descending towards the runway. It is approaching 6pm on the Italian north-east coast and a few lights are beginning to flicker, though it would be wrong to suggest I could pick out St Mark's Basilica or any other iconic Venetian landmarks between huddled shoulders and crumpled, curious brows peering through postage stamp-sized plane windows. The bus ride from the airport to Venice Mestre train station is even less scenic. But I have not come to ride gondolas or browse Byzantine mosaics. Venice was simply a gateway to a plethora of former Serie A stars, who any minute would be hunkering down for an aperitivo and wondering why one was going spare. Would Totti call first dibs on mine?

Thankfully, the train from Venice to Ferrara is swift and the scenery pleasant. The June air is still humid at dusk when pacing the mile walk from Ferrara's central train station, along Viale Cavour, past the locals enjoying summer evening drinks, to Hotel Touring. I only begin to sweat when the receptionist reveals she can't find my booking. 'Shit,' I cry internally. And then, like magic, she has it. Never in doubt. Bag flung in the room quicker than you can say 'Golazo!', anxiety replaced by excitable energy and a childlike sense of anticipation, I bounded off to find the castle packed with Serie A legends I'd been promised.

I'd flown to Italy on a bit of a hunch, an opportunistic visit for what I felt would be an insightful and original story. I had stumbled across Operazione Nostalgia by chance, a concept that began as a Facebook page created in 2015. It was the brainchild of Andrea Bini and essentially involved posting pictures and reminiscing about Serie A players from Bini's youth; what he would describe as the Italian glory years of the

1990s and early 2000s. Bini roped university friend and co-founder Luca Valentino into his project and, with the pair's background and expertise in digital and social media, the page flourished. Within six months, they had more than 50,000 followers. They decided, in hope more than expectation, to host an event in Milan. It was a triumph. Bini, Valentino and four ex-footballers were joined in Piazza San Babila, near the Duomo, by 500 fans all donned in vintage jerseys of the clubs they supported. The square was blocked. TV cameras even turned up to see what all the fuss was about. 'If you are able to move the people from online to offline, that is the real engagement,' professes Valentino.

The project continued to grow. Its target audience, most in their mid-30s, similar to the founders themselves, bought into the values of Operazione Nostalgia. As did Max Tonetto, the once-capped Italy midfielder who represented Reggiana, Empoli, Lecce, Bologna, Sampdoria and Roma during his career and came with a wealth of former Serie A contacts. Inevitably, it has evolved into a business. 'It is our life,' says Valentino. 'We developed the company and manage it ourselves.' Despite that, or perhaps because of, Valentino stresses the desire to always stay true to the project's roots. 'We all love football,' he says. 'In the 90s and 2000s, calcio and Serie A was the best league.' The pair realised the context on social media was very different, where it is all about the latest news and the present day. 'For Italy, the present is not very great!' laughs Valentino. 'We felt that there was a need for our generation to remember that period. We like to speak without creating polemic problems. We want to talk about football as a sport and about positive values and great players. But we also talk about the province idols. In that period in Italy, at Brescia were Roberto Baggio and Pep Guardiola, for example. For Lecce, we have Javier Chevanton.'

One of Valentino's favourite players to have participated in an Operazione Nostalgia rally and the ultimate 'province idol' is Dario Hubner, who spent most of his career racking up goals in the lower leagues before joining Cesena in Serie B and finally getting his top-flight breakthrough in Serie A for newly promoted Brescia at the age of 30. Hubner made his debut for Le Rondinelle against Inter at the San Siro on the opening day of the 1997/98 season, at the same time as Brazil sensation Ronaldo, who had just become the world's most expensive player for the second time in a £19.5m move from Barcelona. One of the debutants scored that afternoon in Milan and it wasn't O Fenômeno. Instead, Hubner, the formidable 'Bison of Brescia', notched the first of 16 league goals that season. A cult figure later immortalised in several Italian music tracks, Hubner, who was also renowned for smoking on the substitutes' bench and partial to a Grappa, would later go on to become the oldest player to be named Serie A top goalscorer. He bagged 24 times for Piacenza in 2001/02 at the age of 35 to share the Capocannoniere award with Juventus' David Trezeguet. His record stood until a 38-year-old Luca Toni broke it while playing for Verona in 2015.

Who would meet the criteria of a province idol if this was a Premier League project, I ask? 'For me, at Manchester City it is Paulo Wanchope,' laughs Valentino. 'Or Matt Le Tissier at Southampton!'

A year after Milan, Bini and Valentino went on the road again, this time to Ostia near Rome, where almost 2,000 people and 40 ex-footballers turned up. That was more than enough for a match against each other. The squad included former defender Aldair, a World Cup and Copa America winner with Brazil and Serie A champion with Roma, as well as Italian World Cup-winning midfielder Simone Perrotta. 'A nostalgic afternoon to spend together with friends. All united between beers, porchetta and many smiles,' wrote Italian journalist Francesco Pietrella about the first 'Nostalgia Derby'. In 2017, they went further south to Lecce, doubling the number of fans. And come 2018, as the project continued to snowball, Parma got in contact to set up a legends game against an Operazione Nostalgia Stars team at the club's iconic Stadio Ennio Tardini home. Parma fielded a side boasting popular names from their heady days in the 1990s, when the club won four European trophies (the UEFA Cup twice, the Cup Winners' Cup and the Super Cup) with Hernán Crespo, Juan Sebastián Verón, Mario Stanić and Diego Fuser among those to pull on the yellow and blue hoops. 'Eight thousand people at the Tardini. Verón, Crespo, crazy!' remembers Valentino. 'We thought we were already near the top but in 2019, La Liga called us.' Fernando Hierro, Christian Karembeu and Fernando Morientes featured in a team of La Liga stars. 'We had Del Piero as captain,' smiles Valentino. They also had Edgar Davids.

The Covid pandemic meant any plans the pair had to stage an event had to be put on hold for four years, making the return in June 2023 extra special. Operazione Nostalgia's online presence grew during that time to become stronger than ever, with more than a million followers on Facebook. It is a project that has allowed them to rub shoulders with some of the game's greatest players. But for Valentino, it has also provided an opportunity to satisfy some of the misgivings of his childhood. One season as a youngster, he and his friends collected stickers from packets of bubble gum. They were so close to completing the collection but just two stickers proved elusive; Sergio Volpi and Paolo Poggi. That is until now. 'We brought this trauma that we couldn't finish this album,' he passionately explains, finally able to scratch the itch 25 years later by signing both players up for the Operazione Nostalgia fixture. 'Now people can come just to take a selfie with these players and say they have completed it! This is one of our secrets – nostalgia but in a positive way in terms of emotion and memories.'

The founders were determined to return with a bang after their absence and the setting for the opening gala duly delivers. All I really knew about Ferrara before this trip was that it sits between Venice and Bologna and is home to the football club SPAL, who in 2023 were back in Serie C, the Italian third tier, after a brief climb and three-year stay in Serie A. Valentino, however, kept mentioning a castle – the pin location he sent me on WhatsApp even read 'Sala Stemmi Castello Estense' at 'Piazza Castelo' – yet the lira does not drop until I turn the corner from the hotel to be met by the sight of grand medieval towers growing from the moat that navigates the whole perimeter of an actual, real-life castle. On the cobbled street outside one gated entrance to a bridge that crosses the water, 30 to 40 fans wait with mobile phone cameras primed. A bouncer stands, arms folded, guarding the stone entrance next to a lady ticking names off on a clipboard. Sheepishly, I make my way through the expectant entourage and offer my credentials. They exchange words in Italian, before turning sideways to allow me to slip through the gate and across the bridge.

A buoyant Valentino welcomes me and leads us through an archway, where the floor opens into a magnificent courtyard with tables draped in white linen and tons of diners dressed in fine gowns and black tie. My chinos and casual shirt look a little undercooked, until I scan the floor and spot Francesco Totti sporting just a T-shirt. There he is, in the flesh, sitting at a table all of ten yards away. It takes a while to figure out the dynamics of the guest list. There are friends, media, sponsors and, of course, the players and their families. All are extremely welcoming to this random Brit who has come to crash the party. Across the table is former Italy goalkeeper Marco Amelia, who spent a year at Chelsea under José Mourinho as back-up to Thibaut Courtois and Asmir Begovic, having previously represented Livorno, Palermo, Genoa and AC Milan. Amelia is handsome and confident and dominates conversation on the table in both Italian and English. He regales stories, told in both languages just for my benefit, from his playing days and we discuss Guglielmo Vicario's impending move from Empoli to

Tottenham Hotspur. Amelia, now working as a TV pundit, says he believes the Italian could become one of the best goalkeepers in the Premier League.

Amid the chat and the drinks flowing, I can't help but peruse the grand courtyard, especially to observe Totti. Eyes bulging, jaw on the floor, my advances are less than subtle. Throughout the night, I exchange nods of acknowledgement with a myriad of other former Serie A stars, trying to place their now mature faces to the kits and colours they wore more than two decades ago.

Javier Zanetti even appears on stage to give a talk about his PUPI Foundation – PUPI being both a play on his nickname, 'El Pupi', and Por Un Piberío Integrado, which translates as 'for an integrated childhood'. It is a project which aims to provide food, education, health and aid to impoverished and disadvantaged children in Buenos Aires, where the former Argentina and Inter wing-back grew up, while also helping young people to integrate with society. Zanetti, just like he did as a player, moves with purpose and authority, a figure to be respected. Yet, always there, just in my peripheral vision, is Totti. Even at a private function for players, sponsors and media, people are approaching him and asking for selfies.

I'd been promised several interviews over the weekend but mentions of speaking to Totti or Alessandro Del Piero, the other huge star to be captaining a team at Saturday's match, were coyly shrugged off and now I could see why. The guy is worshipped like a king. A true one-club man, a seventh-generation Roman who spent his whole career playing for his boyhood side and became both their top goalscorer and record appearance-maker in the process. The guy who led Roma to a first Scudetto in 18 years and only their third ever league title, won two Coppa Italia and also a World Cup with Italy. A nearly 50-year-old multi-millionaire who has spent his entire life living in the capital, his hometown. That just doesn't happen in this game. It's part of what is so enchanting about Totti, that he could have gone to any club in the world in his prime, yet he chose to stay with I Giallorossi and sport the same jersey as those heroes who appeared in the posters on his childhood bedroom wall, especially former captain and midfielder Giuseppe Giannini, one of Totti's inspirations and a player he would go on to share a dressing room with.

I came to discover how two university friends created a flourishing, feel-good football business but, in a wider context, the opportunity to spend time in the presence of these greats also feels so appealing. If my intention is to convey some of the most soulful aspects of the game, then stories do not come more wholesome than that of Francesco Totti and his enduring Roman love affair. Real Madrid president Florentino Pérez spent several years chasing the Italian, wishing to add the playmaker to his stable of 'Galacticos'. The Spanish giants even tried to tempt him with an incredible package, a reported €12m a year, dwarfing the €5.8m salary he was on at Roma. The La Liga club offered him personal and club image rights that the player's management estimated could reach €15m in 12 months. Not only that, Pérez also promised Totti the No.10 shirt the departing Luís Figo was set to leave behind by joining Inter Milan on a free transfer. Perhaps starring for the Spanish giants would also have beckoned a Ballon d'Or but Totti's destiny was to never leave Roma behind.

'You never even dreamed of a career ending like this. Too big even to conceive,' he wrote in his autobiography, *Gladiator*, asking whether he had done enough to 'repay Rome'. 'Of course, you guided them to the Scudetto and that's a rare feat. But the river of love that you've been swimming in since the day of your debut, the affection with which it supports you and protects you, the faith that it has in you – not trust, faith! – can these know their end?' Totti explained he would not be able to live with hearing that, without him, Roma had lost a derby with Lazio or were suffering in the table. 'You'll hit the locker, making a dent in it, you'll massage your sore fist and you'll murmur something in your hesitant Spanish to your shocked team-mates,' he added. 'You'll want to be 2,000km away from there to organise the Giallorossi's rescue. You'll want to but you won't be able to.'

Having consistently rejected advances from Madrid, when Totti and Pérez met again later in his career, the Real president jokingly asked the Italian to sign a shirt for him, saying: 'The only player to say no to Real Madrid!' But while those encounters may have made Totti feel guilty for even momentarily pondering a different future, he had been turning down requests to leave Rome before he even kicked a ball for the club. Aged 12, scouts from Milan, who had just won their first Serie A title of the Silvio Berlusconi era, identified the prodigious youngster at a youth tournament in

Rome. Milan sporting director Ariedo Braida came to Totti's house and attempted to persuade his parents to allow their son to move six hours north, offering them a job and a 150m lire cheque to do so, the equivalent of €75,000 in those days. But the boy stayed in Via Vetulonia, in his family home above the mechanics. The rest is a beautiful history.

Totti's playing career lasted almost 25 years. From coming on as a substitute for his debut against Brescia as a 16-year-old in March 1993, to being given a standing ovation by Roma's Stadio Olimpico crowd when entering the field as a 40-year-old in the second half of a 3-2 win over Genoa in May 2017. After the final whistle, a tearful Totti was handed a signed No.10 shirt and read a speech to his adoring fans. 'Over the years, I've tried to express myself through my feet, which have made everything simpler for me ever since I was a child,' he professed. 'At some point in life, you grow up. That's what I've been told and that's what time has decided. Damned time.' Totti said he desperately wanted to not have to wake from his dream of representing Roma. 'Allow me to be afraid,' he finished.

There is a romance about Francesco Totti but there is a rawness, too. When the air of immortality fades, in many ways the hero becomes more relatable. Totti in his Hollywood prime was the guy who could marry a showgirl on live television and celebrate goals with T-shirts proclaiming his love for her but in the years between retirement and this dinner, the wounds opened and the details of a marriage falling apart were analysed in the tabloids like one of his defence-splitting assists. In an interview with *Corriere della Sera*, Totti spoke about how his retirement and the Coronavirus death of his father, Enzo – the quiet soul who would bring croissants and pizza to Roma's Trigoria training complex – followed by the break-up of his marriage, had led him to depression. 'I was fragile,' he revealed.

Totti, it turns out, shares the same fears and anxieties as us mortals. Where once fans could not help but stand and applaud the magician, now they just wanted to give him a hug. At dinner, however, Totti is content among old friends. Inside these ancient walls, he continues to be worshipped like a god. And despite all the attention, he somehow ghosts effortlessly into the night, leaving the adoring public with a taste of how those man-markers of the past felt when they thought they had him. Tomorrow, he will prove his sorcery with a football never dies.

As the sun rises from behind Castello Estense, the hazy morning rays glinting off its turrets and the castle's 14th-century architecture reflecting from the moat below, it is even more impressive than when lit up at night. Once inhabited by the House of Este, which governed Ferrara from 1264 to 1598, and later a grand court palace (and, of course, dining spot for veteran Italian footballers) the castle stands proudly in the centre of the city after being refurbished in 2002. Picking up some pastries and an espresso from Duca D'Este, I enjoy breakfast in the cobbled square that surrounds the fortification, while marvelling at the impressive clock tower and reading up on Ferrara's grand and complex history.

Its beautiful walled centre was granted UNESCO world heritage status in 1995. According to the official tourist information site, Ferrara was 'the first modern city' and one that was among the 'culturally most important to the Italian Renaissance city states'. It was revered at the time as one of the European capitals of culture, arts, politics and gastronomy and a reference point for artists and poets. Yet, at this time in the morning, there is a peaceful calm, making it hard to imagine furious citizens protesting about tax increases, causing Nicolò II d'Este to commission the fortress in 1385 to protect his family.

The organisers invite me to head over to Hotel Carlton, where the players are staying, after breakfast to arrange some interviews but, after making the short stroll through Piazza della Repubblica, passing the quaint community garden, and along Via Giuseppe Garibaldi, I find myself at the back of an energetic crowd gathering around the hotel entrance. Garibaldi, an Italian patriot, general and 19th-century revolutionary who played a crucial role in the Risorgimento, the unification of Italy, may be regarded as the country's national hero, worthy of a monument in the city, but the mass of people in football shirts blocking the street bearing his name would no doubt argue the same modern-day status could be bestowed upon these players they wish to get a glimpse of mingling the other side of the hotel windows. Luckily, Nando, a big man with an enviously thick black beard acting as the player liaison, ushers me past the crowd and security guards at the doorway and into the hotel lobby, where some players and family members are relaxing.

Nando gives me the all-clear to grab whoever I want for a chat and says he will help translate if necessary. So, as Georgios Karagounis wanders through, I ask if he would mind answering a few questions. He politely obliges. I'm intrigued to know what the former Inter midfielder believes makes the Operazione Nostalgia event so special for the players involved. Why are they all so keen to take part? 'It is good to see a lot of friends after a long time,' he explains. 'It is great for the audience, too, because they come from all around Italy and we build a huge party.' Karagounis is well travelled, having won Euro 2004 with Greece and played in Portugal with Benfica and in the Premier League with Fulham, and pauses for a moment before delivering a considered final thought: 'It is a great community. It doesn't matter the colours and maybe it would be great if this message would go across all the football universe.'

There seems to be a genuine buy-in from the players for the event. Valentino previously explained the size of the rally meant they now needed signed guarantees from those involved. They couldn't promise 14,000 paying spectators these stars and one of them not show up. But from the ex-prós I have spoken to and observed, there is a real desire to take part.

The players are taken in twos and threes to and from the fan park, about a mile away, to sign autographs, pose for photos and generally mingle with supporters. It is a searingly hot day and many seem to be returning to the hotel dripping with sweat and needing to change clothes. The loudest and most enigmatic of the bunch is Sebastien Frey. He is without the bleached blond hair or flowing locks that defined him at various points in his playing career but the former goalkeeper still boasts an imposing frame. It is now softened by his light beard, spiked hair rigidly gelled into position and shirt unbuttoned down to his chest. He cuts a welcoming, smiley figure.

Frey's career took him from Thonon-les-Bains, on the banks of Lake Geneva in France, to Cannes and the French Riviera and then Milan, with Inter. He was worshipped at Verona for helping them stave off relegation during a loan spell in 1999/00, replaced Gianluigi Buffon at Parma and then earned something of a cult status at Fiorentina. It was in Florence, after suffering a serious knee injury, that he was introduced to Buddhism by former team-mate Roberto Baggio, himself known as the 'Divine Ponytail', in part because of his strong faith in Nichiren Buddhism. Frey stated at the time that practising the religion helped him feel more relaxed and sure of himself and he recovered to play for the best part of the next decade, winning two caps for France and having spells at Genoa and Turkish outfit Bursaspor before retiring in 2015.

However, he tells me retirement has not stopped him playing regularly in charity and exhibition games with Totti and co. 'It is always a big pleasure to play with or against some players,' he beams. 'We make a lot of jokes. It is very funny, because when you play against some players, you have one idea about their personality. Now, we are all ex-players and you discover the personalities of some players that maybe you didn't like before! Now, we are all friends and we don't represent the present of football. Now, we are just playing to enjoy the moment and for some good association. It is a very good atmosphere.' Frey has already been to the fan village and mixed with supporters of all tastes. He sees it almost as a duty, an honour, to fulfil their wishes for photographs or signatures and, of course, to perform for them on the pitch. 'I don't want to fight with nobody,' he adds, with a hearty grin, before insisting he is here to win the match. 'With a smile, that is the most important thing!'

Like many of the fans here, though, who spend their money to come and reminisce about the old days, there is a sense Frey and his fellow ex-pros believe they hail from a more romantic era of Italian football. That is despite the Azzurri being crowned European champions in 2021, beating England in a penalty shoot-out at Wembley. 'For us, it is very important,' Frey continues. 'We are talking about all the ex-footballers. I recall the history. I think in the 1990s and 2000s we did something special, because today we are not playing anymore and all the people still continue loving us and respecting us a lot and we are very proud of this. I am very happy because of this.' Frey is also keen to stress how this rally brings fans of all clubs together. Despite playing for Inter, he has signed plenty of autographs for fans in rival Milan or Juventus shirts.

Totti has been warming up for the big match by playing padel tennis with Vincent Candela, who is no doubt giving his former Roma team-mate a tough match. Candela is fresh off the back of being named the inaugural winner of the Sports Legends Cup at the 2022 World Cup in Qatar, beating Italian World

Cup winner Marco Materazzi in a competition that also included ex-Brazil striker Ronaldo, Gabriel Batistuta, John Terry, Kaka and Clarence Seedorf. It was organised by Paris Saint-Germain president Nasser Al-Khelaifi, who also just happens to be a keen player and whose Qatar Sports Investments company has since acquired the World Padel Tour.

Many of the other players are grabbing their pre-match meals or taking the chance for a quick catnap. So I opt to make my own way down to the fan village to soak up some of the pre-match atmosphere, passing by the Stadio Paolo Mazza en route. Situated within the city walls and hidden by the residential buildings around it, as the corner of SPAL's ground appears at the end of an avenue of trees it has something of a vintage feel to it. After all, Valentino says they chose this stadium because of its 'English' characteristics, 'English' being the way Italians often refer to a football ground with stands that feel close to the pitch and without an athletics track. Were it not for the unmistakably Italian floodlights careering high above the blue and white terraces and sun-baked seats, this could easily be mistaken for a stroll past Stockport County's Edgeley Park.

The streets around the stadium are dotted with supporters. But, as the fan village draws closer, the sheer number of people making their way over in contrasting kits is striking. Thousands flood between the stalls representing clubs the length and breadth of Italy, snacking and sipping beers on a glorious summer afternoon. Most have complied with the organisers' call to come in vintage jerseys, which makes meandering through the crowds feel like a nostalgic and somewhat comforting time hop.

A group of four lads are donned in Parma's iconic yellow and blue hoops, each sporting a different player's name on their back. There is Thuram, Di Vaio, Crespo, Cannavaro. Other names evoke different memories; Maldini, Weah, Baggio, even Thomas Häßler. There are classic Sampdoria, Inter and Fiorentina numbers, some represent Empoli, Udinese, Perugia, Brescia and Palermo. And among plenty of Francesco Totti Roma shirts and Juventus tops bearing Alessandro Del Piero's name, there are several gems to unearth. One proud dad has kitted his son out in a 1994 Padova shirt with Alexi Lalas on the back. Such is the wear on the printed letters, it must have been his father's original. Undoubtedly, he is the only fan at the event honouring the first American to play in Serie A.

Unable to place its red and black stripes, one kit catches my eye and provokes a certain curiosity. This belongs to a now-defunct club, the shirt's owner, Luca Aielli, explains, whose most recent reincarnation as SS Virtus Lanciano 1924 ended with voluntary liquidation following their relegation from Serie B in 2016. It was an almost five-hour journey for Aielli to visit from Lanciano but a worthwhile trip to share the experience with fellow fans 'without rivalry', as he puts it. For him, the attraction is the opportunity to meet some of the players he regarded as legends during his childhood.

Chatting to Luca and other fans in their various club hues gives me football shirt envy, so I shuffle past the small-sided cage games taking place, beyond the table football and video consoles tent and, after perusing a couple of attractive yet lavishly priced vintage jersey stalls, head for the club merchandise table in the corner. Immediately drawn in by the blue and white stripes of SPAL – that's an abbreviation of Società Polisportiva Ars et Labor for you Latin speakers, and Sports Club Society of Art and Work for the rest of us – I pick out a player-worn shirt purely because it fits best. On my last check, No.97 Ludovico D'Orazio is on loan at Serie C side Latina, but his old SPAL shirt will be getting a good outing in Greater Manchester.

As kick-off approaches and the hordes of multi-coloured fans enter the stadium, there is a friendly and jovial atmosphere simmering. Once Totti emerges from the tunnel to warm up, however, that canvas of kits erupts into a chant of 'Il Capitano'; it is a wholesome welcome, not just from the Roma supporters in carmine red and gold but from a majority of the 14,000 ticket holders now taking to their seats. Each subsequent player is beckoned on to the turf with applause and chants of their own, before returning to the changing rooms to apply some last-minute Deep Heat and make sure those old injury niggles are appropriately taped up.

As a recognisable mop of tight curly hair bounces past me, one fan screams out 'Tommasi!' and the unsuspecting figure turns in my direction. I've been awarded the privilege of being allowed to stand pitchside. Suddenly appearing face to face with Damiano Tommasi, I take the opportunity to introduce myself. 'Welcome to Verona,' is the response, before Tommasi laughs, shakes his head and corrects himself. 'Welcome to Ferrara!' It's a forgivable mistake, for Tommasi is now the mayor of Verona and must utter that phrase multiple times a day. Tommasi's first foray into politics came as president of the Italian Footballers' Association in 2011, spending almost a decade in the position before running for mayor of the city in which his football career began. Indeed, he has always demonstrated a strong social conscience. It was a young Tommasi who chose to undertake charitable work with the civil service while playing for Hellas Verona, instead of the alternative military option, stating: 'I did not want to serve my country by holding a rifle.' And it was Tommasi who asked to be put on minimum wage while enduring a long injury lay-off at Roma, earning a papal blessing. The midfielder helped orchestrate the great Giallorossi side of 2000/01's Scudetto triumph and collected 25 Italy caps throughout his career. Poignantly, he was also awarded the L'Altropallone prize in 2000 – an honour that calls itself the 'alternative to the Ballon d'Or for sports people' and is awarded to those who commit their time and effort to good causes and charitable work.

Tommasi, then, is a thoroughly decent bloke and has been in his current mayoral position since 2022 after being elected as head of a centre-left coalition between the Democratic Party and Sinistra Italiana, the Italian left, in Verona. The combined parties saw off right-wing opposition, in a city that traditionally swings that way, to make them the first left-leaning office in 20 years in Verona, which had been declared an anti-abortion city under previous mayor Federico Sboarina's leadership. Tommasi said the victory showed 'politics can be done without insults or responding to provocations' and he kept his promise to cycle the

Stelvio Pass, the second-highest route of its kind in the Alps and one famed for a marathon climb that includes 48 hairpin bends.

At 49, though, and only four years on since he last laced up his boots in Europa League qualifying for San Marino outfit La Fiorita, a player once renowned for his tenacious midfield displays will not be pulling out of any tackles tonight. 'Always,' he grins when asked if the game will be competitive, before easing into a now customary more political answer. 'It is a special event because we come back to our past and meet a lot of old friends. It is a special day to see all these people with different shirts sit in the stands.'

As an expectant crowd wait patiently for the players to return, a performer in an Inter Milan shirt takes to the centre of the pitch and belts out a rendition of 'An Italian Summer' or, as many Italians refer to it, *'Notti Magiche'* (Magical Nights). It is the official song from Italia 90 and the No.1-selling single in the country that year. That was, no doubt, helped by the Azzurri's success in finishing in third place on home soil. Translated to English, it reads like this:

> *Magic nights, chasing a goal,*
> *Under the sky of an Italian summer.*
> *And in your eyes, the desire of winning.*
> *One summer, one more adventure.*

It's as close to an Italian version of New Order's 'World in Motion' as I can imagine, though Mario the performer has managed to crowbar the names of all the players featuring in this evening's match into the lyrics. As he comes off the pitch, Mario admits he was nervous but I reassure him that the whole stadium seemed to enjoy it. Even the security guards were humming along. 'You don't have something like this in England?' he asks, pointing out the different club shirts sitting next to each other in the crowd behind us. 'That's the beauty of football.' After a successful performance, he is back to acting like a fan himself and explains his next mission is to get a photograph with former Inter striker Diego Milito.

With the players kitted up and congregated in the tunnel, Mario's selfie will have to wait. I'm primed all of two yards in front of them, ready to get my own snaps, except, as Totti and Del Piero shuffle to the front, captain's armbands on, a horde of other fully grown men jostle for position around me. Totti playfully ruffles an unsuspecting linesman's hair and then shares a joke with Del Piero before they stroll out, studs clinking on the concrete, inches from my toes, up on to the pitch to a chorus of cheers and chants, through a guard of honour put in place by the young mascots and, finally, into position for kick-off. Vincent Candela, for reasons unknown, has drawn his own name and number on the back of his shirt in black marker pen. Arturo Di Napoli's wife and children stand on the touchline, all wearing Salernitana shirts with his name on.

The game is played at a fairly languid pace until the sprightly Antonio di Natale, at the age of 45, rises high into the red Ferrara sky and sends an impressively acrobatic bicycle kick narrowly over the crossbar. Inter's treble-winning forward Milito then kick-starts a flurry of goals, showing that composure and a striker's instinct never leave you. 'Diegoooo ...' screams the announcer. 'Milito!' is the crowd's response. Totti is Totti. Effortlessly majestic, he clips a wonderful pass to the wing and a chorus of his name rings out around the stadium. He continues to saunter around midfield at jogging pace, weaving in and out of tackles, meandering past opponents and spraying no-look passes with both feet. It is opposition skipper Del Piero, though, who levels from the penalty spot. The former Juventus icon, affectionately known as 'Alex', has explained how he was charmed by witnessing fans of rival clubs chant his name at a previous Operazione Nostalgia rally. Now it is booming around the Stadio Paolo Mazza once more. Luca Valentino, the co-founder, explains: 'Del Piero, at the last event, said "Guys, I have seen everything on the pitch but this was the first time there was a part of the stand with a fan of Inter Milan making a song for me!" He said only at Operazione Nostalgia can that happen. That is a satisfaction for us.' 'To see the touched eyes of Del Piero and Totti gives us chills,' adds Andrea Bini, who created the project. 'They are players that have passed through the stages of all the world and to make them emotional is not a common thing.'

Totti, determined not to be outdone by old foe Del Piero, crashes an effort against the crossbar and then turns provider with a precise, curling pass inside the full-back which former Roma team-mate David Pizarro flicks beyond goalkeeper Marco Amelia. Operazione Nostalgia favourite Javier Chevanton nets either side of a smart finish from ex-Juventus defender Paolo de Ceglie as a Mexican wave rolls around the ground. But, with the game poised at 3-3, it is former

Chile international Pizarro who deservedly grabs the winner for Del Piero's side. At the age of 43, he is one of the standout players, both technically and in terms of physical fitness. The players enjoy a lap of honour, soaking up the adulation of the adoring crowd. I spot Mario weaving between legends with a homemade cardboard cut-out of the Champions League trophy, eventually earning Diego Milito's attention for the selfie he has been longing for.

Marco Amelia, the former Chelsea goalkeeper, pays an emotional tribute to another former Blue, holding aloft a Juventus shirt bearing Gianluca Vialli's name, the former Italy striker and assistant manager to Roberto Mancini during their European Championship success in 2021 having passed away a few months earlier from pancreatic cancer aged just 58. It is a humbling, sobering moment in an otherwise celebratory evening.

As the crowds disperse, I head down the tunnel to chat with some of the welcoming SPAL staff I met earlier. Owner and president Joe Tacopina is down there, now on to his fourth Italian club after roles at Roma, Bologna and Venezia, though a name more familiar with the wider world for having represented Michael Jackson and New York Yankees baseball star Alex Rodriguez and for being US president Donald Trump's personal attorney. Totti and Del Piero have already slipped out while others, including Diego Milito, are saying their farewells to old friends and team-mates, the changing room littered with electrical tape and empty drinks bottles. It is reminiscent of any amateur ground up and down the country. Except here, a few moments ago, were hundreds of international caps packed under one roof.

I've got an early flight to catch from Bologna in the morning and want to wish Valentino well before heading off. He's looking tired but relieved; the latest Operazione Nostalgia rally has gone off without a hitch. In fact, you would say it has been a roaring success. You can bet the next one will be even bigger. The fans have gone home happy, I tell him, and the players, too, it seems. 'It's exactly the soul of our project,' he says. 'To see thousands of people enjoying it together without rivalry and to give them the emotion to see for the first time or once again their idols so close. It's our mission and we are incredibly proud to have reached so far. The values are the positive ones of a sport so vital as football; aggregation, joy, emotions and also sacrifices. Football should promote these values. It's true that, nowadays, the attention is more on other aspects, sometimes not so positive, so I think this is what fans and players appreciate of our projects. We bring back to reality these positive values, memories and emotions.'

Valentino is off to find a well-deserved drink and it's time for me to leave, slipping out of an almost empty stadium through a slightly ajar gate. The floodlights have been turned off now and the features of the ground are only distinguishable thanks to a few dimly lit lamp posts on the street. I didn't get a chat with Totti but perhaps that worked out for the best anyway, watching him up close doing his talking with his feet, the way I fell in love with him in the first place. Glancing back at the stadium evokes the same emotions I get leaving a football game anywhere in the world. Win, lose or draw, as the adrenaline subsides and you mould back into civilian life, another chapter closes and the pitch, the players and the chants from the terraces turn, instead, to memories; a wholesome dose of nostalgia.

Chapter 15

Can't Smile Without You

REACHING OUT for a hand twice the size, immediately sensing it's the right one by the tough, dry skin, thickened and forged through years of moulding stone. The calluses may look uncomfortable but they are also comforting, tugging and guiding you through a seemingly never-ending huddle of grown-ups at hip height, the end of their scarves forming a blue and white tassel curtain that flits across your forehead. You want one, desperately. To fit in, to feel part of this movement. To be like Dad. And you get it. The man with a stall in front of the terraced houses, pushing gum into a cheek with his tongue to barter over a bigger sale. Finally, it's yours. Mapping the club crest with your fingertips, Dad snaking it around your shoulders and tucking it inside your jacket before setting off through the crowd again. The smell of burgers grilling, onions sizzling, cigarette smoke wafting and mingling with a background soundtrack of loud, indistinguishable chatter and the occasional cry of 'C'mon you Spuuurs'. It overloads the senses. You're moving with purpose now, Dad reading a paper ticket like an Ordnance Survey map, striding towards a hole in the wall, where metal turnstiles rhythmically clink. The stone steps are steep, your legs struggle to keep up, so you break into a skip, scarf dangling from the bottom of your coat, only looking up to catch the glare of the floodlights spilling out above huge, imposing stands.

The grass is greener than you imagined, the players far away but tall and defined. You can make them out from the posters on your wall. 'That's Darren Anderton. There's Teddy Sheringham!' They are the superstars, the ones recognisable to everyone slipping into their seats, but your real hero is sitting next to you. He seems immortal, impenetrable. There is so much going on, words you've never heard before, ones you think you're not allowed to say. You could be here with 35,000 other people or kicking a ball through the pouring rain in Knebworth Rec, just the two of you and you would feel just as safe, just as satisfied. You talk about everything and nothing at all, you ask a thousand questions and have a thousand more. You sit, stand, cheer. People around you shout, sing, groan, clap. The net ripples and they leap to their feet, thousands of plastic seats recoiling and slapping against their backrests. Those weighty, workman's hands lift you on to your seat so you can see the pitch again. The players are hugging; the fans, too. Adrenaline shoots through your veins. This is the best feeling ever. You're in now, you're hooked.

I don't know when I fell in love with Tottenham Hotspur Football Club, or football in general, but I do remember moments of giddy excitement. Going to White Hart Lane for the first time (and every time, to be honest) was one of those. Dad coming home from work with my first Spurs kit was another. All I had until that Pony number was the previous season's shorts my mum found in a charity shop. After that, I must have asked for a shirt on every birthday and Christmas. A garish, lime green goalkeeper kit with Ian Walker's name on the back was a particular highlight. It didn't matter that we didn't win as many games as Manchester United or that Chris Armstrong didn't score as many goals as Alan Shearer. I worshipped that team and those guys pulling on the same shirts as me like they were the bastions of beautiful football.

Supporting a football club is a deep emotional connection that you can't really explain. For me, it was only ever going to be following what my dad did, although I also loved to imagine what it would be like to play for a European club like AC Milan, Ajax or even Panathinaikos, whose shirt I picked up from a market stall once on holiday. My dad and my uncle, Dave, grew up in Southgate, north London, so naturally Tottenham was the local choice. Dad started going to White Hart Lane as a teenager with his mates in the 1970s. They would get the 298 bus from the Cherry Tree pub in Southgate down to Wood Green, then jump on the W3 to Tottenham. The whole day out, from bus fares to matchday programme and tickets, would cost about £1.50. He went to every home game the season Spurs spent in Division Two in 1977/78, winning promotion and seeing the emergence of a young Glenn Hoddle. Young, free and reckless, it's what he calls his 'golden era' as a fan.

'I would wear Doc Martens, flares, a denim or Harrington jacket, a "silk" scarf tied around each wrist and a wool scarf round my neck,' he recalls, fondly. 'As the journey progressed, the buses would take on more and more Spurs fans, with the levels of noise and excitement gradually building. By the time we were dropped off at the end of White Hart Lane, we were buzzing. Occasionally, we would stand at the Paxton Road End, to be behind the goal, but usually we would be on the upper east terrace, commonly known as The Shelf. We would run up the stairs from the turnstiles, desperate for that first view of the pitch and keen to get a good spot as near to the centre of the pitch as possible. The atmosphere on The Shelf was amazing. Singing, shouting and jumping up and down was obligatory.'

For me, it was Dad. But those early bonds can be forged in so many varied ways; you might have lived round the corner from Burnley's Turf Moor, been sent a Southampton scarf by your auntie, grown up in Australia watching Brian Clough's Nottingham Forest on the television or seen Blackburn win the title in 1995. There were Rovers fans knocking around Hertfordshire when I was growing up. My best mate even did the unthinkable and switched from Blackburn to Manchester United when the Premier League trophy changed hands the following season.

Spurs didn't have a regular haul of trophies to celebrate, so I would watch my dad's VHS of the 1981 FA Cup Final and bask in his tales of being behind the goal where Ricky Villa scored the winner in the replay against Manchester City, screaming at him to pass it until being overcome by joy when Villa slipped the ball through Joe Corrigan's legs and into the net. I would love to experience that taste of success more often, of course, but as you get older, you appreciate the game in different ways.

When my grandad, Fred, first moved to London from York he would go and watch Tottenham or Arsenal, whoever was at home on a particular weekend, just to take in a match. In his retirement, he would spend his afternoons cutting any Spurs-related snippets from the day's newspapers to show my brother and me. His weekends were taken up ferrying us around the south-east of England to play football. If we didn't have a game, it would be spent kicking a homemade ball (normally rolled-up socks) up and down his living room with us while watching the Premier League scores pop up on Ceefax. I guess, in that sense, football is a metaphor for life as a parent or grandparent. He wasn't too fussed how York City or Tottenham had got on; he never showed it, at least. It meant more to him that we enjoyed it.

I went the other way, to Manchester, making following my boyhood club in person harder, although I'm fortunate to watch plenty of games, both in the UK and Europe. Bar two League Cups in my football-viewing memory, there has been little to crow about. But the hill I will die on is that football is about the journey, rather than the actual silverware. Sod the celebration police; if you win a derby, hold out with ten men against the odds, come from behind to reach the next round of the cup, just enjoy it. Very few teams win things, anyway. In fact, one of the best days of my life as a supporter was being in Tottenham for the Champions League Final in 2019. The run to the final was both magical and mind-boggling; Fernando

Llorente in Manchester, Lucas Moura in Amsterdam. Wow! We couldn't make it to Madrid but the weather in north London was scorching, there were 60,000 Spurs fans singing and dancing on Tottenham High Road, some up trees and on top of bus stops. I was on my brother's shoulders, jigging to Moussa Sissoko chants. The game itself was dreadful; Tottenham were out of it after 30 seconds when Liverpool were awarded a penalty. They went on to win 2-0. But the feeling, beforehand, of shared excitement and belonging is something that will always stick with me.

My father-in-law will testify to that. I married an Everton fan, so our kids are screwed either way if they decide to follow one of their parents. But Paul, as a season ticket holder since the 1960s, has lived through the glory days as a Toffee. He has witnessed four First Division titles – including three as a regular match-going fan – and even European success. However (and this is, at least, what he tells them), going to the match with his daughters means more than seeing Everton win the UEFA Cup Winners' Cup in 1985. As Everton's final season at Goodison Park approached, they asked him for his greatest game, expecting the answer to be the Cup Winners' Cup semi-final second leg against Bayern Munich. After a goalless first leg, the German giants took the lead on Merseyside, only for Everton to fight back and win 3-1. 'That was a great team, a great manager and a magnificent atmosphere,' recalls Paul, giving an honorary mention to Everton's 1-0 win over Liverpool at Goodison Park in the FA Cup fifth round in 1967, when he was 12. 'That was incredible. Alan Ball scored the winner.'

Instead, however, the game he chose was when Everton came from 2-0 down to beat Crystal Palace 3-2 and secure their Premier League survival in May 2022. 'A one-off game like that was vitally important for Everton staying up, which was the most important thing – maybe more important than winning a trophy, in a way,' he says. 'To be 2-0 down and come back to win 3-2 was really dramatic. I felt it meant more to me because Hannah and Natalie were with me. And we shared the emotion of the whole game, the ups and downs, jumping and dancing around together when we scored. Other games, like Wimbledon in 1994 – that was very similar, 2-0 down, came back to win 3-2. But without your family with you, it makes that much difference to how important it is to be part of.'

I wouldn't like to call them a jinx but the girls started wanting to attend Everton games after seeing their dad's excitement at going to Wembley for the 1995 FA Cup Final win over Manchester United. The Toffees haven't won anything since. 'One of the saddest things for me, really, is that, in all these years, they have never seen us win a trophy,' says Paul. 'My dad introduced me to Everton and we won quite a lot of things while he was still going. I have always been very proud they both go and proud of my family background, which goes right through on my father's side. His father supported Everton and his father did and *his* father was Everton's first goalkeeper, in 1878. He played the first league game – George Bargery. There is a long stream of Evertonians and, by coincidence, my mum's family are all Evertonians as well, so there was absolutely zero chance of me ever supporting anybody else! When I had Hannah and Natalie, I wasn't consciously trying to get them interested in football but they just gradually absorbed my enthusiasm, I think. I thought at some point they might drop off – there are other things in the world – but they have always been determinedly loyal. It is special when we all go together; it means a lot. The fact you have these highlights through a season, and lowlights as well, that's all part of it. It means so much to do that with a family, a group of people you are close to or a mate you have been going with for 30 years.' Paul ponders for a moment. 'I couldn't deal with a daughter who had been a Liverpudlian,' he laughs.

For me, Tottenham Hotspur will always by my first love but I enjoy embracing different football experiences these days. Non-league visits are one of my favourites. It's a million miles from those White Hart Lane trips as a youngster but just as rewarding, just as enthralling. The local derby between Trafford FC and Wythenshawe was a particular highlight of 2024, in the Northern Premier League Division One West. Football with mates, mates of mates, people standing near you that you think are mates of mates and you end up chatting to them regardless. Mates with kids, kicking a ball to one another on the concourse until it hops over the barrier and on to the grass. 'Give us it back, lino!' Mates with babies, wrapped up from head to toe on a mild November afternoon and passed from one friend to another as mum or dad grab another beer. 'Just to keep warm …' Hey, they do Pomona Island here. A local derby, nearly 600 people packed into Shawe View to see Trafford win 2-0. Thirty years on and you're still asking questions. 'Is that Adam Le

Fondre?' It isn't. One mate tells everyone he was in the sauna with the centre-half at David Lloyd on Friday afternoon. 'He's a top lad.' Another isn't even interested in the game; it's just an excuse to have five pints at 3pm on a Saturday afternoon. Someone's on the Bovril. 'It smells like non-league.' You cheer the goals and chat in between. You pile out and go your separate ways after two hours where nothing else matters. Not even the football, really. It's just a reason to be together, a shared emotion. Once, it was a way to bond with Dad. Now, it's a chance to connect with friends. A chance to experience something different, every time, because no game is the same, no crowd identical. A chance to get lost in something, knowing millions of people are doing the same, each in their own little worlds. Shawe View, White Hart Lane, San Mamés, Stade Bauer …

Now it's me holding my little boys' hands, guiding them through crowds and bringing them home exotic football jerseys from my travels. I get as much joy watching my four-year-old trying to do a drag-back on a frosty Sunday morning in Urmston as I do watching Tottenham Hotspur at what is, in my completely unbiased opinion, the finest stadium in England (stick that in the cabinet!). It fills my heart in a way I can't put into words when he asks if we can take his ball to the park for a kickaround. It warms my soul when my one-year-old shouts 'Goal!' as he tries to get involved, too. As the wonderful and inspirational Chris Gardner, the man played by Will Smith in *The Pursuit of Happyness*, told me: 'Those little boys, they crawl all over you now like you're the monkey bars at the playground. One day soon, before you know it, you're going to have to look up. By the time they are 12 years old, you are going to be looking them in the eye!' Life moves fast and so does football. I'm excited for them, for the friends they will make, the bonds they will forge and the places and cultures they will discover through this crazy little game, if they want to.

And that's just it, really, isn't it? Football is a way to express yourself, to make friends, believe in something and enjoy a sense of belonging. This game means a million different things to a million different people. It's meant a million different things just to me, depending on the context. It can be beautiful and sometimes it can be disappointing. It can be liberating, infuriating, bewildering and intoxicating. It makes you happy and it makes you sad, it makes you want to cry tears of dejection and tears of joy. It strips you back to raw emotions, fires the passion inside you and it bearhugs your soul. Because it always means *something*. And it always will.

Bibliography

Books:

Burns, J., *Maradona: The Hand of God* (London: Bloomsbury, 2010).

Cruyff, J., *My Turn, the Autobiography* (United Kingdom: Pan Macmillan, 2017).

Evans, C.J., *Los Leones: The Unique Story of Athletic Club Bilbao* (United Kingdom: Pitch Publishing, 2024).

Holden, K., *Played in Germany: A Football Journey Through a Nation's Soul* (United Kingdom: Duckworth Books, 2024).

Kendall, H., *Love Affairs & Marriage: My Life in Football* (London: De Coubertin Books, 2013).

Kok, A., *Johan Cruyff: Always on the Attack* (United Kingdom: Simon & Schuster UK, 2022).

Kuper, S., *Barca: The Rise and Fall of the Club That Build Modern Football* (United Kingdom: Hachette UK, 2021).

Ludden, J., *Once Upon a Time in Naples* (Manchester: Parrs Wood Press, 2005).

Moffet, S., *Japanese Rules: Why the Japanese needed football and how they got it* (United Kingdom: Yellow Jersey, 2003).

Totti, F., *Gladiator* (United Kingdom: De Coubertin Books, 2021).

Williams, T., *Va-Va Voom: The Modern History of French Football* (London: Bloomsbury, 2024).

Wilson, J., *The Barcelona Legacy* (United Kingdom: Blink Publishing, 2018).

Winner, D., *Brilliant Orange: The Neurotic Genius of Dutch Football* (London: Bloomsbury, 2001).

Journals:

Esposito, A., 'Tourism-driven displacement in Naples, Italy', *Land Use Policy, Volume 134* (2023) 10.1016/j.landusepol.2023.106919

Selected websites and newspapers:

www.athletic-club.eus

www.redstar.fr

9News

BBC News

BBC Sport

Cambridge Rules 1848

Corriere della Sera

Corriere Milano

El Mundo Deportivo

El Pais

ESPN

FourFourTwo

Get French Football News

Il Riformista

Il Romanista

La Gazzetta dello Sport

Reuters

Sky Sports

The Athletic
The Berliner
The Guardian
The *New York Times*
The Times

Documentaries

Mighty Penguins (2023) Fever Media: https://vimeo.com/812497747/7a9fb565fb?

"Welcome to Berlin Motherf*cker!": Derby Days Berlin (2019) Copa 90: https://www.youtube.com/watch?v=IF_1k_0ACj8